This is the seventh volume in the popular Cummings Foundation for Behavioral Health series beginning in 1991 that addresses healthcare utilization and costs. The Nicholas & Dorothy Cummings Foundation, in association with Context Press, is pleased to continue the tradition of distributing complimentary copies to the directors of American Psychological Association approved doctoral programs, to selected leaders in psychology, and to key persons in the field of behavioral healthcare.

It is hoped you will find this series useful in your work. The Cummings Foundation for Behavioral Health requests that after you have finished reading it, you donate it to the library of the institution with which you are affiliated.

Additional copies for individuals only, may be obtained as long as supplies last by sending $5.00 to cover postage and handling to the following address. Regretfully, repeat, multiple, and bulk requests cannot be accommodated.

Janet L. Cummings, Psy.D., President
The Nicholas & Dorothy Cummings Foundation, Inc.
561 Keystone Avenue, #212
Reno, NV 89503

Library and Institutional copies may be ordered from CONTEXT PRESS for a charge of $29.95 plus shipping and handling.

Early Detection and Treatment of Substance Abuse within Integrated Primary Care

Early Detection and Treatment of Substance Abuse within Integrated Primary Care

A Report of the Fourth Reno Conference in a Series of Reno Conferences on the Integration of Behavioral Health in Primary Care, with this conference devoted to the Early Detection and Treatment of Substance Abuse within the Primary Care Setting

Editors:
Nicholas A. Cummings, Ph.D., Sc.D.
Melanie P. Duckworth, Ph.D.
William T. O'Donohue, Ph.D.
Kyle E. Ferguson, M.S.

Cummings Foundation for Behavioral Health:
Healthcare Utilization and Cost Series,
Volume 7
2004

CONTEXT PRESS
Reno, Nevada

Early Detection and Treatment of Substance Abuse within Integrated Primary Care

Hardback   pp. 195

Library of Congress Cataloging-in-Publication Data

Reno Conference on the Integration of Behavioral Health in Primary Care:
Beyond Efficacy to Effectiveness (4th : 2003 : University of Nevada)
    Early detection and treatment of substance abuse within integrated primary
care / editors, Nicholas A. Cummings ... [et al.].
        p. cm. – (Healthcare utilization and cost series ; v. 7)
    "A Report of the Fourth Reno Conference in a Series of Reno Conferences
on the Integration of Behavioral Health in Primary Care, with this conference
devoted to the Early Detection and Treatment of Substance Abuse within the
Primary Care Setting."
    ISBN 1-878978-47-0 (hardcover)
    1. Substance abuse–Diagnosis–Congresses. 2. Substance
abuse–Treatment–Congresses. 3. Primary care (Medicine)–Congresses. I.
Cummings, Nicholas A. II. Title. III. Series.
    RC563.2.R46 2003
    616.86'075–dc22

                                                            2004002527

© 2004 CONTEXT PRESS
933 Gear Street, Reno, NV   89503-2729

Printed in the United States of America

The Healthcare Utilization and Cost Series
of the Cummings Foundation for Behavioral Health

Volume 1 (1991):
> *Medical Cost Offset: A Reprinting of the Seminal Research Conducted at Kaiser Permanente, 1963-1981*
> Nicholas A. Cummings, Ph.D. and William T. Follette, M.D.

Volume 2 (1993):
> *Medicaid, Managed Behavioral Health and Implications for Public Policy: A Report of the HCFA-Hawaii Medicaid Project and Other Readings.*
> Nicholas A. Cummings, Ph.D., Herbert Dorken, Ph.D., Michael S. Pallak, Ph.D. and Curtis Henke, Ph.D.

Volume 3 (1994):
> *The Financing and Organization of Universal Healthcare: A Proposal to the National Academies of Practice.*
> Herbert Dorken, Ph.D. (Forward by Nicholas Cummings, Ph.D.).

Volume 4 (1995):
> *The Impact of the Biodyne Model on Medical Cost Offset: A sampling of Research Projects.*
> Nicholas A. Cummings, Ph.D., Sc.D., Editor.

Volume 5 (2002):
> *The Impact of Medical Cost Offset on Practice and Research: Making It Work for You.* A Report of the Second Reno Conference, May 2002.
> Nicholas A. Cummings, Ph.D., Sc.D., William T. O'Donohue, Ph.D., and Kyle E. Ferguson, M.S., Editors.

Volume 6 (2003):
> *Behavioral Health as Primary Care: Beyond Efficacy to Effectiveness.*
> A Report of the Third Reno Conference, May 2003.
> Nicholas A. Cummings, Ph.D., Sc.D., William T. O'Donohue, Ph.D., and Kyle E. Ferguson, M.S., Editors.

The Reno Conferences

Co-sponsored by the University of Nevada, Reno and
The Nicholas & Dorothy Cummings Foundation

The First Reno Conference on Organized Behavioral Healthcare Delivery was convened at the University of Nevada, Reno in January 1999.

The Second Reno Conference on Medical Cost Offset was convened at the University of Nevada, Reno in January 2001.

The Third Reno Conference on Medical Cost Offset and Behavioral Health in Primary Care was convened at the University of Nevada, Reno in May 2002.

The Fourth Reno Conference on Substance Abuse in Primary Care was convened at the University of Nevada, Reno in May 2003.

The Fifth Reno Conference on Disease Management in Primary Care will conven at the University of Nevada, Reno in May 2004.

Preface

This book consists largely of expanded papers that were first presented at the University of Nevada, Reno on May 16-17, 2003. This conference was generously supported by grants from The Nicholas and Dorothy Cummings Foundation and the University of Nevada, Reno.

Substance abuse is a major public health concern, affecting millions of people in the United States. According to the 2002 *National Survey on Drug Use and Health*, approximately 72 million Americans use tobacco products, 16 million are heavy drinkers, and 20 million use illicit drugs (SAMSA, 2003). Substance abuse can result in severe health problems; families suffer; people are victimized on account of substance-related crime; and most tragically, thousands of innocent children die each year in impaired driving accidents. Over and above the human cost, substance abuse problems cost the United States billions of dollars, annually. Given its far-reaching impact on the welfare of society, healthcare professionals should make substance abuse a priority.

Most patients with substance abuse problems present in primary care settings, oftentimes with other complaints. Thus, substance abuse can seem elusive during routine visits. Nonetheless, when professionals know what to look for and there is adequate infrastructural support with respect to triage, implementing substance programs with an eye on early detection and intervention can dramatically improve health outcomes and create significant financial benefits. The chapters in the present volume are testament to this fact.

We have made use of two chapters by the senior editor, "Who is the Substance Abuser?" and "Different Tugs from Different Drugs", both of which were originally published in Cummings, N. A., & Cummings, J. L. (2000). *The First Session with Substance Abusers: A Step-by-Step Guide*. San Francisco, CA: Jossey Bass (A Wiley Company). We are grateful to John Wiley & Sons, Inc. for their permission to reprint these chapters. We also made use of the senior editor's popular American Psychological Association presidential address titled, "Turning Bread into Stone: Our Modern Antimiracle," that was later published in the *American Psychologist* (1979, 34, pp. 1119-1129). Incidentally, following his address, over 7,000 requests were made for this piece and the article was republished by the *American Psychologist* an unprecedented three times. This article was reprinted with the author's permission.

This book owes much to many people. First and foremost our special thanks are due to the chapter authors who furnished this volume with their excellent work. We are exceedingly grateful to Emily Neilan for her outstanding effort in preparing this manuscript and keeping us on schedule. Lastly, we would like to thank our families and friends for their patience and support during this project.

Reference

Substance Abuse and Mental Health Services Administration. (2003). *Overview of findings from the 2002 National Survey on Drug Use and Health*. (NHSDA Series H-21, DHHS Publication No. SMA 03-3774). Rockville, MD: Author. Retrieved October 26, 2003, from http://www.samhsa.gov/oas/p0000016.htm#

Contributing Authors

David O. Antonuccio received his B.A. (1975) in psychology (honors) and economics from Stanford University. He received his M.A. (1979) and Ph.D. (1980) in Clinical Psychology from the University of Oregon. He is currently Professor in the Dept. of Psychiatry and Behavioral Sciences at the University of Nevada School of Medicine. He served on the Nevada State Board of Psychological Examiners from 1990 to 1998. His clinical and research interests include the behavioral treatment of depression, anxiety, and smoking. Among his many publications is the self-help book for smokers entitled *Butt Out*. He holds a diplomate in Clinical Psychology from the American Board of Professional Psychology and is a Fellow of the American Psychological Association. He was named Outstanding Psychologist in 1993 by the Nevada State Psychological Association (NSPA), received an Award of Achievement from NSPA in 1999 for his work on depression, and was named the 2000 recipient of the McReynolds Foundation Psychological Services Award for outstanding contributions to clinical science.

Janet L. Cummings received her doctorate in clinical psychology from the Wright State University School of Professional Psychology and is a licensed psychologist in the state of Arizona. She has over 15 years of clinical experience. Dr. Cummings has authored 6 books, including a book on substance abuse assessment and treatment, as well as numerous journal articles and book chapters. She is an adjunct professor at the University of Nevada, Reno and has taught other mental health professionals in workshops throughout the United States and the United Kingdom. Dr. Cummings is a member of the American Psychological Association, the Arizona Psychological Association, the American Association of Forensic Examiners, and the American Society for the Advancement of Pharmacotherapy. She is a National Board of Cognitive-Behavioral Therapists Diplomate in Psycho-therapy, a Distinguished Practitioner in the National Academies of Practice, and a Lifetime Member of Strathmore's Who's Who.

Nicholas A. Cummings, Ph.D., Sc.D. is Distinguished Professor, University of Nevada, Reno and President, Cummings Foundation for Behavioral Health. He chairs the boards of both the University Alliance for Behavioral Care (U/ABC) and The Nicholas & Dorothy Cummings Foundation. He is the founder of over two dozen organizations, such as the California School of Professional Psychology (four campuses), American Biodyne, National Council of Schools of Professional Psychology (NCSPP), and the National Academies of Practice (NAP). He is a former president of the American Psychological Association and the recipient of the Gold Medal for a Lifetime of Achievement in Practice. He is the author of over 400 journal articles and book chapters, and he has authored or co-edited 28 books.

Melanie P. Duckworth, Ph.D., is an associate professor in the Clinical Psychology Training Program at the University of Nevada, Reno. She received her doctorate in Clinical Psychology from the University of Georgia in 1992. She completed an internship in Clinical Psychology and a one-year postdoctoral fellowship in Behavioral Medicine at the Brown University School of Medicine. Dr. Duckworth's current research examines posttraumatic stress reactions, coping styles and strategies, and psychological disability in the context of interpersonal violence, motor vehicle accidents, and chronic medical conditions.

Kyle E. Ferguson is pursuing his Ph.D. in clinical psychology at the University of Nevada, Reno. He received a master's degree in behavior analysis from Southern Illinois University and a bachelor's degree from the University of Alberta. Among other publications, he coauthored the books, *The Psychology of B.F. Skinner* and *Taking Anger Along for the Ride and Steering Clear of Rage*, and is coeditor on several books, *Handbook of Professional Ethics for Psychologists*, *Behavioral Health as Primary Care: Beyond Efficacy to Effectiveness*, and *The Impact of Medical Cost Offset on Practice and Research*.

J. Harry Isaacson, MD, FACP is currently the Vice Chairman, Department of General Internal Medicine Cleveland Clinic Foundation, and Director of Clinical Education Cleveland Clinic Lerner College of Medicine of Case Western Reserve University.

Dr. Isaacson attended the University of Michigan Medical School and completed his Internal Medicine Residency and Chief Residency at the University of Vermont. He has taught a number of national workshops related to substance use disorders, and has been involved with national organizations focused on improving physician training in the identification and management of patients with substance use disorders.

Peter E. Nathan is the University of Iowa Foundation Professor of Psychology at the University of Iowa. He received the PhD in clinical psychology from Washington University in St. Louis. He is an editor with Jack Gorman of *A Guide to Treatments that Work* (1998, 2002, Oxford University Press) and the author of *Practice guidelines: Not yet ideal* (American Psychologist, 1998) and *Research on psychotherapy efficacy and effectiveness: Between Scylla and Charybdis?* (Psychological Bulletin, 2000).

William T. O'Donohue is the Nicholas Cummings Professor of Organized Behavioral Healthcare Delivery in the Department of Psychology at the University of Nevada at Reno. He is also president and CEO of the University Alliance for Behavioral Care, Inc., a company selling integrated care services. He also holds adjunct appointments in the Departments of Philosophy, Psychiatry and at the University of Hawaii, Monoa. He received a doctorate in clinical psychology from the State University of New York at Stony Brook and a master's degree in philosophy from Indiana University. He is editor and co-editor on a number of books, including *Management and Administration Skills for the Mental Health Professional*; *Integrated Behavioral Healthcare*; *Positioning Mental Health Practice with Medical/Surgical Practice*; *The Impact of Medical Cost Offset on Practice and Research*; and *Treatments that Work in Primary Care*.

Dr. David Oslin is an Assistant Professor of Psychiatry at the University of Pennsylvania Medical Center and the Philadelphia Veterans Affairs Medical Center. He holds joint appointments in the Section of Geriatric Psychiatry and the Center for Studies on Addiction. He completed residency training at the University of Maryland and fellowship training at the University of Pennsylvania. He is the recipient of a career development award from NIMH and is conducting research on the treatment of late life major depression that is complicated by other disorders such as alcohol dependence. He was recently selected to serve as the Co-Chair for the Huss Research Chair in late life addictions sponsored by Hazelden. He serves as an ad hoc reviewer for several journals and is a member of numerous professional and scientific societies.

Christine (Tina) Runyan, Ph.D., is an investigator at the VERDICT and an Assistant Professor in the Dept. of Medicine at the University of Texas Health Science Center at San Antonio. Dr. Runyan received her Ph.D. in clinical psychology from Virginia Tech and completed post-doctoral training in clinical health psychology at Wilford Hall Medical Center. Her primary research interest is examining ways to integrate health delivery systems in order to improve the recognition and early intervention of behavioral and psychiatric disorders in primary care clinics. Her other areas of interest include behavioral and lifestyle approaches for disease prevention, population health, clinical informatics, and the integration of clinical psychology with public health. Before joining the VERDICT in August, 2003, Dr. Runyan worked as a health psychologist and consultant for the Air Force Medical Service developing and implementing a model for the integration of behavioral health providers into primary care clinics.

Ian Shaffer MD, MMM is currently the Chief Medical Officer at MHN, a managed behavioral healthcare organization. At the time of writing this chapter he was Chief Operating Officer of University Alliance for Behavioral Care, Inc., a company focusing on the integration of primary and behavioral care. Dr. Shaffer, a child psychiatrist and addiction medicine specialist has written numerous articles and several book chapters on the delivery of behavioral health care while serving as the Chief Medical Officer of Value Behavioral Health. Dr. Shaffer has served as a member of the National Advisory Committee for the Center for Mental Health Services and was Chairman of the Managed Behavioral Health Association.

Table of Contents

Preface ix

Contributing Authors xi

Chapter 1 17
**Primary Care: An Entry Point for the Detection and Treatment of
Substance Abuse**
> *Kyle E. Ferguson, Melanie P. Duckworth, William T. O'Donohue, & Nicholas
> A. Cummings*

Chapter 2 33
Turning Bread Into Stones: Our Modern Antimiracle
> *Nicholas A. Cummings*

Chapter 3 49
Who is the Substance Abuser?
> *Nicholas A. Cummings & Janet L. Cummings*

Chapter 4 63
Presenting Problems: Different Tugs from Different Drugs
> *Nicholas A. Cummings & Janet L. Cummings*

Chapter 5 93
**Substance Abuse Treatment within Primary Care: Frontline Detection
and Intervention**
> *Nicholas A. Cummings & Janet L. Cummings*

Chapter 6 111
Issues in Addressing Substance Abuse in Primary Care
> *Ian Schaffer*

Chapter 7 121
Early Detection and Treatment of Alcoholism in Primary Care
> *Peter E. Nathan*

Chapter 8 133
**Opportunities for Improved Detection and Treatment of Alcohol Misuse:
Using Behavioral Health Consultants in Primary Care**
> *Christine N. Runyan*

Chapter 9 153
Late Life Alcoholism in Primary Care
David W. Oslin

Chapter 10 169
**Early Detection and Treatment of Prescription Drug Abuse in
Primary Care**
J. Harry Isaacson

Chapter 11 181
Integrating Behavioral Interventions for Smoking into Primary Care
David Antonuccio

Primary Care:
An Entry Point for the Detection and Treatment of Substance Abuse

Kyle E. Ferguson
Melanie P. Duckworth
William T. O'Donohue
University of Nevada
Nicholas A. Cummings
University of Nevada, Reno and the
Cummings Foundation for Behavioral Health

Substance abuse is clearly a significant public health problem that affects not only the United States but is rampant across most of the world. It is one of the most serious health problems because it can have so many negative consequences for both the abuser and those individuals associated with the abuser. Substance abuse can result in health problems ranging from minor problems to death; substance abuse can stress or destroy families and friendships; it can impair occupational functioning; it can result in financial stress or ruin; and it can increase social burden through criminal engagement and victimization. Mark et al. (2001) found that just one substance abuse problem, heroin addiction, cost the US $21.9 billion in 1996—with 53% of this total due to productivity losses; 24% due to criminal costs; 23% due to medical costs; and .5% due to social welfare costs. Of course, the most tragic consequence of substance abuse is lost life. As unfortunate as the death of the substance abuser are the deaths of innocent third parties who suffer and die as a consequence of drinking-related traffic fatalities. These wide ranging negative consequences render substance abuse a serious public health problem and a priority for health care professionals.

Three relatively recent developments have served to further highlight the importance of substance abuse:

1. Substance abuse is increasing across nearly all age groups. Epidemiologists are finding more problems in both the young (pre-teens) as well as the old (65+).
2. With the advent of designer drugs, some illicit substances are becoming easier and cheaper to manufacture and market; harder for law enforcement to monitor and control; and most problematic from a mental health perspective, more reinforcing and addictive.

3.   Some substance abuse is becoming closely associated with relatively
     new and serious medical problems including AIDS and Hepatitis C.
     The pathway for disease transmission from the substance abuser to
     other substance abusers and non-abusers results in an almost
     inestimable potential for the spread of such diseases.

Substance abuse, because of the range of associated biological, psychological,
social, and financial consequences, has received a significant amount of lay and
professional attention. Alcoholics Anonymous, Narcotics Anonymous, Mothers
Against Drunk Driving, and other grass-roots movements have sprung up and have
gained considerable recognition as organizations aimed at substance abuse intervention and prevention. The work contained in the current volume confirms the
commitment of health care professionals to identifying, evaluating, managing, and
preventing substance abuse. Professionals are hard at work constructing etiological
theories for substance abuse problems, devising diagnostic tools, and creating/
establishing a wide variety of prevention and intervention programs. Nonetheless,
it is fair to make three claims about the current state of the field:

1.   There is a need for much more scientific evaluation of the quality of
     procedures used to identify and treat substance abuse problems.
2.   Generally, the empirical tests of existing therapies, while sometimes
     compromised by design and methodological concerns, do not suggest
     the effectiveness of such therapies.
3.   Substance abuse problems, in the main, represent unsolved scientific
     and clinical puzzles that require innovative thinking and novel
     intervention approaches.

The existing substance abuse literature is characterized by controversies related
to causation, assessment, and treatment of substance abuse problems. Controversies
related to causation center around the single and interactive contributions of
biological (e.g., genetic inheritance), psychological (e.g., anxiety, depression, or the
"addictive personality"), sociocultural (e.g., peer pressure or belief in "magic pill"),
and environmental (e.g., poverty) factors to substance abuse.

The largest controversy in assessment revolves around the psychometric
soundness of the various assessment procedures employed in the detection and
classification of substance abuse problems. Are measurement procedures reliable
and valid? Is a multi-method assessment approach valued? Are reports from
significant others gathered? Are assessment procedures employed consistently
across individuals?

The substance abuse literature is also characterized by controversy. The major
controversies from this literature are outlined below.

1. *Inpatient versus outpatient treatment.* Does the patient require isolation (particularly from their sources for their substance) and medical supervision or does the less intrusive outpatient treatment format facilitate the patient's move from old, maladaptive lifestyle behaviors to new, healthier lifestyle behaviors?

2. *Professional versus lay therapists.* Do lay therapists, particularly ex-addicts, have better therapy skills (e.g., catching minimization, lies, etc.) than psychologists and psychiatrists? Should one of these professionals be primary and the other adjunctive?

3. *Medication versus environmental therapies.* To what extent are substance abuse problems better treated by pharmacological interventions such as Methadone and Antabuse rather than psychological therapies that incorporate cognitive-behavioral techniques?

4. *Treatment versus treatment plus relapse prevention.* To what extent should the initial therapy be supplemented by maintenance therapies such as the relapse prevention approach developed by Marlatt and colleagues (see Larimer, Palmer, & Marlatt, 1999, for a recent review)?

5. *Abstinence versus controlled use.* Should the goal of substance abuse therapy be complete abstinence or controlled drinking?

6. *Treatment versus non-treatment of co-morbid psychological problems.* Should co-morbid psychological problems be treated in conjunction with substance abuse problems? Are there treatment gains associated with targeting co-morbid conditions (e.g., bipolar or PTSD) before targeting substance abuse problems? Are there treatment gains associated with targeting substance abuse problems before targeting co-morbid conditions? Is simultaneous treatment of these problems most effective?

7. *Single versus polysubstance abuse treatment.* Multiple addictions or polysubstance abuse appear to be the rule rather than the exception (Miller & Gold, 1993). How different are the treatment requirements of the single substance abuser from those of the polysubstance abuser?

Together, these controversies underscore how essential it is that substance abuse treatment approaches be mindful of Gordon Paul's (1969) key question regarding therapy: "What treatment, by whom, is most effective for this individual, with that specific problem, under which set of circumstances, and how does it come about?" (p. 44). The controversies that exist across substance abuse theory, assessment and treatment domains also serve to direct the significant substance abuse research agenda. Tests of single and multidimensional explanatory models of substance use and abuse are needed. Considerable effort should be directed toward the development of more sensitive, inexpensive, and consumer friendly detection and diagnostic devices. More effective prevention programs are needed, with particular emphasis placed on primary prevention programs for children. Identification of core variables related to the development of substance abuse is needed so that childhood prevention programs are targeted, time-limited, and effective. The development of cost-effective treatment programs and relapse prevention programs for the management of substance abuse problems should be considered critical to the nation's public health and welfare.

This book summarizes the state of the art of substance abuse detection and treatment in primary care. It is the thesis of this book that the primary care setting is an attractive entree point for the substance abuser and that strengthening efforts around substance abuse detection and treatment in the primary care setting is a viable alternative to more traditional substance abuse identification and treatment approaches. The following points support these contentions:

1. Treatment in primary care is typically regarded as less stigmatizing. Substance abuse problems are typically highly stigmatizing problems.
2. Primary care settings have good potential to detect substance abuse problems and relapses given these settings are equipped for the detection of both physiological and behavioral indices of substance abuse problems. Substance abusers often have health problems (e.g., fractures, gastritis, and substance seeking problems) that bring them into the primary care setting. In presenting to primary care agencies for management of other health problems, the substance abuser affords health care professionals additional opportunities to detect and manage substance abuse problems.
3. Primary care settings offer a potentially more effective and safe management of these problems as both medical conditions and mental health problems can be simultaneously managed in these settings. Primary care offers "one stop shopping".
4. Abusers will continue to access primary care for the rest of their lives and thus follow up and booster sessions can be given to manage relapse.
5. Primary care medicine tends to both value and practice evidence based treatments (although imperfectly). Substance abuse treatment has been an arena which seems to have attracted a lot of fads and fanciful treatments. However, primary care medicine has the potential to offer treatments that have the best empirical support.
6. Primary care has the best potential to produce efficient psychotherapy. Through better detection, offering more acceptable therapy, being better able to co-manage psychological and physical problems, and practicing evidence base therapies, primary care has the best potential of reducing overall health care costs by providing the most appropriate therapy to the patient.

To provide the reader with an overview of the field of substance abuse, a variety of classes of substances are addressed in this book. Particular emphasis has been placed on maladaptive patterns of alcohol use. We place such emphasis on patterns of alcohol use and abuse because it is the most widely researched substance and because of the often severe and far-reaching negative consequences of alcohol abuse.

Alcohol: Definitions and Models of Use and Abuse

The National Institute on Alcohol Abuse and Alcoholism (NIAAA, 1990) separates drinkers into three groups: 1) individuals who are able to drink with few, if any, problems (most social drinkers fall into this category); 2) non-chemically-dependent drinkers who have sufficient enough alcohol-related problems to warrant attention (e.g., skipping work on account of a hangover after a night of binge drinking); and 3) individuals who are chemically dependent and thus suffer from the disease alcoholism. According to the NIAAA, alcoholism is characterized by tolerance (i.e., requiring more of the substance to obtain a comparable high, or conversely, the same amount producing less of the desired effect), chemical dependence, lack of control over binges, and withdrawal symptoms (i.e., unpleasant sensory experiences, such as nausea, chills, depression, all of which are attributable to deprivation of the drug). Approximately 10-11 million citizens of the United States would be considered to have an alcohol use disorder using these criteria (NIAAA, 1990, p. ix).

Professionals who promote the NIAAA definition of alcoholism typically embrace the abstinence model of substance abuse treatment. The most well known abstinence model is that of Alcoholics Anonymous (AA). In AA's 12-step program, alcoholics are required to quit at the outset and maintain sobriety for the remainder of their lives. This complete and sustained abstinence requirement can be summed up by the expression "one drink, one drunk," an expression that has been attributed to AA. Although the most popular and most frequently court mandated, AA has not been shown to be the most effective treatment for treating alcoholism. In fact, the various treatment approaches for alcoholism are considered to be equally effective or ineffective.

Although the DSM-IV (1994) employs similar criteria as the NIAAA, it does not use the term alcoholism, nor does it use the term addiction as seen elsewhere in the literature. Rather, the DSM-IV breaks maladaptive substance use down into two groups of behaviors: dependence and abuse. Substance dependence refers to a maladaptive pattern of substance use where three or more of the following manifest within a 12-month window of time: 1) tolerance; 2) withdrawal; 3) more of the substance is taken than intended (i.e., on a micro level, the person loses control and binges); 4) failed attempts at controlling its use (on a more macro level, encompassing overall patterns of behavior); 5) increase in frequency of drug-related behavior (e.g., more physician visits to obtain prescriptions, prostitution, theft); 6) marked disruption in social, occupational, or recreational activities; and 7) the individual continues to use the substance in the face of marked impairment in activities of daily life (APA, 2000, pp.110 – 111).

Substance abuse refers to problematic patterns of substance use, though physiological dependence is not present. Again, as is the case with dependence, the window in which symptoms is observed is 12 months. Over and above significant impairment and/or distress, one or more of the following must manifest before the diagnosis of substance abuse can be made: 1) failure to carry out role-related duties and obligations; 2) frequent substance use that places the individual or those around him or her in harm's way (e.g., impaired driving, frequent accidents, unsafe care of an infant); 3) recurrent legal problems related to substance use (e.g., Drinking While Under the Influence [DUI] violations; alcohol-related assault charges; breaking and entering while intoxicated); and 4) the individual continues abusing the substance in spite of substance-related problems (APA, 2000, pp.114 – 115). Although substance use does not lead to physiological dependence, it acutely impairs judgment and promotes impulsivity, making any of the above four problems more likely.

Using DSM-IV criteria, Grant (1996) found that an estimated 18% of the US population satisfied the diagnosis for alcohol abuse or dependence at some point during their lives. For some individuals, patterns of alcohol consumption might become problematic during a specific developmental period. For example, many individuals who meet the diagnostic criteria for alcohol abuse while attending college simply "grow out of it" after graduation, with the change in environment that follows college graduation (e.g., familial obligations that come with marriage and parenthood (Marlatt & Witkiewitz, 2002)). For other individuals their prognosis is less promising. Individuals who become dependent on the substance will usually have a lifelong struggle with alcohol.

Endorsing the DSM perspective on problematic patterns of alcohol use does not preclude one from adopting the disease model, it does open the way to alternative approaches to the abstinence model. Conditioning, social learning, and harm reduction models are three such alternative approaches.

The conditioning model views problematic drinking behavior as learned behavior. As such, excessive drinking is believed to have resulted from direct contact with particular contingencies of reinforcement. Because excessive drinking is seen as learned behavior, it is believed that individuals can unlearn these intemperate patterns and learn more acceptable drinking behaviors. This therapeutic perspective is called controlled drinking or behavioral self-control training (BSCT; Hester, 1995). Among other aspects, BSCT is characterized by the following:

1. *Setting limits on the number of drinks per day.* This supposedly mitigates against binging by reducing "free operant" behavior (i.e., drinking whenever they want).
2. *Self-monitoring drinking patterns.* Problem drinkers are largely insensitive to the contingencies under which their drinking is a function. Self-monitoring brings them into better touch with these contingencies, with the expectation that such knowledge will affect their behavior (so called rule-governed behavior).
3. *Changing the rate of drinking (e.g., fewer drinks/hour).* Similar to the first point, this imposes limits over free operant patterns of behavior.

4. *Practice assertiveness by refusing drinks.* On some occasions an individual may over drink so as not to offend a very generous "drinking budding." Assertive training is designed to teach the problem drinker how to behave with his or her best interests in mind, without overly offending the other person on account of behaving too aggressively.

5. *Rewarding oneself for achieving goals.* This is designed to strengthen a more adaptive coping repertoire. A good habit thus replaces a bad one.

6. *Identifying those antecedents that evoke heavy drinking (e.g., argument with a co-worker) and those that evoke moderate drinking.* This training is designed to promote generalization as individuals begin identifying triggers in both cases, and as a result, begin making changes in their own lives in accordance with their observations.

7. *Learning other coping skills, functionally incompatible with drinking.* Insofar as step 6 identifies triggers, step 7 targets what to do when faced with those negative cues in the environment.

8. *Avoiding relapse back to heavy drinking patterns.* Substance abuse treatment is incomplete if it does not address the abstinence violation effect (AVE). Accordingly, individuals should be taught how to cope with an occasional relapse (e.g., see it discretely rather than as a global phenomenon in his or her life).

The social learning model emphasizes the role of significant others in modeling drinking behavior. A parent might serve as a model of drinking behavior for his or her child. A peer might model drinking behavior for his or her friend. Over and above establishing the drinking behavior in the observer, models for drinking behavior also serve as discriminative stimuli for drinking greater amounts. When others model patterns of heavy drinking, the likelihood that the observer will view heavy drinking as "acceptable" drinking, behavior increases. Countless studies show, for example, that problem drinkers tend to drink more around "drinking buddies." Each member of the coterie serves as a model for and imitates the drinking behavior of other members. Part of the treatment from a social modeling perspective, therefore, will necessarily entail a change in social contexts. Changing social contexts need not entail dramatic changes around the venue or the cast of characters implicated in problematic patterns of alcohol use. Changing the social context might involve changing the individual's role and participation in such social contexts. Like the conditioning model, the social learning model allows for controlled drinking. Individuals, for example, can still drink moderate amounts of alcohol. For example, an individual might be taught to assertively refuse drinks proffered by other drinkers. Additionally, because drinking is seen as a modeled way of coping with life's problems, such individuals might be taught other more effective coping skills (e.g., problem solving skills training, relaxation training).

The harm reduction approach emphasizes a reduction in use of the harmful substance such that negative health effects are appreciably diminished. It is impor-tant to note that, unlike the conditioning and social learning models, the harm reduction approach is a population-based approach that derives from a public health perspective. This public health perspective that underlies the harm reduction approach is nicely characterized in the following statement made by the World Health Organization (2001):

> The prevention of alcohol dependence needs to be seen within the context of the broader goal of preventing and reducing alcohol-related problems at the population level (alcohol-related accidents, injuries, suicide, violence, etc). The goals of therapy are the reduction of alcohol-related morbidity and mortality, and the reduction of other social and economic problems related to chronic and excessive alcohol consumption.

For individuals who manifest physical dependence, alcohol consumption often becomes a pervasive and longstanding problem. Chronic alcohol use increases the risk of a host of health complications. Below are a number of individual, social, and economic problems that are directly related to excessive and chronic alcohol consumption.

Physiological consequences of chronic alcohol use. Alcohol affects all of the major organ systems and bodily tissues. The hepatic, circulatory, and central nervous systems are especially prone to damage after years of excessive and chronic alcohol use.

Cirrhosis of the liver. Cirrhosis of the liver is common with excessive chronic alcohol use. Cirrhosis entails the destruction of healthy liver tissue, supplanting it with scar tissue. Among others factors (e.g., hepatitis B and C), alcohol is the number one cause of cirrhosis in the United States (Lieber, 2001). Each year about 28,000 lives are lost to this disease (Centers for Disease Control [CDC], 2003). Regarding health care utilization, alcohol-related liver disorders are associated with 101,200 hospitalizations, and $1.8 billion in health care expenditures (Kim et al., 2001).

Coronary heart disease. When used in moderation, alcohol is associated with reductions in coronary heart disease (CHD). However, when used in excess (i.e., over 30g ethanol per day) the risk of developing CHD increases dramatically (Criqui, 1987).

Korsakoff amnestic syndrome. Korsakoff amnestic syndrome (KAS) is a severe memory disturbance affecting a person's ability to formulate new memories (i.e., anterograde amnesia) and as the disease progresses, affecting an individual's ability to recall older memories (i.e., retrograde amnesia) (Langlais, 1995). KAS is especially common with heavy drinkers who have abused alcohol for decades. KAS is related to Thiamine deficiency. Major liver damage, as caused by chronic and excessive use of alcohol, interferes with the body's ability to process Thiamine. Moreover, because alcohol is of high caloric value in and of itself, many alcohol abusers fail to get enough of this vitamin because they are simply not eating enough of a well balanced diet.

Fetal Alcohol Syndrome. Central nervous system damage from chronic drinking can also affect the very young. Research has demonstrated unequivocally that significant amounts of alcohol ingested during pregnancy places the fetus at heightened risk of developing Fetal Alcohol Syndrome (FAS). These features and associated intellectual impairment appear to be caused by severe oxygen deprivation induced by repeated ethanol consumption. The FAS brain develops cumulatively as a result of this recurrent state of intrauterine hypoxia (Mukherjee & Hodgen, 1982, p. 702). FAS affects the intellectual and physical development of the fetus and worst of all, it is an irreversible condition. Among other features, newborns show a characteristic 1) narrowing of the eyelids, 2) the grove running from the lip to nose is usually absent, 3) they have a short upturned nose along with 4) an underdeveloped jaw, giving them a flat face, and 5) marked microcephaly. As these individuals reach school age, they begin to show psychomotor backwardness and severe learning disabilities (Victor & Ropper, 2002). FAS tends to be underreported in the literature. Recent estimates suggest that, among 1,000 live births, less than one of those would meet the criteria for FAS (CDC, 1997). FAS is likely underreported for two reasons: 1) physicians do not always screen pregnant mothers for substance abuse or dependence and 2) pregnant mothers might be dishonest or may not discuss their drinking patterns with the physician because they truly do not see themselves as having a problem.

Alcohol and traffic fatalities. Nearly half of all traffic fatalities are alcohol-related (i.e., either the driver or nonoccupant had a blood alcohol concentration, BAC, over 0.01g/L; National Highway Traffic Safety Administration, NHTSA, 1989). In 2001 alone, alcohol was implicated in almost 20,000 motor vehicular deaths (NHTSA, 2002). Sadly, approximately 25% of all traffic deaths, involving children under 15 years of age, were alcohol-related; two-thirds of which involved a legally drunk driver (i.e., BAC=0.10g/L in most states; CDC, 1991). In a recent federal report, it was estimated that alcohol-related vehicular crashes cost Americans over $50 billion each year (Blicoe et al., 2002).

Alcohol and suicide. Major Depressive Disorder and alcohol dependence have the highest correlations with those who have successfully committed suicide (Hendriksson et al., 1993). Men in their 50s and 60s are particularly susceptible, especially after exhausting their social supports on account of their drinking (Szanto et al., 2001). Also related to alcohol abuse/dependence and suicide is the age of onset of the disorder. Namely, a person who starts drinking in his or her teens is four times as likely to attempt suicide than an individual who abuses alcohol late in life (Buydens-Branchey, Branchey, & Noumir, 1989).

Alcoholism and the workplace. Individuals who are dependent on or abuse alcohol are absent from work 4-8 times more often than nonabusers (U.S. Department of Labor, 1991). When they are at work, alcohol abusers are markedly less productive when compared to nonabusers. In fact, productivity losses on account of alcohol are estimated at over $100 billion annually (U.S. Chamber of Commerce, 1990).

Alcohol and violence. About a third of the time, reported violence between partners is alcohol-related, where the male is usually intoxicated at the time of the assault (Leadley, Clark, & Caetano, 2000). Alcohol is also implicated in many cases of child sexual abuse (Widom, 1993). Namely, the perpetrator is usually under the influence when he or she abuses the child. While many perpetrators are under the influence of alcohol when they commit crimes, alcohol also plays a major role in increasing the likelihood that a person will become victimized. It is widely known that alcohol impairs judgment, disrupts balance, and affects reaction time. In a recent study that reviewed 80 studies of violent offenders, alcohol did not only play a major role with about half of the perpetrators but with about half of the victims as well (Roizer, 1993). Date rape, for example, almost invariably involves alcohol for both victims and perpetrators.

Organization of this Volume

Chapter 2. Although the incidence of substance abuse is increasing, the problems of addiction have been largely ignored in psychotherapy and mental health. Professionals either see addiction as falling outside their scope of practice, deferring to specialty care, or they have simply given up hope on account of the fact that traditional psychotherapeutic or biomedical treatments have been largely ineffective or worse, iatrogenic (e.g., a methadone addiction [i.e., treatment] exacerbating a heroin addiction). Cummings, in his presidential address delivered to the American Psychological Association, provides evidence for why traditional approaches have failed. In lieu of these, he proffers a competing approach based on over a decade of research he calls "Exclusion Therapy." Cummings's chapter will describe the basic structure and rationale for this psychological model of treating addictions.

Chapter 3. Cummings and Cummings describe the characteristics of an addict. Contrary to popular belief, addicts are not restricted to prostitutes, inner-city youths, and violent felons. As it turns out, everyone from all walks of life is susceptible to developing an addiction. Moreover, there is a confluence of several points of view that make detection of an addict particularly difficult when they present to therapy. First, from a cultural point of view, addicts might be overlooked because their substance use is (wrongly) deemed appropriate given the fact that they belong to a particular cultural or ethnic group where use of the substance is pervasive (e.g., drinking wine with every meal). Second, from a patient's point of view, addicts are extremely apt at identifying substance abuse in others though, on account of "denial," fail to see it in themselves. Third, from their family's point of view, they might have a vested interest in the person remaining an abuser, so-called "enabling." Perhaps, these individuals benefit from their enabling role (i.e., "co-dependency"). Fourth, from the medical point of view, because "physical cravings" on withdrawal have to manifest before one is said to have an addiction, many substance abusers who do not fall into this category are overlooked, even though substance use markedly interferes with daily functioning. By contrast, in response to these, Cummings and Cummings provide what they call "a pragmatic point of view." The authors propose a hybrid model, incorporating elements from both medical and psychological models, targeting these erroneous points of view.

Chapter 4. Most patients with substance abuse problems present in primary care settings, oftentimes with other complaints, peripherally related. Accordingly, given that substance abuse can be elusive during routine visits, early detection and treatment are key. In Chapter 4, Cummings and Cummings describe the types of clinical presentations associated with various drugs of addiction (e.g., stimulants, depressants, opiates, hallucinogens, and poly-substance abuse); the emphasis of which is on detecting these warning signs of addiction.

Chapter 5. Despite the fact that chemical dependency is prevalent in about ¼ of patients seen in primary care, most health care administrators and planners regard substance abuse treatment as specialty care. Given that substance abusers utilize several times the amount of medical/surgical care, this manner of thinking can no longer be tolerated in light of this nation's "health care crisis." A move toward integrating behavioral care with primary care in the frontline detection and treatment of chemical dependency is paramount, if we are ever to mount the inflationary spiral of health care expenses in the United States. Studies have shown that developing and implementing substance programs with an eye on early detection and intervention can dramatically improve health outcomes and create significant financial benefits. In Chapter 5 the authors describe several successful early treatment programs within integrated care settings.

Chapter 6. Primary care physicians often find it a challenge to directly approach a patient with evidence of substance abuse. Given that they are oftentimes over-worked and pressed for time, they simply do not have the means to adequately address substance abuse in their practices. Placing a behavioral health consultant into primary care is a viable solution to this problem. Shaffer's chapter reviews a number of the concerns having to do with integrating behavioral health consultants into primary care and how these may be approached. This chapter also explains the activities of the behavioral consultant, particularly in regards to decreasing barriers to entering into substance abuse treatment.

Chapter 7. Alcohol misuse is a major public health problem contributing to premature morbidity and mortality in the United States. Runyan's chapter describes a successful integrated care model used in the United States Air Force that employs behavioral health specialists in the early detection and treatment of alcohol misuse. This approach is an excellent example of how to execute the public health perspective at the level of polices and procedures. Runyan also discusses the potential benefits of integrated care on the part of administration, primary care physician, and patient.

Chapter 8. Alcohol abuse and dependence are among the most common and most serious disorders affecting primary care patients. They are also among the most likely to lead to referrals to primary care physicians by self or others. Common early complaints by these patients can include depression and anxiety, sleep problems, family and marital discord, vague somatic symptoms, and difficulties in concentration and problem-solving. Nathan's chapter will discuss how the CAGE can serve as a useful instrument in the early detection of alcohol abuse and dependence. While referral to an alcoholism specialist for treatment is often indicated, primary care physicians themselves have reported some success after learning to use motivational interviewing to heighten patients' motivation to confront their abusive drinking.

Chapter 9. Oslin's chapter reviews the most recent literature on the treatment of at-risk alcohol use and alcohol dependence among older adults. Several recent intervention studies have been completed and will serve to shed light on best practices for the broad array of treatment needs that seniors face. Topics to be covered include the treatment of at-risk drinking, the treatment of alcohol dependence, the treatment of alcohol dependence concurrent with other behavioral health problems and policy implications for identifying and treating older adults.

Chapter 10. According to the National Household Survey on Drug Abuse (National Institute on Drug Abuse [NIDA], 2001), approximately 4 million people over the age of 12 are using prescription medications for non-medical purposes.

Opioids, commonly prescribed for pain management due to their analgesic properties, are among the most commonly abused prescription drugs. Opioids alleviate pain by working directly on the brain and spinal cord (CNS). Functionally, opioids lower a person's awareness of pain. For the chronic pain sufferer, opioids prescribed on an "as needed" or per (PRN) basis are especially problematic. Many patients take so much medication that they literally "knock themselves out" in their attempt to rid themselves of the pain. Persons using prescribed pain medication may develop a drug tolerance. Surveys with chronic non-cancer pain patients indicate that tolerance can occur in up to 75% of cases (Jamison et al., 1994). Once tolerance develops, withdrawal in the form of intense pain will occur after the person stops taking the drugs. Patients on opioid therapies have significantly more hospitalizations and more surgeries than patients not taking opioids (Turner et al., 1982). Moreover, patients using opioid have a higher rate of unemployment relative to patients using non-opioid therapies in managing their pain (Jamison et al., 1994).

Another class of medications that are commonly abused is central nervous system depressants, including barbiturates and benzodiazepines. These medications are primarily used as sleep aids and for anxiety management. Prolonged use of high doses may lead to drug tolerance and withdrawal symptoms should use of the medication end too abruptly. Many of the withdrawal symptoms are comparable to alcohol withdrawal (e.g., delirium tremens). CNS depressants are often implicated in accidents (e.g., falls), as a person's reaction time, balance, and psychomotor reactivity are compromised (Sorock & Shimkin, 1988).

Prescription drug abuse is common among patients seen in primary care settings, yet prescription drug abuse is often overlooked by physicians. Primary care physicians can play a major role in reducing prescription drug abuse by learning to identify drug-seeking behavior, by educating patients about their medication regimens, and by setting firm but reasonable prescribing guidelines for their practices. In Chapter 10 of this volume, Isaacson describes how physicians can take a more active role in early detection and treatment of prescription drug abuse, placing only a minimal additional burden on primary care physicians.

Chapter 11. Despite the fact that over 90 causes of death have been attributed to smoking, about 50 million adults continue to smoke in the United States (Shultz et al. 1991). According to Centers for Disease Control (2003), cigarette smoking is related to approximately 440,000 deaths each year (1 in every 5), costing the nation

$150 billion annually, $75 billion in medical expenditures and $80 in indirect costs (i.e., lost productivity). Relatively speaking, smoking ranks first among the most prominent contributors to premature death, outranking poor diet/inactivity patterns, alcohol, and firearms (McGinnis & Foege, 1993).

Since the Surgeon General's first report on smoking in 1964, studies demonstrating the adverse effects of smoking have proliferated. According to the American Lung Association (2003), smoking causes 87 % of lung cancer cases and is implicated in most cases of emphysema and chronic bronchitis. Over and above respiratory ailments, smoking also plays a major role in coronary heart disease and stroke, especially when combined with other poor lifestyle patterns (The Vestfold Heartcare Study Group, 2003). As with other substances, smoking can result in deleterious health effects for persons other than the smoker. Smoking is associated with fetal defects and growth delays (Higgins, 2002), with babies of mothers who smoke during pregnancy having a 27% higher mortality rate during the prenatal period than mothers who do not smoke (Cushner, 1981).

Smoking is considered the most preventable cause of death and illness in America. Although the nicotine patch stands as the most widely employed treatment for smoking, the effectiveness of nicotine replacement therapy is greatly enhanced when used in conjunction with behavioral interventions. In Chapter 11 of this volume, David Antonuccio reviews patterns of nicotine use and provides an overview of pharmacological and behavioral interventions for smoking that includes estimates of treatment effectiveness. A step-by-step guide to behavioral smoking cessation is also included.

Conclusion

Substance abuse is a major public health concern affecting the lives of millions of Americans. Although the science of substance abuse treatment remains highly controversial, there is mounting evidence that identifying and treating substance-related problems in primary care settings can produce beneficial outcomes. This makes sense when one considers the fact that most substance abusers frequently turn up in primary care. In spite of the motivation behind the visit, primary care professionals have a unique opportunity to prevent substance abuse from running a chronic course. For this reason and the fact that treatment in primary care is looked upon as less stigmatizing, primary care settings are the ideal entree point for detection and treatment of substance abuse.

References

American Lung Association. (2003). *American Lung Association state of tobacco control: 2003 Report.* Retrieved January 22, 2004, from http://www2.lungusa.org/tobacco/

American Psychiatric Association. (2000). *Quick reference to the diagnostic criteria from DSM-IV-TR.* Washington, DC: Author.

American Psychiatric Association. (1994). *Diagnostic and statistical manual of mental disorders* (4th ed.). Washington, DC: Author.

Blincoe, L., Seay, A., Zaloshnja, E., Miller, T., Romano, E., Lucter, S., & Spicer, R. (2002). *The economic impact of motor vehicle crashes, 2000.* Washington, D.C.: National Highway Traffic Safety Administration, U.S. Department of Transportation. Retrieved May 12, 2003, from http://nhtsa.dot.gov/people/economic/econimpact2000/index.htm

Buydens-Branchey, L., Branchey, M. H., & Noumair, D. (1989). Age of alcoholism onset: I. Relationship to psychopathology. *Archives of General Psychiatry, 46,* 230-255.

Centers for Disease Control. (2003). Deaths: Final data for 2001. *National Vital Statistics Report.* Retrieved January 22, 2004, from http://www.cdc.gov/nchs/data/nvsr/nvsr52/nvsr52_03.pdf

Centers for Disease Control. (2003). *Targeting tobacco use: The nation's leading cause of death 2003.* Department of Health and Human Services.

Centers for Disease Control. (1997). Surveillance for fetal alcohol syndrome using multiple sources—Atlanta, Georgia, 1981–1989. *Morbidity and Mortality Weekly Report, 46,*1118–20.

Centers for Disease Control. (1991). Alcohol-related fatalities among youth and young adults – United States, 1982-1989. *Morbidity and Mortality Weekly Report, 40,* 178-179, 185-187.

Criqui, M. H. (1987). The roles of alcohol in the epidemiology of cardiovascular diseases. *Acta Medica Scandinavica Supplementum,717,* 73-85.

Cushner, I. M. (1981). Maternal behavior and perinatal risks: Alcohol, smoking, and drugs. *Annual Review of Public Health, 2,* 201-218.

Grant, B. F. (1996). DSM-IV, DSM-III-R, and ICD-10 alcohol and drug abuse/harmful use and dependence, United States, 1992. *Alcoholism: Clinical and Experimental Research, 10,* 1481-1488.

Hendriksson, M. M., Aro, H. M., Marttunen, M. J., et al. (1993). Mental disorders and comorbidity in suicide. *American Journal of Psychiatry, 150,* 935-940.

Hester, R. K. (1995). Behavioral self-control training. In R. K. Hester, & W. R. Miller (Eds.), *Handbook of alcoholism treatment approaches: Effective alternatives* (2nd ed.) (pp. 148-159). Needham Heights, MA: Allyn and Bacon.

Higgins, S. (2002). Smoking in pregnancy. *Current Opinion in Obstetrics & Gynecology, 14(2),* 145-51.

Jamison, R. N., Anderson, K. O., Peeters-Asdourian, C., & Ferrante, F. M. (1994). Survey of opioid use in chronic nonmalignant pain patients. *Regional Anesthesia, 19(4),* 225230.

Kim, W. R., Gross, J. B., Poterucha, J. J., Locke, G. R., & Dickson, E. R. (2001). Outcome of hospital care of liver disease associated with hepatitis C in the United States. *Hepatology, 33,* 201-206.

Langlais, P. J. (1995). Alcohol-related thiamin deficiency: impact on cognitive and memory functioning. *Alcohol Health Res. World,19,* 113-121.

Larimer, M. E., Palmer, R. S., & Marlatt, A. (1999). Relapse prevention: an overview of Marlatt's Cognitive-Behavioral Model. *Alc. Res. Hlth., 23(2),* 151-160.

Leadley, K., Clark, C. L., & Caetano, R. (2000). Couples' drinking patterns, intimate partner violence, and alcohol-related partnership problems. *Journal of Substance Abuse, 11*, 253-263.

Lieber, C. S. (2001). Alcohol and hepatitis C. *Alcohol Res. Health, 25(4)*, 245-54.

Mark, T. L., Woody, G. E., Juday, T., & Kleber, H. D. (2001). The Economic Costs of Heroin Addiction in the United States. *Drug Alcohol Depend., 61*, 195-206.

Marlatt, G. A., & Witkiewitz, K. (2002). Harm reduction approaches to alcohol use: Health promotion, prevention, and treatment. *Addictive Behaviors, 27*, 867-886.

McGinnis, J. M., & Foege, W. H. (1993). Mortality and morbidity attributable to the use of addictive substances in the United States. *Proceedings of the Association of American Physicians, 111*, 109-118.

Miller, N. S., & Gold, M. S. (1993). A neurochemical basis for alcohol and other drug addiction. *Journal of Psychoactive Drugs, 25*, 121-128.

Mukherjee, A. B., & Hodgen, G. D. (1982). Maternal ethanol exposure induces transient impairment of umbilical circulation and fetal hypoxia in monkeys. *Science, 218*, 700-702.

National Highway Traffic Safety Administration. (2002). *Traffic safety facts 2001: Alcohol.* Washington, D.C.: U.S. Department of Transportation, National Highway Traffic Safety Administration. Retrieved May 12, 2003, from http://www.nrd.nhtsa.dot.gov/pdf/nrd-30/ncsa/tsf2001/2001alcohol.pdf.

National Highway Traffic Safety Administration. (1989). *Drunk driving facts.* Washington, D.C.: U.S. Department of Transportation, National Highway Traffic Safety Administration.

National Institute on Alcohol Abuse and Alcoholism. (1990). *Seventh special report to the U.S. Congress on alcohol and health* (U.S. Department of Health and Human Services Publication No. ADM 90-1656). Washington, DC: U.S. Government Printing Office.

National Institute on Drug Abuse. (2001). *Research report series: Prescription drugs/abuse and addiction.* Retrieved May 12, 2003, from http://www.drugabuse.gov/Infofax/PainMed.html

Paul, G. L. (1969). Behavior modification research: Design and tactics. In C. M. Franks (Ed.), *Behavior therapy: Appraisal and status* (pp. 29-62). New York: McGraw Hill.

Shultz, J. M., Novotny, T. E., & Rice, D. P. (1991). Quantifying the disease impact of cigarette smoking with SAMMEC II Software. *Public Health Reports, 106*, 326-333.

Sorock, G. S., & Shimkin, E. E. (1988). Benzodiazepine sedatives and the risk of falling in a community-dwelling elderly cohort. *Archives of Internal Medicine, 148*, 2441-4.

Szanto, K., Prigerson, H. G., & Reynolds, C. F. (2001). Suicide in the elderly. *Clinical Neuroscience Research, 1*, 366-376.

The Vestfold Heartcare Study Group. (2003). Influence on lifestyle measures and five-year coronary risk by a comprehensive lifestyle intervention programme in patients with coronary heart disease. *Journal of Cardiovascular Risk, 10(6)*, 429-437.

Turner, J., Calsyn, D. A., Fordyce, W. E., & Ready, L. B. (1982). Drug utilization patterns in chronic pain patients. *Pain, 12*, 357363.

U.S. Chamber of Commerce. (1990). *Corporate initiatives for a drug free workplace.*

U.S. Department of Labor. (1991). *What works: Workplaces without drugs.*

Victor, M., & Ropper, A. H. (2002). *Manual of neurology* (7ᵗʰ ed.). New York: McGraw-Hill.

Widom, C. S. (1993). Child abuse and alcohol use and abuse. In S. E. Martin (Ed.), *Alcohol and interpersonal violence: Fostering multidisciplinary perspectives* (pp. 291-314). Rockville, MD: U.S. Department of Health and Services, Public Health Service, National Institutes of Health, National Institute on Alcohol Abuse and Alcoholism.

World Health Organization. (2001). *The World Health Report 2001 – Mental health: A new understanding, new hope.* Geneva: World Health Organization.

Turning Bread Into Stones:
Our Modern Antimiracle

(first published in 1979)

Nicholas A. Cummings, Ph.D., Sc.D.
University of Nevada, Reno and the
Cummings Foundation for Behavioral Health

We are told in the New Testament (Matthew 4:3) that while Christ was wandering in the wilderness, the Devil tempted Him by saying, "If indeed thou be the Son of God, cast those stones into bread." That would have been the ancient miracle. Let us move forward in time almost 2,000 years to 1975, the last year for which the National Institute Of Alcoholism and Alcohol Abuse (NIAAA) and the National Institute of Drug Abuse (NIDA) have figures.

In 1975, alcoholism, its treatment, and its related problems cost the United States $43 billion (NIAAA, Note 1). During that same year, drug abuse and drug-abuse-related problems cost this country $10.5 billion (NIDA, Note 2), for a combined total of $53 billion, or 2.5% of the gross national product for that year.

Economists have asked how long our society can support such a price before productivity is affected. Many experts think we have already turned that corner. Startling as it may seem, 1 of every 11 adult Americans suffers from a severe addictive problem. Drug addiction is epidemic among teenagers: One of every 6 teenagers suffers from a severe addictive problem. At any given time on our nation's highways, an average of 1 of every 12 drivers is too drunk to drive. We must not over look the iatrogenic contribution: At any given time, 1 of every 7 Americans is regularly taking a psychotropic drug prescribed by a physician. Worst of all, the overmedication of our elderly is a national disgrace. Often in clinical practice what appeared to be early senile confusion clears up once the elderly individual is removed from mind-altering prescription drugs that have special side effects for older persons, or from several sometimes incompatible medications prescribed by three or four physicians concurrently.

Our Drug-Oriented Society

We have indeed become a drug-oriented society. I am not making any judgment about that; this may be good or bad, depending on your perspective. It may be that the mental health movement has promised the American people a freedom from anxiety that is neither possible nor realistic, resulting in an expectation that we have a right to feel good.

We may never know to what extent we ourselves have contributed to the steep rise in alcohol consumption and to the almost universal reliance by physicians on the tranquilizer.

What this translates to is that addictive problems are going to take up more and more of our practice. In a recent survey, 23% of a random sample of psychotherapy patients seen in a large metropolitan mental health center were suffering problems substantially exacerbated by alcohol or drug abuse, and only 3.5% of these were so identified by their own therapists (Cummings, Note 3).

Our drug-oriented society has spawned new industries, and I will only give you three examples. The "free zone" in Miami is the passageway for contraband from Colombia: Literally pounds of cocaine and tons of marijuana come into Miami daily. It is called a free zone because the authorities are totally helpless to stop the drug traffic, and we see entire boatloads of drugs seized and the seamen deported only to show up again within days with another boatload.

In California, where the giant redwoods used to grow but have now been logged, the five most remote northern counties have experienced an economic depression. A new industry is replacing the lumber industry: the growing of marijuana in 7-10-acre plots deep in the forest and hidden from the narcs (narcotics agents). I had the opportunity to visit one of these marijuana-growing communes recently, something you cannot do alone because the foils, traps, and snares that have been created to fool the narc are as complete as the foils, traps, and snares that are set up in the hills of the rural South where moonshiners are avoiding the revenuer. The marijuana growers even seem to dress and talk the same, but there is one important difference: In the South you seldom see 5- and 6-year-olds stoned out of their minds, like I did in the northern counties of California.

I will mention only one other new industry you may not have heard of: Chronic cocaine use so degenerates the nasal membranes that in California, plastic surgeons are inserting plastic passages in the nostrils of chronic cocaine users who have destroyed their natural passages. I could list many more new industries resulting from society's drug orientation, not the least of which is our multi-million-dollar drug paraphernalia industry.

A Psychological Model of Addiction

The medical profession is totally unprepared to deal with addiction. The medical model treats addiction to one substance by substituting another substance. In this way we used heroin to cure morphine addiction. We now use methadone to cure heroin addiction, Valium to cure alcoholism, amphetamines to cure carbohydrate and sugar addiction. I would suggest to you that the medical model, which plays a kind of addictive musical chairs, is a total failure because it actually escalates the problem in severity. Attempts to educate physicians about the dangers of substitute addiction or overmedication are difficult, if not often futile. The prescription pad is the number one item in the physician's armamentarium and is one of the very few truly licensable medical activities.

I would like to present to you a psychological model that has its roots 16 years ago in San Francisco in the treatment of the runaways to the Haight-Ashbury district of San Francisco and the Telegraph Avenue area of Berkeley. At that time I was codirector of the Golden Gate Mental Health Center, a privately financed community mental health agency. I was treating these runaways, under California law, which allows teenagers to receive treatment for addiction or sex problems without parental consent, something that could not be obtained in these cases.

In one way I was fortunate to be in San Francisco, because we felt the shock waves of a drug oriented society fully 10 years before the rest of the nation. You may laugh at what happens in California, but whether you talk about the patio, the barbeque pit, the divorce rate, the hot tub, the cocaine party, or Levis, today's California fad becomes commonplace throughout the nation within 5-15 years. The drug cult and the waves of drug taking we saw in San Francisco in the mid 1960s are now commonplace across the land.

What I would like to do is describe a treatment approach that began some 16 years ago and introduce it by some formal comments about the causes of addiction. We just do not know what they are. We know a lot about addiction, none of which satisfactorily explains causality, but the interesting thing is that one does not need to know cause in order to intervene. There is a growing body of evidence which indicates that some people are born with a genetic predisposition to become addicted (Kandel, 1976). For others it is congenital and in utero; for example, very small amounts of alcohol imbibed by the mother during certain months of pregnancy predispose a child to alcoholism (Julien, 1978). So compelling is this evidence that a couple of years ago, the Food and Drug Administration considered requiring a label on bottles of alcohol stating that even small amounts of alcohol are dangerous to pregnancy. This would have been a very unpopular move, and I think that is why it was dropped. There is alcohol and drug addiction that is acquired (Blum et al., 1972; Peele & Brodsky, 1975). These causes are difficult to demonstrate, and the bottom line has yet to be written in any of them. Apparently, some people must have had a genetic predisposition, because the first time they took a glass of beer at the age of 11, they were alcoholics. Others seem to acquire the addiction. There is no question that the frequent ingestion of any addictive substance is sufficiently reinforcing so that everyone takes the risk of addiction. Yet not everyone becomes addicted, even children born of women who are heroin addicts. Although 92% of these infants show severe withdrawal upon birth, 8% do not, and the presence or absence of withdrawal has nothing to do with the amount of heroin the mother has taken. These are all questions for which we do not have the answers, so in treating my clients, I tell them the answers don't matter. In our program we stress the concept that addiction is something for which the individual can and has to take responsibility. I give the following example to my clients: We do not know what causes diabetes. We know it is a failure of the isles of Langerhans in the pancreas to produce insulin, but why one person's isles of Langerhans fail and another's do not is irrelevant to treatment. Some families seem to be predisposed to the disease, and others do not; in many cases individuals seem to acquire it through prolonged obesity. In any case, the answer is abstinence from sugar. The first, first, first thing one must do when confronted with an addict is convince that person that the prerequisite intervention in the addiction is abstinence from the chemical to which one is addicted.

In our program we stress that the concept of addiction as a disease is useless because it implies that one is helpless and cannot do anything about it. We say that least important of all is the debate over what is habitual and what is addictive. The medical definition of an addictive substance has to do with whether or not physical withdrawal occurs when a person is deprived of that chemical. I submit to you that the physical withdrawal from heroin is 72-90 hours. The psychological withdrawal is the rest of your life. The same thing is true with alcohol, amphetamine, tranquilizer, or barbiturate abuse: The psychological reinforcement is the crucial factor. An excellent example is the history of thousands of heroin-addicted combat troops in Vietnam who readily gave up their narcotics use once they were back home and the psychological factors encouraging their addiction were removed (Peele, 1978). I say to my clients, "Do not ask whether a chemical is addictive or habituating," and they understand when I point out that although cocaine is regarded in medicine as not addictive, it is so highly reinforcing that cocaine dependency will not be abated even though the drug costs $2,500-$3,000 an ounce, will burn out your nasal passages, and produces such behavioral side effects as paranoia and grandiosity.

I would like to give a fascinating example of "addiction" in a hospital during the days when alcoholics were placed in locked wards. In this instance the hospitalized moved their cots into the bathroom while the staff looked on, baffled. After several days it was found that these alcoholics had substituted water for alcohol. If one drinks eight gallons or more of water per day, the pH level of the blood is altered and one becomes intoxicated. The consequence of this was that the patients had to move their cots to the bathroom to be near the spout and the toilet, because eight gallons of water per day results in constant drinking and urinating. So I say to my clients, "Do not ask me about what is addictive and what is not. If you are an addictive personality, you can even get addicted to water."

So it is irrelevant whether addicts lack endorphins, the natural substances in the brain that mitigate against pain and help us survive unpleasantness, and whether this is genetic, in utero, or acquired. I now want to describe to you how we treat addiction, a method that after several years of trial at the Golden Gate Mental Health Center became the backbone of the addiction treatment program at Kaiser-Permanente in San Francisco, and one that is used in several other programs throughout the United States (Cummings, Note 4, Note 5).

I tell my clients that addiction is not merely popping something into one's mouth but a constellation of behaviors that constitute a way of life. An addict can be likened to an unfinished house that has only an attic and a basement. When one falls out of the attic, one falls all the way down to the basement because there are no intervening floors to stop the fall. My addicts know exactly what I mean, because they know only two moods: elation and depression. They do not know what normal is. They do not experience the limited, normal mood swings common to other persons, because when they start to fall out of the attic, they run quickly to the bottle, the pill, the needle, anything to prevent falling clear down to the basement. So, indeed, the first thing we have to teach them is how to build a floor in that house, because you cannot live just in elation or depression. As one philosopher put it, those who are chronically depressed are damned to pursue pleasure constantly for the rest of their lives.

I remember that during the early days in the Haight-Ashbury, adolescent runaways came to me because they did not want to go to the city clinics, which were required to report addiction. Many got their money from Philadelphia, or Atlanta, or wherever their parents would send the money on the promise they would not come back home and embarrass the family. Others, both girls and boys, sold their bodies on the street to make their bread; still others stole or sold dope. At that time I realized what it costs to keep a habit going, and this is where the title of my address comes from. Using the vernacular I learned from my teenage runaways 15 or 16 years ago, it takes an awful lot of bread to make a stone. This is our modern antimiracle. In the beginning I treated addiction in the traditional, ineffective fashion, using the premise that one need not confront and prohibit the addictive behavior; through insight and understanding the client will come to lose the compulsive craving. This was before I recognized that addicts are extremely adept at playing this psychotherapy game and do not need the collaboration of an incompetent therapist to perpetuate their addiction under the guise of seeking help. I will never forget the time a young man in one group said to me, "Nick, you are never going to help us as long as we are hitting." I asked what he meant and he wisely indicated that "whether we see you once a week, twice a week, three times a week, or every day, hitting is so pleasurable, we can wipe out all the psychotherapy you give us with one pill or a touch of the needle." He was right, and for the first time in my professional career I learned that all insight is soluble in alcohol or drugs. So in that group we made a commitment to total abstinence for a period of three months. They all agreed but came in the following week and tried to talk me out of it. I said no, that we had made a commitment and I insisted we honor it. They did, and it was the first group of teenage runaways that I was able to help not only to give up drugs but also to become reconnected to life. After that I began to develop with these and other teenagers a system of treatment wherein the client earns his or her way into the treatment situation and continues to earn a place in that treatment situation by making gradual steps agreed on in advance. Failure to meet agreed-on standards results in various degrees of exclusion, and finally one may be thrown completely out of the program. This is why Wolfgang Lederer, seeing a demonstration, named it *exclusion therapy*. I did not like the name at first, but I have since come to regard it as a proper title based on truth in packaging. We anticipated therapeutic contracts before these became popular or standard, and today I make a detailed contract with every client very early in our sessions. As I show below, the technique is a combination of (a) therapeutic contracts, (b) reality therapy, (c) operant conditioning, (d) insight therapy, (e) brief psychotherapy, (f) communication theory employing the double-bind and para-doxical intention, and (g) group therapy, all melded into a system of "psycho-judo," wherein the addict's own massive resistance is used to propel him or her toward giving up the addictive life-style. Although individual sessions are used to establish a transference and to motivate the client toward health, the job really gets done in the group as these persons who, as teenage or adult addicts, are fixated at the adolescent level of rebelliousness and acting out. At this level peer pressure has its greatest impact, and the newfound peer pressure toward health of the group is the ultimate ingredient in solidifying a determination to clean up.

Intervention Phase 1: Withdrawal

Addicts do not come to us to be helped for their addiction. They come to us because they are about to lose something or have lost something. It may be a spouse, a job, a driver's license, freedom (threat of jail), or health (e.g., cirrhosis of the liver, esophageal hemorrhaging). Essentially, they come wanting the therapist to bring back the halcyon days when drugs worked and made them feel mellow. The therapist must start with the full realization that the client does not really intend to give up either drugs or the way of life. During the first half of the first session the therapist must listen very intently. Then, somewhere in midsession, using all of his or her rigorous training, therapeutic acumen, and the third, fourth, fifth, and sixth ears, the therapist discerns some unresolved wish, some long-gone dream that is still residing deep in that human being, and then the therapist pulls it out and ignites the client again. This is not easy, because if the right nerve is not touched the therapist loses the client. Some readers will erroneously regard our approach to treating addiction as harsh or punitive in its stark sense of reality. Whitaker's (Note 6) admonition is important here: Because the therapist's distance can be destructive in psycho-therapy, we tend to emphasize closeness too much. A good therapist is one who can commingle closeness and distance as is appropriate at the moment. An inept therapist is one who has only one approach, either closeness or distance. Because addictive persons have character disorders, they behave in infuriating ways. To become angry (even unconsciously) at some-one with a character disorder results in the forfeiture of the therapist's ability to help. Exclusion therapy provides a time-limited microcosm of the real world that enables the therapist to be close when needed but distant enough to avoid anger when the client behaves in an infuriating manner.

Some will also erroneously prejudge exclusion therapy as manipulative. Haley (1976) pointed out that all good psychotherapists manipulate. The inept therapist is often the one who cannot admit this, so that manipulation is to the benefit of the therapist rather than of the client. As I show below, game playing is a cardinal feature of addicts, whose negative or destructive games must be countered with positive or healthy games.

Once the client is motivated to continue in the first session, I advise my client, to his or her amazement, that I will not make a second appointment until he or she is clean. For the heroin addict this mean 3 days, for the alcoholic it means14 days, for the barbiturate addict it means 10 days, for the amphetamine addict it means 7 days. Most clients today are what I call cafeteria addicts; they take anything placed before them, and while remaining constantly stoned, they pride themselves that they are not really addicted to any one substance. The cafeteria addict is required to stay clean for 10 days, and the withdrawal really drives home the fact that he or she has become dependent on being stoned. I say to them, "I will not even give you a second appointment until you call me up and say to me, 'Nick, I'm clean.'" Because of the addicts' negativism, the refusal to see them sets up a challenge they cannot ignore. They become determined to go clean in order to foil the therapist, who expresses out loud doubts that they can really do it. Heroin addicts are amazed that I will not put them in the hospital. What I do is find a friend who has never been on drugs, and I give that person a crash course in taking care of somebody who is going through withdrawal. Then I call the client and the sitter every two hours, day and night for three days. On each call I have the client tell me what is being experienced, and I tell them exactly what they will feel during the next two hours. This removes the terror from the unknown. Then there comes a point somewhere around the 60th or 70th hour when I am able to report to the client that he or she has crested: "From now on, every time we talk you are going to feel a little better. You won't be out of the woods for a couple of more days, but you will feel better every time we talk."

When I am asked why I do not hospitalize patients who are withdrawing, I answer with an axiom: "Degree of pain is directly proportional to the proximity of the sympathetic physician. In other words, the hospital is where all the drugs are, and if you scream enough and hurt enough, at 3:00 in the morning some intern or nurse will not be able to resist giving you the needle, and that means if you are on your second day you may have to start at Square 1 again." I say to them, "It hurts more in the hospital because the drugs are there." They hear me.

Addicts use what I call the street-paver syndrome. Have you noticed that when a street is torn up to replace underground utilities, the street pavers put the pavement back, but never at quite the same height? It is either half an inch too low or half an inch too high, so passing cars hit a bump. Similarly, addicts will always comply, but not quite. The heroin addict will demand an appointment one hour before the 72 hours are up. The alcoholic will call one day before the 14 days are up. When the heroin addict calls, I say, "Don't call me now, I can't give you another appointment. You call me in an hour." When the alcoholic calls, I say, "Your time is up at 3:30 tomorrow afternoon." They reply that I am the craziest doctor they have ever encountered, and they slam down the telephone vowing never to call again. One hour or 24 hours later to the moment they telephone. No matter what the therapist is doing, it is imperative that the client be seen that day. I am often scheduled as late as 10:00 or 11:00 at night and must see them after that. The client recognizes the commitment of the therapist and never forgets it. I have clients all over California who shake their heads and say, "My second appointment with that guy was at 1:30 in the morning. How do you turn down a guy like that?"

Our treatment has been devised into a set of easily appreciated and understood axioms that reduce the "analgesic experience," as Peele (1978) has called the life-style of the addict, into easily understood phrases which may seem simplistic but which, to the addict, are like words of wisdom. The addict uses what has been called "the cutoff," a form of denial in which the addict tunes out anything that touches on his or her addiction. These simple axioms have a propensity to break through the cutoff. Scare tactics are counterproductive. Telling an alcoholic that cirrhosis will kill is enough to drive him or her to drink.

When addicts first come in, they are determined not to see you. They are there because their spouse, their boss, their probation officer, their doctor, somebody has said, "You've got to do something about this addiction." They come in determined to convince the therapist that they do not need to be seen. During the course of the first interview, after having ascertained the precious deeply buried wish, I say, "It's a shame that you have this dream, but you are not ready to give up your addiction and I can't see you." The first response from this person who came in determined not to continue is rage and a demand to be seen. Addicts are determined to do the opposite of whatever you tell them, and here is where the double bind is useful. When you tell them you won't see them, they get furious. One must start with whatever the client brings to the first session, so the therapist takes seriously the need to get out of trouble. But the client must be helped to see the long-term problem and that the future under the present life-style is bleak. This is done not by reasoning, which will be tuned out, but by outmaneuvering the negativism. With every intent of helping the client, the therapist suggests possible solutions that can be provided but makes these contingent on fulfilling the required number of days of abstinence. The client is thus placed in another double bind. The therapist states unabashedly that he or she will do every thing possible to help the client out of trouble once the addict is truly a client, a status that is not attained until the client has been clean for the requisite number of days and has earned a second appointment.

During this phase the therapist will be confronted with two related games addicts play. The first of these is, "I can quit any time but I don't want to." The therapist agrees that the client is indeed not ready and would not be able to quit even if he or she wanted to, for if the person were truly not an addict, quitting for the prescribed period would be easy. The client digests this as 'a challenge or counters with a related game: "I cannot quit." The first game is, "I am not really addicted," and the second is, "I am no longer responsible." Using psycho-judo again, the therapist agrees with the client, sighs that the client seems hopelessly addicted or unmotivated, and urges him or her not to really try because it would be an exercise in futility. At this point the client needs an assurance, and the therapist cites one or two examples of successful cases that were similar to the present client but again sighs that this would not seem to apply to him or her.

In the 16 years we have been using this technique, four of five addicts so challenged will respond by meeting the requisite number of days of total abstinence. Of the remainder, about half will call six months to a year' later to announce they have fulfilled their required period of withdrawal. We have even had addicts return triumphantly as much as two years later, having carried the therapist's telephone number with them for that entire period.

Once the client returns for the second interview, the successful withdrawal is lorded over the therapist, who immediately concedes having been wrong about the client, congratulates the client on the victory, and admits how delighted he or she is to have miscalculated the strength and determination of the client. At this point the client has had the first experience in self-mastery and has put the first plank in the floor that is to be eventually built between the attic and basement, as discussed above.

On the second appointment the therapist is able to build on the client's feeling of self-mastery and to agree on a contract wherein each succeeding session is dependent on the client's continuing to remain clean. Each session is begun by asking if the client is clean. If not, there is no session that day, and the client returns the following week at the scheduled time. The client is not permitted to telephone, admitting he or she has had a fall, and then not come in. It is part of the necessary procedure that the client take responsibility for the fall and experience the therapist's reaction. The therapist does not disapprove; he or she merely complies with the agreed-on terms. Interesting things happen during this period: The client attempts unsuccessfully to draw the therapist into the kind of struggles he or she has carried on with coaddicts (parents, spouse, boss, lover, friends).

The next task is to motivate the client for the group program of 24 sessions. This requires 4-12 sessions, depending on the individual. The therapeutic contract for the group program involves an agreement to attend all 24 sessions, to be excluded for any sessions prior to which the client has had a fall, and to be permanently excluded on the fourth fall. Furthermore, the client must pay for all subsequent sessions after permanent exclusion. Because of insurance, this will often mean no money or as little as one dollar, but the weekly bill is a regular reminder that the client is a member in exclusion. This has very frequently motivated the client to return and try again, some thing the excluded addict can do after the 24 sessions have been completed and the group disbands.

At this point a note of caution is important. Some addicts, though the minority, require hospitalization for withdrawal, and it is a matter of considerable expertise to differentiate these. The close collaboration with an internist skilled in the treatment of severe withdrawal is essential. Some alcoholics are on the verge of delirium tremens when first seen. Other alcoholics, as well as barbiturate and Valium addicts, are subject to convulsions on withdrawal. Most of these can be treated without hospitalization by providing the sitter with a "hummer," a dose of the chemical from which the client is withdrawing, to be administered when the client demonstrates signs of impending convulsion. It is important that the existence of the hummer be kept a secret from the withdrawing client, because knowledge of it will surely trigger a convulsion as a means of legitimately obtaining the chemical.

It is interesting that heroin withdrawal, with its severe chills, cramps, and other symptoms, does not present these medical complications. Special mention must be made of Valium withdrawal which persists for as long as six weeks, with recurring waves of severity during which the individual may wander or have convulsions that he or she will not remember. Another drug with a prolonged withdrawal period is methadone, which is given to heroin addicts presumably as an alternative to the isolation and criminal behavior which become so important in the addictive life-style. I have seen the bone aches in methadone withdrawal persist well into the second month.

Intervention Phase 2: The Games

The 10 members in each group all start at once. There is enough flow that new groups are starting at regular intervals. Once the clients have been motivated to come in, the therapist must bear in mind that they have made a 6-month commitment only, after which it is their fond hope that they will become social drinkers or weekend joy poppers. There is an interesting thing about addiction, and it takes the 24 sessions before these clients realize it. Once addicted, no matter how long one remains clean, the addiction remains at the highest achieved level of tolerance for the rest of one's life. This is very easily demonstrated with "foodaholics." A foodaholic may take 20 years to get to 400 pounds. Once a fat cell is formed, it never disappears. Losing weight makes it empty, but it sits there like a flat plastic bag, waiting to be replenished. The foodaholic can shrink back to 175 pounds, but if he or she begins overeating again it is only a matter of a couple of months before the body reaches its greatest attained weight of 400 pounds, because new fat cells do not have to be created. Something similar seems to happen with the addictions to chemicals. This is most easily demonstrated by a heroin addict who took years to build up a $300-a-day habit. That addict can be clean for 5 or 10 years, but if he or she starts to shoot up again, the $300-a-day habit will resume within a brief time. An alcoholic can build up to a quart a day of bourbon over many years. If that person quits and then starts to drink again, the result will be a quart-a-day craving within two weeks. The more you drink, the more you can because your tolerance goes up, except for Valium. Valium has no overdose level. It is the most commonly prescribed drug in America, with 11 billion tablets consumed in the United States in 1975. The only ways one can die on Valium are to swallow enough pills to choke or to mix Valium with alcohol. Valium is usually prescribed in 5-mg pills. Those who are addicted to Valium (another so-called nonaddictive drug) get 20 or 30 physicians to prescribe these 5-mg pills, and they take 700-900 mg per day. A nurse I worked with was taking 1,100 mg of Valium per day, and it was difficult to believe she could carry on her work. On one hand she was a zombie, and on the other hand all she was doing all day was swallowing pills. Debbie has now been clean for seven years.

Once in the group program, the phase called "the games" begins. All addicts play games. The major game played is "the rescue game." All addicts become the focal point of everybody who has a problem. They are called on the phone day and night by friends who tell them their troubles. They play the rescue game no matter how undeserving the person. They attempt to rescue them because when they themselves mess up and are undeserving, they can then feel entitled to be rescued.

Alcoholics Anonymous (AA) turns a destructive rescue game that enables the person to continue to drink into a positive rescue game called sobriety. I have great respect for AA. In our program, however, our goal is to end the rescue game once and for all and free the alcoholic from having to spend the rest of his or her life going to AA meetings or to a psychotherapist. Addicts play games, and they cannot go from destructive games directly to no games. We spend this phase, Phase 2, in teaching them constructive games.

What are some of the games they play? "The rubber ruler" is one of the most frequent and can take many forms. It can consist of telling the bartender to leave the olive out of the martini, with all kinds of jokes about how many cubic centimeters of gin the olive displaces. The real reason is that after seven martinis, the alcoholic does not want to look at an ashtray and see seven toothpicks, because he or she wants to walk out of the bar and say that only three martinis were consumed.

The foodaholic will believe that the giant-sized bag of potato chips he or she just demolished was only one quarter full, when it was really 7/8 full. The rubber ruler can be either stretched or compressed. An addict will often be convinced he or she has been clean for 1½ months when it has only been about 10 days.

"The vending machine" is an interesting game that alcoholics play. It says, "I have been a good boy, I have been a good girl. Why isn't life making it easy for me?" It begins in childhood, when our parents forgive our F in spelling because we did so well in Sunday school two days earlier, even though the two are totally unrelated. Alcoholics continue such childish expectations and demand miracles after having been dry for two or three weeks. Because they have been good, addicts expect life to open up and give them all they want: a better job, a better lover, freedom from their probation officers, instant health.

Another common game is self-pity, and no addicts will resume their addiction until they first get themselves into the vortex of self-pity that makes the thing possible. Self-pity can be justified by a cross word from a boss, a nagging spouse, or a so-called sick society.   All of these become excuses to resume drug activity. In fact, addicts quite frequently precipitate crises in order to justify their addiction, a common ploy being to incite a previously nagging spouse to begin nagging again as an excuse to end a period of sobriety.

In all of these games one sees the addict's careful point-counterpoint in which guilt, justification, absolution, and, punishment abound in complex acting-out patterns that assure the continuation of the addictive life-style. From morning after remorse to contrition when arrested for drunk driving, the addict not only is full of good intentions but manages to suffer in such a way that he or she can continue to view himself or herself as blameless and misunderstood. So the addict settles for what Peele (1978) called "comfortable discomfort." He or she becomes a kind of successful loser who alternates between elation at having fooled the world and depression at the discovery of his or her low self-esteem and lack of self-confidence.

The addict is adroit at playing "the feeling game," so the unwary therapist may be fooled into accepting the counterfeit feelings as genuine insight, just as the addict's friends have been fooled for years. In fact, everyone has had the experience of being shocked to learn that a friend or neighbor who was known for sincerity, concern, and honest feeling turned out to be an addict who had neglected his or her family for years. The therapist would do well to employ only positive changes in behavior over suitable periods of time as the real yardstick to insight or understanding.

"The file card" is an important game because it is an unconscious determination to resume drinking at a certain point in time, or once certain conditions have been fulfilled. In *While Rome Burns*, Alexander Woollcott has one of his characters telephone his hostess of the night before to apologize for missing her dinner party, saying, "On the way to your home I was taken unexpectedly drunk." No one is taken unexpectedly drunk. Rather, one plants a decision in the back of one's mind to the effect that if my wife nags me the 20th time or if my boss makes me work weekends, I deserve a drink. So once the event happens, the addict begins, to drink, or pop pills, without having to arrive at any further conscious decision, in such a way that the file card, once filed, is automatic although forgotten.

Alcoholics are perfectionists. If I were an unscrupulous employer I would hire nobody but primary alcoholics. I would expect them not to work on Mondays because they would be recovering from their hangovers, and they would miss work on Fridays because they could not hold off for the weekend and would begin drinking on Thursday night. But on Tuesdays, Wednesdays, and Thursdays, I would get two weeks worth of work out of them. They are perfectionists, but their perfectionism is part of the game that feeds their life-style and justifies addiction.

Intervention Phase 3: The Working Through

With the mastery of the destructive games and before the substitution of positive or healthy games, the group members suddenly become zealots. This is "the holier-than-thou stage" out of which many reformed drunks never emerge. It is important that this highly authoritarian outlook be understood and ameliorated, for during this phase the addict becomes merciless toward a fellow group member who may have a fall. Such an outlook toward the world can lead only to new kinds of problems in living.

Once this is worked through, and about halfway through the 24 group sessions, the group members become depressed. They realize there is no short cut, only hard work ahead. The fanaticism disappears, but so does the enthusiasm that carried the client thus far. It is as if the energy goes out of the group, and each group member settles into a profound depression that places him or her at risk. It is interesting that few clients have falls during this period; most of the falls have occurred in Phase 2, when most of the testing of the limits is being acted out. Furthermore, the therapist's vigilance is alerted at this period, and the group members who have now been working together for several months accept the assurance that once this depression is weathered, better days are coming.

Intervention Phase 4: Self-Responsibility

In the final phase the client seems to finally accept responsibility. This is in the form of a conviction, heretofore aggressively resisted, which concludes that abstinence is for life, not the six months of the group program. With the acceptance of this fact comes a kind of peaceful resolution with oneself and a sense of mastery.

This phase appears just at the point when the addict despairs that he or she will never emerge from the profound depression. It happens suddenly, and clients describe it as an experience similar to learning to type or mastering a foreign language: Proficiency is preceded by a seemingly interminable period of more or less mechanical struggling. Then one day one is typing or speaking the language. In our case, the intervening floor in the house has been built and the client is no longer subject to panicky mood swings that send him or her scurrying for the bottle, the needle, or the pill.

A key ingredient has been the therapist, whose unrelenting firmness, fairness, and honesty have provided a role model and whose deep commitment and concern have ameliorated the client's chronically low self-esteem and interpersonal distrust, so aptly described by Chein, Gerard, Lee, and Rosenfeld (1964).

Special Cases

Exclusion therapy is applicable to foodaholics as well as to therapy addicts and compulsive gamblers. These require special therapeutic contracts, but space limitations permit only brief mention of them. Exclusion therapy is not applicable to tobacco addiction.

There are two types of foodaholics: carbohydrate addicts and sugar addicts. The two types of addiction are often mixed in one person, but it is surprising how frequently the pure forms of addiction are found. Since the therapist cannot insist on total abstinence (one has to eat), the client is required to lose five pounds for a second appointment and two pounds per week to qualify for the subsequent sessions. Foodaholics usually insist on losing more than the required amount, a sure sign they will fail, so the therapist must point out, "Even when you are losing weight you insist on gluttony in reverse."

Foodaholics will reach what has been termed in the group a "sound barrier," the weight that the client will seemingly be unable to go below. It was so named because once beyond the barrier it is difficult to recall why it was so difficult, somewhat analogous to what the field of aviation experienced with supersonic flight. The sound barrier is mostly psychological, for the client changes from the psychological outlook of a fat person trying to lose weight to that of a thin person who is still somewhat overweight. The temporary bouts of hypoglycemia experienced by foodaholics as they lose weight are not restricted to them. All withdrawal results in recurring periods of hypoglycernia, not only because the alcoholic is used to a high quantity of alcohol or sugar in the blood but also because the glycogen function of the liver has been disrupted by prolonged use of a chemical. In fact, the so-called "rush" in drug taking is essentially the result of drugs triggering the sudden discharge of stored glycogen.

It is important that the therapist never recommend a diet to the foodaholic, stressing instead that the client understands his or her body a lot better than the therapist does and has long ago learned what will lead to weight loss. This prevents the game that foodaholics play with their physicians, getting them to prescribe a diet that the patient will effectively sabotage.

In the United States we have unfortunately created a legion of therapy addicts who constantly pursue psychotherapy, individual growth, and every new fad that emerges, in the firm belief, somewhat analogous to the Santa Claus fantasy, that the next encounter will produce the desired insight and state of narcissistic peace. We call these persons couch freaks, growth grogs, or woe-is-me artists. Exclusion therapy is very successful in helping these heretofore repressed individuals realize that the cure for constipation is not diarrhea. Space does not permit an adequate description of the special technique required in these cases.

Conclusion

Exclusion therapy is not an elegant theory of the addictive personality or a hypothesis about the cause of addiction. It is a viable system of intervention that has proven successful in a variety of settings in the United States during the past 16 years.

With our own clients at the Kaiser-Permanente center in San Francisco we have followed a randomly selected sample over the years and have maintained active follow-up. Of this sample of 639 clients who have been in the program, 73% are living drug-free lives. Of these, 349 have been clean for 5 years, and 123 have been clean for more than 10 years. Almost half of the total sample experienced at least one fall, for which they came to the clinic for several individual sessions. Occasionally, someone request that he or she repeat the entire group program, and this is granted. Others have entered traditional therapy and gained the kind of insight that was not possible as long as they were drunk or stoned.

If the estimate is correct that 23% of clients seen in psychotherapy are suffering from either addictive problems or emotional problems that are exacerbated by alcohol or drug abuse, then psychotherapists must be prepared to discover, confront, and intervene in these conditions. Medicine has not been successful in meeting the wave of addiction and problems exacerbated by drug abuse because the very nature of the medical model inadvertently encourages either iatrogenic addiction or the substitution of one addictive substance for another. Like the efforts of most workers in the field of alcohol and drug abuse, traditional therapy, based on the assumption that insight must precede abstinence, is even worse than no intervention inasmuch as it kindles the addict's fantasy that something will happen for him or her.

In mental health clinics in the San Francisco area, 40%o of those seeking psychotherapy are manifesting or hiding alcohol or drug abuse problems, and my own estimates indicate that within a decade, a figure of 40% for the nation as a whole should be expected. Professional psychology must be prepared to meet this epidemic. The psychological model of intervention remains the most viable, and I hope I have done something in this address to enable psychology to meet the challenge that these problems will continue to present in even greater degree in the future.

Footnotes

1. National Institute of Alcoholism and Alcohol Abuse. (1978). *1975 Statistical Report*. Washington, D.C.: Alcohol, Drug Abuse, and Mental Health Administration Clearinghouse.
2. National Institute of Drug Abuse. (1978). *1975 Statistical Report*. Washington, D.C.: Alcohol, Drug Abuse, and Mental Health Administration Clearinghouse.
3. Cummings, N. A. (1975). *Survey of addictive characteristics of a random sampling of patients presenting themselves for psychotherapy* (In-House Paper). San Francisco: Kaiser-Permanente.
4. Cummings, N. A. (1969). *Exclusion therapy: An alternative to going after the drug cult adolescent*. Paper presented at the meeting of American Psychological Association, Washington, D.C., September 4.
5. Cummings, N. A. (1970). *Exclusion therapy II*. Paper presented at the meeting of the American Psychological Association, Miami, September, 7.
6. Whitaker, C. (1979). *The present imperfect*. Paper presented at the Fourth Don D. Jackson Memorial Workshop (sponsored by the Mental Research Institute, Palo Alto, California), San Francisco, August 3-4.

References

Blum, R. H., et al. (1972). *Horatio Alger's children*. San Francisco: Jossey-Bass.

Chein, I., Gerald, D., Lee, R., & Rosenfeld, E. (1964). *The road to H*. New York: Basic Books.

Haley, J. (1976). *Problem solving therapy*. San Francisco: Jossey-Bass.

Julien, R. M. (1978). *A primer of drug addiction* (2nd ed.). San Francisco: Freeman.

Kendel, E. R. (1976). *Cellular basis of behavior*. San Francisco: Freeman.

Peele, S. (1978). Addiction: The analgesic experience. *Human Nature, September*.

Peele, S., & Brodsky, A. (1975). *Love and addiction*. New York: Taplinger.

Who Is the Substance Abuser?

Nicholas A. Cummings, Ph.D., Sc.D.
Janet L. Cummings, Psy.D.
University of Nevada, Reno and the
Cummings Foundation for Behavioral Health

[This material is used by permission of John Wiley & Sons, Inc. and originally was published in Cummings, N. A. & Cummings, J. L. (2000), *The First Session with Substance Abusers: A Step-by-Step Guide*. San Francisco, CA: Jossey Bass (A Wiley Company).]

When asked who is the substance abuser, most people, including mental health professionals, readily conjure up stereotypical images:

* The raucous middle-aged man with a big belly, bulbous nose, and pasty skin, reeking of alcohol
* The furtive young grunge who is rushing the compact disc player he has just stolen to the nearest "shooting gallery" to exchange it for a fix
* The streetwalker supporting her habit through prostitution
* The inner-city youth who spends most of his time in a "crack house," wherever it might be this week, or "dealing" to the often well-dressed occupants of the cars that pull up to the curb where he stands every evening
* The violent felon, twice imprisoned for assault, whose crimeridden life is liberally laced with all kinds of drugs, as well as alcohol

The hard-core addict is easy to spot. Harder to spot but nevertheless more common is the substance abuser who is a next-door neighbor, a coworker, or even a colleague. Consider the case of Florence, who I (Nick) saw just two years ago.

Florence had a Ph.D. in social psychology and was a full professor at a prestigious university. She also was the principal investigator and project director of a brilliantly conceived and executed program for inner-city adolescent girls. She spent every Saturday morning on-site with her abused adolescents.

Recently, on the way to the center, which was in the heart of the inner city, she was severely beaten and robbed. Once out of the hospital, where she was treated for severe wounds and three broken bones, her doctors referred her for treatment of posttraurmatic stress disorder (PTSD). She chose to see me, even though it meant traveling a considerable distance every week for her sessions.

It was obvious that she was a brilliant and compassionate psychologist, well deserving of the reputation she had in the field. I was initially quite taken with the way she spoke of her involvement in the amelioration of the severe abuse to which inner-city girls were subjected. And at first I admired how quickly she had returned to her Saturday work in the inner city. Her doing so was against all medical advice, as her injuries were not yet sufficiently healed.

Then I noted certain inconsistencies that jolted me out of my Mother Teresa countertransference. Her ready return to the inner city was not in keeping with her diagnosis of PTSD. She looked twenty years older than her age of fifty-four. Her skin had a distinct alcoholic pallor along with premature wrinkles. Her hands revealed a tremor in spite of her attempts to hide it by clasping them. Was Florence a substance abuser who already manifested organic signs?

Through a series of interviewing techniques based on the approach that we will discuss in later chapters, I learned that Florence used her weekly trips to the inner city as the opportunity to buy her week's supply of drugs. She lived alone, and every night she smoked crack. Then she would go to bed with a bottle of wine, a behavior known among addicts as sucking on a lemon. Having finished the wine, she would eventually fall asleep. But a stupor is not restful sleep, and the next morning Florence would "crank" herself with uppers (amphetamines) she had also purchased from her corner pusher.

I pointed out that for someone who was trying to improve the lot of people in the inner city, she was participating in one of its most unfortunate aspects. In full denial, Florence reminded me that she was an excellent social psychologist and understood too much about the problems to ever get addicted.

Florence heaped rationalizations upon each other with the intensity of one who must avoid facing the truth. I responded that I had read the story. It was called Rain, and it was written by W. Somerset Maugham. It was about a missionary who set about to save the soul of Sadie Thompson, a prostitute. Instead, he found himself partaking of the "sexual depravity" he had been condemning, and he took his own life. I asked if, indeed, she was not taking her own life little by little, the hard way.

Florence determined at that session to enter treatment and go clean. But it was not to be. Three days after our appointment, she was readmitted to the hospital, this time with advanced cirrhosis and pancreatitis, as well as other conditions, all related to her prolonged substance abuse. She died before I could see her again.

We purposely chose to present the case of Florence to demonstrate that the substance abuser not only may be anyone but also may be a person we like, respect, and admire. She may even be one of us.

Errors in Points of View

Before looking extensively at the unlikely array of patients you will certainly see and, we hope, appropriately identify, it is important to see how the inherent biases of those people most involved result in their missing or purposely overlooking the chemical dependency surrounding us. Because of the issues hidden in these points of view, therapists are often thrown off the track and are thus prevented from providing useful help.

The Cultural Point of View: It's All Relative

In addition to differences among families in tolerance or acceptance of substance abuse, there are cultural differences in what is deemed OK. In the inner city, drugs are easier to obtain than bottled water, and children play while their single teenage mothers smoke crack. Children as young as eight are recruited as runners, and gang membership is a matter of survival. But our African American and Hispanic colleagues who work side-by-side with us treating substance abuse have made it very clear that factors stemming from poverty, resignation, or despair do not properly define a culture. They remind us that cultural tolerance in no way lessens the ravages of substance abuse on children and adults. We have relied on these colleagues to help us sift acceptable from unacceptable behavior in the light of cultural variables. But they have hammered into us over and over that when we are confronted by the denial of an addict, our need to confront that denial is necessarily ubiquitous-it knows no cultural boundaries. A therapist who holds the point of view that drug addiction differs according to culture or skin color can dilute and hamper the work he has to do.

True, there are cultural differences as to the definition of social use, but the patients who come to us have already slipped far down the slope of addiction, or they would not be seeing us. You must be cognizant that an addict will attempt to excuse his addiction by proffering the claim that his behavior is considered socially acceptable by his ethnic or cultural group. Our job is to treat addicts, not to engage in philosophical discussion of what is culturally or ethnically acceptable social behavior.

These considerations are integral to establishing a therapeutic alliance with the chemically dependent patient, and we will be discussing them in detail. In addition to the biases developed from our families and culture, there are other points of view that obscure what is happening in the first session.

The Patient's Point of View: It Ain't Me

To the patient, the addict is always the other guy. It is very interesting that when patients identify the other guy, they can be amazingly accurate. This is because those who are chemically dependent read a great deal on the subject (some are even reading this book) and understand it as only one who has been there can; but then they do two things, both of which they do well: (1) they project their knowledge onto those around them who are abusers, and (2) they bolster their own denial by comparing themselves to those exhibiting levels of addiction more advanced than their own. They thus succeed in avoiding even a modicum of self-understanding.

Friends, including behavioral health practitioners, are often startled when someone ostensibly close to them enters a drug rehabilitation program after years of chemical dependency unnoticed by anyone. They are even more startled when one or two in their circle enumerate accurately the telltale signs that had been present for months or years. Persons who had noticed may be skilled practitioners who understand addiction, or they are recovering addicts, but more often they are persons who are living in denial of their own addictive problem.

After Florence died, a member of her psychology faculty was outspoken in deriding his colleagues for having overlooked the signs that Florence had been exhibiting. Actually, Florence had kept her chemical abuse successfully hidden; nonetheless, he loudly proclaimed that had her colleagues been more vigilant, she might still be alive. Not quite a year later he was admitted to a drug rehab program for his own abuse of many years' standing. In having concentrated for years on Florence's subtle symptoms he had avoided looking at himself, and in deriding the faculty he may have been uttering his own unconscious plea for help.

When a substance abuser gets into trouble, she can always find another addict who is in even greater trouble, implying that it is the other person who is the addict, not she. If arrested for driving under the influence (DUI, there is the excuse, "I am not like the other people appearing before the court today who are here for the second or third DUI." When the second or third DUI arrest occurs, the excuse is, "I'm not the drunk who caused an accident or ran over a pedestrian." So pervasive is denial that every arresting officer jokes that all drunk driving can be explained by the universal lament, "Honest, offisher, I only had two beersh." (The person's blood alcohol level tells the true level of alcohol consumption, contradicting the legendary two beers.) Similarly, the person fired for being drunk or stoned on the job or for frequent absenteeism rationalizes, "At least I got another job right away, so I don't have a problem like the unemployed guy. I just had a boss who had it in for me." The "boss who had it in for me" excuse is good for a succession of job losses, up to and including the final one, after which the drunk or stoner is too far gone to get another job. Thereafter, he repeats over and over to anyone who will listen (usually his own inebriated friends) the story of the unfairness of that terrible last boss. Even now he is denying the problem!

In explaining how facile this denial can be, we can use the analogy of a person whose calorie craving has resulted in his being overweight, a very common phenomenon in American society. The woman who is obese will make certain there are no full-length mirrors in the house. By seeing only the reflection of her face, she can pretend she is only a little overweight. If when going by a large plate-glass window she inadvertently catches the reflection of her full body, she will experience initial shock at seeing her true girth. Then denial will resume, and she will remind herself that plate glass always distorts. A fat man sitting in a room when another obese man walks in will smirk to himself, "My belly isn't as big as that guy's." Actually, his is probably a lot bigger, and that is why he desperately needs the denial.

The Family's Point of View: Blame the Addict for All Trouble

Because a spouse or other family members are clamoring for treatment of the chemically dependent relative does not mean that they want the effective or appropriate treatment for that person. There are many exceptions, of course, but practitioners are amazed how often a family that is demanding treatment turns around and sabotages it when arrangements are made. A family member-especially the spouse, lover, or parent-is more often than not the patient's enabler, defined as the person who makes possible the continuation of the offender's addictive behavior. It is not uncommon for more than one member of the family, or even the entire family as a unit, to behave as enabler. Examples of enabling behavior abound.

An alcoholic in our program had been dry for six weeks when his spouse, who never drank, joined the Wine of the Month Club and received a case of fine wine early each month. She would open each case and array the bottles on a counter in the laundry room. By the third month, the patient, who had then been dry for over four months, unable to resist any longer, opened the first bottle and was within one day back to his previous binging behavior. The wife was furious; she complained to the therapist that treatment was not working and informed him she had no intention of paying the overdue bill for his services.

We were consulted by the juvenile court when a frequent school problem got out of control. A group of high school students were caught smoking pot a block from the school during the noon recess. They were suspended from school, and the matter was remanded to the juvenile authorities, as the inhabitants of the apartment building where this took place had called the police.

Along with their lawyers, the parents stormed the school and the officers, charging the authorities with everything from false arrest to brutality (one girl had tried to scratch the arresting officer's eyes and had to be restrained).

Schools and police know this scenario well in all of its variations, and they refer to it as the "everyone else but not my darling" syndrome. No wonder that Carroll O'Connor, the actor who lost a son to heroin, admonishes unequivocally, "Get between your child and drugs any way you can." There are certainly parents who do this, but the enabling parent is all too common today. Those parents who really want to respond appropriately may find it difficult in the current "blame the schools" climate. Psychotherapists need to be cognizant of the parents' plight and be prepared to assist sincere parents, especially when their tough love may be required.

There are principally two reasons for enabling behavior. The first is that the enabler has issues that require the continuation of the substance abuse on the part of the spouse, lover, parent, or child. These issues may range from a need for a feeling of safety-"he won't be able to leave me—to a need to be in charge, which the addict's debility accords. When the situation gets out of control, the enabler seeks help for the addict but aborts that help just as soon as the status quo has been restored. The "Wine of the Month" case is such an example. The wife insisted her husband seek treatment when the alcoholic behavior resulted in his losing his job. After he had been sober long enough to obtain a new job, she sabotaged the treatment.

The need to maintain a family mythology is the second reason for enabling. Although the foregoing case of the outraged parents would fit into that definition, the family mythology is usually more pervasive, as the case of Megan illustrates.

Megan, a beautiful, classic blonde in her late twenties, was the second wife of a handsome, successful, and debonair middle-aged man, Bob. There were two young children as beautiful as their parents, and the home was perfect and worthy of being featured in House Beautiful. Bob liked cocaine and had the income to indulge in it frequently. On occasion, and especially on weekends, he would mix cocaine (an upper) with alcohol (a downer), a form of "speedballing" that would result in abusive behavior; sometimes he would beat the children, but mostly he would batter his spouse.

Megan had a need to present an idyllic picture to her parents and to the world, and indeed, "perfect" was the word used by friends and others to describe this family. Megan created a family mythology to sustain the illusion. The children were indoctrinated with the excuse that Daddy worked hard and could not help "blowing off steam," and they were never, never to mention to anyone that Daddy hit them or their mother.
On one occasion, when Bob had battered her to the extent that make-up would not cover the bruises, Megan crashed the car into an abutment so that she could attribute the bruises to the automobile accident. The children dutifully maintained the family mythology, even after Bob overdosed and had to be hospitalized. Megan whisked him off to an expensive private rehab program in a distant city so that all could be hushed up.

Megan was an enabler, and she taught her children to be enablers. It was only after Bob died of an overdose that Megan was finally distraught enough to tell her therapist the truth. She had to grapple with the guilt that, perhaps, without her enabling behavior Bob might have had to get help before he eventually died of his abuse.

Whether family members are sincere or are enablers, they need to be involved in the substance abuser's treatment. We are often asked how one can tell the sincere family member from the enabler. This is difficult, because all family members are *sincerely in denial*, even the ones who are not the primary enablers. The primary enabler needs treatment to understand and change that behavior, and family members who are not enablers need help in addressing the guilt feelings stemming from their mistaken belief that they are causing the addictive behavior. The latter issue is very common for children of all ages (even after adulthood) who have been taught by an enabling parent to take responsibility for mom or dad's chemical dependency.

It is important that the enabler not be misdiagnosed as sincere, and vice versa, a differentiation that you cannot easily render without meticulous clinical consideration. A rule of thumb is to regard the family member or members who are making the most noise and avidly blaming the addict for everything as the most likely to emerge as primary enablers. The nonenablers are more circumspect and are likely to be as weary of the enablers as they are of the addict. The nonenablers do not need the addict in order to validate themselves, whereas this is the presenting issue with the noisy, complaining enablers. The enablers clamor, "I would be happier and more successful and would have no troubles," without the addict. These same enabling family members will be the first to "rescue" the addict from the therapy by sabotaging the treatment just as it begins to produce results. Without family involvement, few addicts succeed in treatment. So important is this consideration that we have devoted all of Chapter Eight to the enabler.

Probably the most frequently encountered family problem is that of spouses who have finally left their addict and have decided to rebuild their lives without him. There is a tendency to respond to the patient's plea and return to the marriage after too short a period of sobriety. The enabler will do so out of need to return to the halcyon days of a false but safe relationship; the sincere spouse will feel guilty that not to do so would jeopardize the spouse's recovery. Without counseling, both types of spouses will invariably make the wrong decision.

The second most frequently encountered family problem involves the exasperated parent or parents who have finally thrown out the adult child who is abusing drugs. The temptation to let the son or daughter prematurely return to the home with the first sign of recovery is intense. Probably these parents have been enablers all along, but in any case, the parents must be counseled that an important part of any person's recovery is for her to become self-supporting.

The Medical Point of View

To satisfy the medical definition of addiction there must be "physical cravings" on withdrawal, as manifested by an array of physical symptoms; withdrawal from opioids (for example, opium, its derivatives, and its synthetic variations: morphine, dilaudid, percodan, heroin, and so on) has always served as the model. This definition has proven not only inadequate but also unfortunate, in that it does not explain the severity of many addictions. It has led the medical profession and the public to believe that any substance that has not been declared medically addictive is not a matter of concern. As noted previously, the assurances by both the government and the medical profession lulled many into believing cocaine was not an addictive substance. History and clinical experience have demonstrated that faulty assurances coming from ostensible authorities served as an inadvertent and tragic impetus to the cocaine epidemic.

Historically, it would seem that under the medical definition, every substance is presumed nonaddictive until proven otherwise. Innocent until proven guilty is important in criminal justice; it is nonsensical in the physical world. This is not mere rhetoric, for every new sedative, pain reliever, or mind-altering drug that has become part of our pharmacopoeia was initially heralded as being nonaddictive and without side effects. In the absence of any evidence, it may be impossible to predict that something will be addictive, but there is also an overriding responsibility not to prematurely declare that something is nonaddictive. Time reveals the fallacy of such declarations as one by one, everything from benzodiazepines (for example, Valium) to methadone shows up on the street for sale to addicts who clamor for them. Even Ritalin, a stimulant prescribed and perhaps overprescribed for attention deficit disorder (ADD) and attention deficit hyperactivity disorder (ADHD), has a street value, and it is often peddled to middle schoolers by the very children for whom it is prescribed. These boys often manage to build up a stash that allows them to sell the surplus for as much as two and three dollars a tablet. Only time is necessary to reveal the consequences of continuing to assure the public that each new mind-altering drug is not addictive.

Of importance to you in the first session is to be mindful that a prescription drug, dispensed legally and responsibly, may have become an addictive substance with prolonged use. Too many therapists erroneously believe that prescription drugs are safe, when in fact there are far more people in the United States addicted to medically prescribed "safe" drugs than there are addicted to heroin, cocaine, and other illegal drugs combined[1]. Be wary of the patient who complains that only a certain drug is helpful; she may be addicted to that drug.

We have prepared Chapter Three to alert you in the first session to the kind of person most likely to become addicted to particular drugs. In addition, we have grouped drugs according to class; we do this because once a person is addicted to a drug, he is addicted to all drugs in that class. The medical profession is too often oblivious to this transfer to an addictive equivalent; physicians often use drugs of the same class as substitutes for another drug to which the patient was obviously addicted.

The Psychological Point of View

The psychological point of view that regards all addictions as being learned behaviors would seem to stand in direct contradiction to the medical point of view that insists in all cases that there be a physiological basis. To the behaviorist there are no "addictions" in the strict sense, as the behaviors so labeled are really habituations that can be unlearned. Treatment, therefore, is reconditioning, deconditioning, negative response extinction, or whatever term might be applicable to explain the unlearning.

Under discussion here are not the excellent behavioral techniques being used in rehab programs that respect the physiological aspects of substance abuse, but rather those approaches that deny cellular changes in addiction and offer the patient the hope of becoming a "controlled" drinker. This term seems in itself to be an oxymoron, for the only persons who count drinks and are obsessed with controlling their ingestion of alcohol are the alcoholics, who invariably lose count and, therefore, control.

Most of us were trained in the context of the psychological definition of addiction, and as such are prey even before the first session to the patient's insistence and belief that she can, with a little help from us, succeed in restoring chemical equilibrium. Throughout this book we caution you against espousing a purely psychological model of substance abuse. It is as seductive to the psychologist as the solely medical model is to the physician.

It is the ubiquitous fantasy of substance abusers that they can become "social" users, and they really do not need a misleading psychological theory to bolster their denial of the importance of abstinence. We recall a patient who had been through three unsuccessful controlled drinking programs before entering our program. He was doing well, and he had been abstinent for over seven weeks. Then he missed the evening group in the eighth week. He telephoned two days later, stating he had been practicing his controlled drinking when somehow he seemed to have forgotten a lesson or two and found himself "unexpectedly drunk" for several days.

A Pragmatic Point of View

Both the medical and psychological models are important in the treatment of substance abuse, but only in combination with each other, not singly. In this section we look at such a combined model, pragmatic and effective, that we have developed and employed successfully for more than thirty years.

The Substance Abuse Practitioner's Point of View: A Synthesis

There are life experiences and cultural influences that provide the learned aspects of substance abuse, and, as will be shown in the next chapter, there are cellular changes in the body of the substance abuser over time that are the physiological basis for the insatiable craving and the pain on withdrawal. Pragmatically, it is often impossible to separate the two components of addiction. Which is the most important? One might as well ask, What is more important when measuring area, length or width? Clearly it is impossible to answer the question as posited, but one can look at individual rectangles and discern that some are long on length and short on width, making the answer for that particular rectangle apparent. There are all manner of rectangles, with varying degrees of length in relation to width, just as there are variations among addicts: some are more influenced by physiology, others more influenced by learning. But let us make no mistake: in every rectangle there is both length and width, and in every addict there are both biological and psychological determinants.

One needs only to stay up one night with a heroin addict who is withdrawing and who is doing it "cold turkey," observing the suffering from both profuse diarrhea and vomiting as well as severely alternating chills and sweat, to be convinced of the physical aspects of withdrawal. Yet denial, which is the most universal and pervasive feature of all addictions, is a psychological phenomenon, as are the effective therapeutic interventions that lead to recovery. Further, the ongoing determination to stay clean (abstinent), known among recovering addicts as surrender, is also a psychological process.

What Do the Numbers Say?

In Chapter Two, we will look at the specifics of drug addiction, including drug preferences, as well as genetic, in utero (prenatal), and environmental-cultural contributors, and finally look at special populations. First, it might be helpful to look at the statistics, enabling the reader to appreciate the specifics of abuse and their extent in the total population.

According to NIDA and the National Institute on Alcoholism and Alcohol Abuse (NIAA), substance abuse is all around us and in a variety of forms. Thirty-five million Americans abuse alcohol, and approximately half that, seventeen Million, abuse marijuana. A startling forty million abuse legal drugs, both prescription and over-the-counter varieties. There are three million heroin addicts, and, following a period when heroin addiction was declining, it is once again on the increase. There are four million persons regularly abusing cocaine or crack cocaine, and five million regularly abuse amphetamines (methamphetamines, crystal meth, and so on). Eleven million regularly abuse barbiturates[2].

Do not attempt to add these up, as there is considerable overlap. Polydrug abuse is the order of the day. Exact numbers are hard to come by, but estimates place chemical dependency in America at a low figure of 15 percent of the total population and a high figure of 20 percent. This means that one in six or one in five Americans is a substance abuser. It bears repeating that 40 to 45 percent of all persons seen by behavioral health specialists have substance abuse problems: either they are addicted, or substance abuse is exacerbating a primary psychological condition[3]. In either case, the substance abuse needs to be addressed as part of treatment. Yet most practitioners rarely address chemical dependency problems, or they take the approach that with continued psychotherapy the chemical dependency will evaporate. Look over your treatment load. In how many cases might you have failed to identify substance abuse? Can you do better?

Perhaps the most significant statistic from NIDA and NIAA is that 71 percent of substance abusers are employed. This means that most will have health insurance, and almost all are potentially in your treatment room, now or in the future. Only 21 percent of substance abusers are unemployed, marginally employed, homeless, or in prison[4]. Under Medicaid even many of these are potentially your patients.

Think for a moment of the implications for your practice. If approximately thirty-five to forty million Americans are addicted, and 71 percent of these are employed and have health insurance, approximately one in three of the patients who walk into your office are likely to be addicted if you only see patients with employer health insurance, or almost one in two if you see persons covered by Medicaid, Social Security Disability, and Medicare. Are you identifying a number even close to that figure? How many addicts are you failing to even suspect, much less identify?

Who Is the Pusher?

No discussion of the addict would be complete without looking at the question of who is the pusher. For the most part the pusher and the user are one and the same. This means that both the addict and the pusher are sitting unidentified in your office. You will never see the drug lord or the mafioso, the ultimate supplier, who is far removed from the grubby level of hard-core addiction. It is the addict sitting unidentified in your office who, in order to pay for his habit, is forced to become a dealer in drugs. Each addict dealer obtains a supply, takes out what he needs for personal use, then "steps on" (dilutes) the remainder, which he then sells. The purity or potency of the chemical depends on how often it has been stepped on before the present buyer acquires it. Those far down on the chain are getting low-grade drugs, and when they are lucky enough to get their hands on high-grade heroin, for example, merely taking the usual dosage results in an overdose because of the difference in potency.

It is not unusual that a patient referred to you has been charged with "possession with the intent to sell." The individual may be a stockbroker in an Armani suit, so unlikely to be a pusher that you accept the patient's protestations that this is a mistake. Yet every brokerage house, large law office, and factory-and every other conceivable employment setting-has its addict pusher. You will be referred a twelve-year-old boy who has been accused of selling Ritalin on the school grounds. The parents are outraged, the boy looks angelic, and in your mind you dismiss the allegations as a mistake. Be reminded that nearly a third of the Ritalin prescribed to school children is being resold by these same children[5]. Many of our schools are awash in recycled Ritalin, and the parents are the last to know it.

The images of the crack dealer standing on the corner in the inner city, the "needle man" (heroin dispenser) in the shooting gallery, the "clerk" in the crack house, the outlaw motorcycle gang peddling speed (amphetamines), the furtive grunge lurking near the school, and the "pizza man" who makes the rounds in an unmarked, nondescript old van are the ones that most persons associate with the pusher. If these are the people you are looking for, you are unlikely to see them in your office.

Most large workplaces have at least one employee from whom drugs are readily available, and these are often trusted employees or even members of the executive suite. We have treated a number of highly successful executives and professionals who had introduced cocaine into their law firm, advertising agency, or brokerage house as a way of supporting their own several-hundred-dollars-a-day addiction. One beautiful and hard-driving account executive confessed after her fall to poverty and disgrace that while she was on top, her money went for cocaine, fast cars, and fast men, in that order, all of which had to be supported by peddling cocaine to her coworkers. But even simpler than that, everyone has an acquaintance who is known for being able to obtain for his friends "whatever candy you want."

With all due respect to the medical profession, the pusher is sometimes as close as the kindly physician who has the reputation among users as a "script doctor."

These script doctors, although in the minority, are still all too common, and they are well known to addicts through their underground. There are three types. The first is the well-meaning physician who wants to alleviate all pain and discomfort. This physician overly prescribes pain killers, sleeping pills, and other mind-altering drugs; he is too naive to realize that the addict is the one who always comes in requesting a specific drug and is obtaining prescriptions from a number of other physicians so that no one physician is aware of the extent of the medications the patient is receiving.

The second type of script doctor is the "impaired" (addicted) physician, who because of her own chemical dependency cannot stand to see someone "strung out" (in withdrawal). Addicts present themselves feigning far greater discomfort than they actually feel, easily obtaining a legal prescription to carry them until they can obtain their illegal drug of choice.

The third type is the unscrupulous physician who is actually illegally trafficking in legal drugs. Because he is issuing an enormous number of prescriptions, this physician needs a "cover," such as a specialization in weight reduction, thus ostensibly explaining the large number of daily prescriptions issued for amphetamines. A variation on this unscrupulous type is the physician who purposely addicts the patient so that thereafter this patient is a source of a steady income stream.

In your first session with a patient, be alert when you find out that the person is the patient of any of the foregoing types of physicians. These doctors are well known in the medical community but characteristically ignored by a profession that is reluctant to report a colleague who is suspect.

I (Nick) was the psychologist who was impaneled to treat most impaired physicians in my community. In that role, I saw the unfortunate and the cynical, but I knew when my physician patients were truly in recovery: they no longer overly prescribed to their own patients. My worst experience was the demise of a close friend, a prominent psychiatrist and a past president of the American Psychiatric Association. He was accused by a number of women of having addicted them with weekly intravenous injections of barbiturates (for example, sodium amytal), thus tying them to his expensive practice in perpetuity. They further accused him of raping them while they were under the "twilight sleep" of the drug, which caused me to wonder if he suffered from his own drug impaired judgment.

I will never know the full story because my friend and colleague denied the charges, but rather than sustaining a hearing by the medical board, he forfeited his license. He was not able to stem the tide of notorious publicity, casting embarrassment on all of us in the behavioral health professions. Of the unfortunately too many times that drug addiction or drug pushing among colleagues has come to my attention, this case is among the saddest for me because of the respect I had for this man's contributions and stature in the field. It remains a constant reminder of how easy it is to miss the problem of substance abuse, especially in the first session.

Footnotes

1. Schuckit, M. A. (1989). *Drug and alcohol abuse: A clinical guide to diagnosis and treatment.* (3rd ed.). New York: Plenum Medical Book Company.
2. National Institute on Drug Abuse and National Institute on Alcohol and Alcohol Abuse (1999). *NIDA and NIAA 1998 statistics.* Rockville, MD: NIDA and NIAA Publication and Distribution Centers; also see the following websites: http://www.nia.nih.gov and http://www.nida.nih.gov.
3. Falco, M. (1992). *The making of a drugfree America: Programs that work.* New York: Times Books.
4. U.S. Department of Labor (1998). *Facts and figures about drugs and alcohol in the workplace.* Washington, DC: U.S. Department of Labor.
5. Moore, T J. (1998). *Prescription for disaster.* New York: Simon & Schuster.

Presenting Problems:
Different Tugs from Different Drugs

Nicholas A. Cummings, Ph.D., Sc.D.
Janet L. Cummings, Psy.D.
University of Nevada, Reno and the
Cummings Foundation for Behavioral Health

[This material is used by permission of John Wiley & Sons, Inc. and originally was published in Cummings, N. A. & Cummings, J. L. (2000), *The First Session with Substance Abusers: A Step-by-Step Guide*. San Francisco, CA: Jossey Bass (A Wiley Company).]

Most psychotherapists, particularly clinicians trained in the behavioral treatment of chemical dependency, know little or nothing about the properties of specific drugs and how they affect different individuals. This lack of information leaves therapists vulnerable to the patient's denial, resulting in a psychological diagnosis that completely overlooks the addiction. There are telltale signs of addiction that are present in the first session but are missed because the psychotherapist does not know what to look for and what to ask about. Which of the following statements are true, and which are false?

- It is impossible to hide drug abuse from a knowledgeable clinician.
- Addiction results in permanent physiological changes that are forever discernible.
- Drug preference varies according to gender, ethnicity, and socioeconomic status.
- Drug addiction can include the medication the doctor gives as a substitute.
- It is possible to reveal the addiction on the first session in spite of the patient's denial.
- Addiction is always to the same family or class of drugs.
- Addicts can have a preference for a drug even before they have tried it.
- Children can be born addicted.

If you answered that each of these statements is true, you are correct. But do you know why each is true, and what to look for in your patients that would reveal what you need to know about that patient within the first session? As we have discussed, substance abuse is widespread in American society. However, when it comes to chemical dependency, one size does not fit all. People have individual, genderbased, cultural, and age-related preferences, tolerances, and susceptibilities. These are so varied, yet so understandable, that knowledge of them gives you a road map to your patients' addictions; these addictions will be glaringly obvious during the first session if you have this knowledge.

Behavioral health practitioners are startled when they realize what a broad scope of chemicals is available for someone to abuse, but this large smorgasbord does not seem to be enough for many abusers. There are "cookers" (underground chemists) busily turning out designer drugs; these drugs are constantly altered in different ways by each cooker, so that the person ingesting designer drugs has no way of knowing what might be the effects of the latest chemical alteration. Yet designer drugs have no end of buyers, in spite of the buyers' awareness that they may be the first to try this new batch. It is interesting that the users of designer drugs are often young people who are otherwise fanatic regarding what they put in their mouths-living as vegetarians who eat only organic foods and are so strict about this that they drink only bottled water. The paradoxes of substance abuse are remarkable!

A Brief Psychophysiology of Addiction

Before getting into the specifics of substance abuse, we think it is important for you to have some understanding of the interplay between the physiology and psychology of chemical dependency. This understanding will alert you to what you can expect to see in the first session, but even more important, what these observations mean for treatment. Understanding the road to addiction, or specifically how people get hooked, gives you the key to how to begin unhooking them.

As a knowledgeable clinician, you can be of far more help to your patients. Simply explaining the addictive craving, its permanency, and what can be done about it gives the patient courage in the first session to go ahead with treatment. Explaining to the patient that he became addicted during his mother's pregnancy because she was ingesting that particular drug makes the remarkable specificity of that addiction understandable and the need for abstinence from the drug acceptable. Being able to give the physiological reason why switching from alcohol to Xanax will not help someone's addiction may be just the precise information the addict needs in the first session for her to decide in favor of psychotherapy instead of medication.

As we will discuss in the following sections, there are specifically three bases of addiction, even though most often they can be separated only theoretically: (1) genetic, (2) in utero (prenatal), and (3) environmental.

Genetic Influences

The genetic mapping of addictions is in its infancy (alcoholism having received most of the initial attention by molecular biologists). It is a difficult process inasmuch as there is not simply one gene marker or even a series of gene markers, but rather a complex array of genetic factors interacting with each other as well as with the environment. The determination of genetic factors in your patient will craft what information you give. It is not only incompetent but also cruel to promise social use to a patient whose addiction is genetically influenced.

One genetic factor is well known and can serve as an example. In metabolizing alcohol, the first step is the transformation of the alcohol molecule into acetaldehyde. This is accomplished by the body's alcohol dehydrogenase enzyme. Interestingly, acetaldehyde is even more intoxicating than alcohol. Most individuals transform the alcohol into acetaldehyde at a steady and timely rate, so they feel the intoxication early on. For them there is an early perception of the effects of the alcohol (blurred vision, unsteady gait, slurring), which results in the signal "I have had enough." Some individuals, however, have a genetically determined slower-acting variety of the alcohol dehydrogenase enzyme. These individuals drink and drink without feeling the effects, only to have large quantities of alcohol suddenly converted to acetaldehyde, with the result that they are now very drunk. We have all known this type of person without knowing there is a genetic basis.

The important consideration for you is that such individuals have a ten times greater chance of becoming alcoholics. This genetic predisposition is found most commonly among Native Americans, where one out of every seven individuals has the slower-acting variety of the alcohol dehydrogenase enzyme, the highest proportion yet discovered among any group. But looking at the predisposition alone does not take into account the influences of environment. What if such a person were born into a home where the family is Seventh-day Adventist or Mormon, religions that forbid alcohol? No matter what a person's genetic background, if she has never tasted alcohol, she is less likely to become alcoholic. However, teetotalers with the genetic predisposition will rapidly manifest addiction if they abandon their religious prohibition.

Prenatal Influences

It has long been known that children born of heroin or crack addicted mothers are heavily addicted at birth and have to undergo withdrawal. This addiction is in addition to other physical and mental consequences and even abnormalities. One of the earliest findings of the methadone programs created by the federal government in the 1970s for heroin addicts was that not only were the babies of women in these programs born addicted to methadone, but the physical and mental ravages they suffered were worse than those seen with heroin babies.

All addictive drugs are addictive to the fetus. The fetus is unable to metabolize chemicals on its own; the substance must eventually leave the fetus and be metabolized by the mother. In addition, even small amounts are relatively enormous to the tiny fetus. These two factors together result in rapid, deep-seated fetal addiction. This is true of all addictive chemicals, many of which have been extensively studied in their prenatal effects.

The best known of these effects is fetal alcohol syndrome (FAS), the most common chemically induced birth anomaly, which surprisingly continues to be missed in its less flagrant form (known as fetal alcohol effects, or FAE) in many child guidance clinics. The number of FAS and FAE children continues to grow because most mothers and many physicians believe that small amounts of alcohol ingested by the pregnant woman are harmless to the fetus. This is not only untrue, but the younger the fetus, the more significant the resulting FAS. Even in cases where prenatal exposure to alcohol has produced no other discernible anomalies, the individual so exposed will nonetheless be at increased risk for alcoholism.

Armed with this knowledge, you will develop sensitive antenna that will look for substance abuse when the first-time patient is pregnant. The misinformation that the placenta and amniotic sack protect the fetus from chemicals ingested by the mother is just that-misinformation. Even more alarming is how widely believed this falsehood is among women and-more amazing-many professionals. But even those who know better seldom ask a pregnant patient about substance abuse.

Once you have determined that your pregnant patient is chemically dependent, immediate referral for prenatal care is mandatory. The care must include immediate detoxification and withdrawal. You may, and even should, work with the prenatal program during the duration of the pregnancy and even beyond.

You must remember that even after the newborn is withdrawn from the chemical to which it was addicted prenatally, it is latently addicted to that chemical for life. Thus, a child born of a heroin addicted mother, once he ingests heroin again, be it at age eleven or thirty, is instantly readdicted. The physiological reason for this will be described later in this chapter.

Environmental Influences

Environmental influences on both physiology and psychology are ever present, but not always apparent. For example, a chronic depression may have its roots in genetics, such as unipolar depressive disorder, but the psychological solution chosen by such an individual may be to seek euphoria. This is often accomplished in childhood through thrill-seeking behavior until the individual in adolescence discovers the euphoria produced by cocaine. The type of cocaine to which such an individual may become addicted will vary with the environment in which the person lives. The inner-city youth will most likely prefer crack cocaine because of its relatively low price and easy availability, whereas the suburban professional will choose powdered cocaine in spite of higher cost because of its purity and stronger effect. In this illustration physiology (genetic depression) has led to a psychological behavior (thrill seeking) which, in turn, is replaced by a chemical addiction whose type is influenced by environment. Similarly, environment can interplay with physiology and psychology, with the result that a class of drugs (uppers, downers, and so on) may become the specific addiction for an individual.

The earlier in life that a person is exposed to an addictive substance, the stronger the likelihood of addiction. This is true not only because peer pressure is greater in youth but also because psychological reinforcement has a more pronounced influence in the growing organism[2]. Furthermore, the individual does not become addicted to just the drug to which she has been exposed but to the entire class of which the drug is a member. For example, the alcoholic is not merely addicted to alcohol but to an entire class of substances known as central nervous system (CNS) depressants. When an alcoholic is exposed to another CNS depressant (for example, benzodiazepines, barbiturates), he is already addicted to that substance. This phenomenon explains why it is a fallacy that chemical dependency can be cured by substituting a substance that is interchangeable in the addictive process. The chemical dependency in such instances is continuous and uninterrupted.

Psychological reinforcement is well known to behavioral health professionals, who tend to focus more on psychological and environmental factors than on genetic and prenatal factors. The peer pressure in adolescence to experiment with alcohol and drugs is alarming, but augmenting this are parental indifference and cultural influences. Parents who in the 1970s were highly involved in the drug culture of the time are ambivalent about confronting the problem with their children. Also potent factors are the ubiquitous drug abuse found amid the poverty and unemployment of the inner city, and the example offered by families in which the parents do drugs in front of the children. In the Irish culture, the son is not regarded as a man until he can drink heavily. The Jewish culture, in contrast, regards heavy drinking as disgusting. (Years ago, when one of the authors diagnosed the alcoholism of the president of a local Jewish congregation, the rabbi telephoned, chastising the psychologist with the pronouncement, "There are no Jewish alcoholics!") More recently, the university has developed a culture wherein 44 percent of college students don't just drink but binge drink[3]. Examples of environmental reinforcement abound.

In assessing the relative importance of biology versus psychology, we must recall our analogy of the rectangle, which is always dependent on both length and width for its area. With particular individuals, we can often discern the relative importance of either biology or psychology, but in most instances, making such a determination is never as simple as calculating area. What is critical for you is to appreciate the importance of both factors, to understand how each is addressed differently in the first session and in subsequent treatment, and to ensure that neither is allowed to become part of the patient's incessant denial.

Physical Alterations

Very few counselors or psychotherapists are aware that brain cells experience permanent changes in response to physiologically addictive substances. Three essentially irreversible changes take place in the body:

1. The body ceases to produce naturally occurring antianxiety and antidepressant chemicals.
2. Brain cells are permanently altered to respond to the same substance in the future.
3. The liver is altered and may be damaged permanently.

Let us look at each of these changes in more detail, as they will determine much of the course of the first and subsequent sessions.

1. *The body gradually ceases production of antianxiety and antidepressant substances.* In the same way that a healthy thyroid will cease to excrete thyroxin if oral thyroid

medication is taken over time, the brain behaves as though there is no longer a reason to produce enkephalins, endorphins, and dynorphans, because the drugs are replicating these substances and thus rendering them redundant. This is especially true for narcotics, and the effect is in a sense permanent. It may be six months to a year after withdrawal that a patient's natural substances are again produced in normal amounts, and this is a trying time, as the patient is without both these natural enzymes and her ingested chemical.

Those working with addicts know that heroin addicts are not to be trusted until after a year of being clean, and alcoholics in Alcoholics Anonymous (AA) are called "babies" until the second year. The risk of relapse is greatest during this period when the abstinent patient is without any buffer. Finally the body begins to produce the natural substances, but any subsequent use of the addictive chemical results in an immediate (rather than gradual) decrease and halt in their production. The sooner the reexposure to the addictive substance after withdrawal, the more dramatic the immediate decrease and halt in the production of the body's (and especially the brain's) natural chemicals. Furthermore, the younger the addict, the more dramatic the halt in production. The tragedy is especially severe for children, whose natural chemical production has not yet matured. It takes a considerable overcoming of the turbulence of adolescence before the body's own mechanisms, both physiological and psychological, have matured. Unfortunately, teenage drug users are skipping their adolescence, with lifelong consequences.

2. *Brain cells affected by addictive substances are designated to respond to the same substance in the future.* This is nature's way of neutralizing an exogenous or poisonous substance: converting it to a necessity. The committed cells do their job well, and for life will crave the substance to which they were designated to respond. As the individual continues abusing, he requires more and more of the substance to produce the "high" (euphoria), because the responding cells are doing their job of neutralizing the chemical. Eventually the increasing number of cells involved will require the addict to ingest quantities of the drug that originally would have resulted in an overdose. This all-important phenomenon is known as drug *tolerance*; once established, it never diminishes. An addict can be chemical free for ten years, but if he resumes the substance abuse, within days his body's level of tolerance will return to the level that was originally achieved over a period of years. Alcoholics who had built up to a quart of whisky a day are surprised to find that even after fifteen years of abstinence, if they start drinking again they require that quart a day within a week or two. Heroin addicts who undergo detox to bring their habit down to a manageable cost are disappointed. Their $300-a-day habit returns within days.

People trying to lose weight experience what also could be called tolerance. Once an adipose (fat) cell has been formed in the body, it never goes away. The cell deprived of calories will lose its mass but will never lose its cellular structure, including its nucleus. This cell remains empty. (Picture a box of one hundred sandwich bags. That box can be held in the palm of one's hand. But fill each bag with a sandwich, and it will require the entire kitchen floor to display the result. Removing the sandwich is like the adipose cell losing its fat; the now flat bag remains.)

Demonstrating the propensity of all cells to survive, the fat cell thereafter craves calories and will usurp calories out of the usual assimilation sequence in order to restore itself. This is why obese persons who have lost weight complain that it takes fewer calories for them to get fat again than it takes thin persons to gain weight in the first place. Eventually, if the person has changed eating and exercise habits for the better, the craving abates, but it never completely disappears. Given one extensive calorie binge, the cells seem to come alive with a full-blown craving.

3. *The liver is altered and often permanently damaged.* The process of converting a chemical from a poisonous to a neutral or useful substance occurs in the liver. In these metabolic processes, many addictive drugs are converted from physiologically damaging chemicals with few or no psychoactive properties into psychoactive substances that are less damaging to bodily organs. It must be emphasized again that the cells designated to do this job will forever want to do their job, and they crave the opportunity to metabolize a particular drug. Furthermore, with continuing abuse, the liver is overworked, rendering the addict susceptible to cirrhosis and other forms of liver disease.

Can There Be Nondrug Addiction?

A controversy rages among the experts over whether "compulsions" for something other than a chemical can be addictive. In recent years there has been a proliferation of activities labeled by therapists as being addictive. These range from compulsive gambling and compulsive shopping to compulsive sexual activity. More recently the public has been bombarded by articles in the popular media that have heralded video game addiction and even Internet addiction. Recently a woman arrested for credit card fraud claimed the defense of Beanie Baby addiction. She claimed she was so compelled to acquire all Beanie Baby dolls, including the rare and expensive ones, that she was driven to fraudulently use other people's credit card numbers to satisfy her craving.

There is no question but that the concept of addiction can be expanded to ridiculous proportions. However, there is now evidence that there can be nondrug addictions that have a previously unrecognized strong physiological component[4]. During the "rush" (excitement of anticipating and then engaging in the behavior), epinephrine, also known as adrenalin, and norepinephrine are at high levels, and endorphins and enkephalins, are released. It is likely that serotonin levels are also elevated at this time. Much of the "addiction" is to the chemicals that the body itself generates. The obvious psychological reinforcers, such as a big win for the compulsive gambler, are also pertinent. Clearly these addictions are in some measure truly chemical; however, the self-generated chemicals may in considerable measure be a triggered response to habituated psychological factors that preceded the eventual chemical reinforcement.

Compulsive gambling and compulsive eating can not only invoke certain physiological effects (the rush of epinephrine for the former, anxiety-sedating effects for the latter) that are addictive, but they can be substituted for the primary addiction in an individual who has become abstinent. Recovering alcoholics are highly susceptible to gambling as a replacement, whereas recovering barbiturate addicts readily replace their drug with food. These two nondrug addictions can also serve as addictions without any other form of addiction preceding or accompanying them. They demonstrate the compelling physiological and psychological cravings that accompany drug addictions. Furthermore, they are treatable through the same approaches that are effective with alcohol and drug addictions, with abstinence being the key for successful recovery. However, many so-called addictions in the popular press (for example, to sex, shopping, video, and the Internet) that have also gained acceptance by some professionals still lack evidence of a strong physiological base. The criterion that cellular change accompanies psychological reinforcement in a true addiction is a credible threshold that so far only compulsive gambling and compulsive eating have convincingly demonstrated. The more fanciful addictions (shopping, video, Internet) seem to be avoidance mechanisms, whereas sex addiction is found in individuals who demonstrate a wide variety of psychological problems.

From the treatment perspective, the "chicken-or-egg" question has yet to be answered, if, indeed, there is an answer. From your standpoint, the important consideration is that of treatment. There is overwhelming evidence that there are lifelong cellular changes that render the abstinent addict just one step away from relapsing into the highest level of tolerance achieved. This seems to be true for compulsive gambling as well as alcoholism, for in time all addictions respond to abstinence with a reduction of the craving that compels the addict to swallow, inject, smoke, inhale, or snort whatever is his or her "bag" (preferred substance).

Let's Look at the Bags

In this section we will discuss the substances that are frequently abused; some of these are legal, others illegal, but all are readily found on the street. The drugs are presented by class, for as we have already mentioned, addiction to one drug easily generalizes to the drugs belonging to the same class. We only briefly address the mechanism by which each drug acts in the body, so as to give you a thumbnail sketch. There are ethnic, cultural, class, gender, and age differences in the choice of drugs (an individual's bag), and although there are distinct trends, you also must remember that there are many surprising exceptions to these modal choices.

It is important to always remember that there is not a single premorbid addictive personality, so do not look for one. The ubiquitous lying, cheating, rationalizing, and conning are manifestations of the addiction. Valuable information can be derived from understanding the bags, so along with typical users, we will describe typical presentations on the first interview.

Uppers (Stimulants)

Drugs used as stimulants primarily affect users by heightening their sensitivity to all forms of stimulation. Consequently users experience grandiose expectations of themselves and others, they overreact to minor events, and they experience intense preoccupation with irrelevant details. We will look at both cocaine and amphetamines.

The primary mechanism of *cocaine* (*crack, snow, snort, nose candy, powder*) is a short-acting but powerful inhibitor of dopamine and of norepinephrine reuptake. Because cocaine is short acting, users need to frequently readminister the drug, which can be snorted, injected, or smoked (freebased). The euphoria likely results from the norepinephrine (NE) system, inasmuch as reuptake blocking causes increased active levels of NE. The "crash" results from the exhaustion of the NE system, which results in drastically reduced levels of active NE. The combination of relatively brief euphoria followed by a severe crash makes repetition compelling and exacerbates the addictive process.

The typical users of crack cocaine are persons of lower socioeconomic status (often minorities) because it is inexpensive and easily available in the inner city. Its low cost per "hit" is deceptive because users require multiple hits to sustain the high and avoid the crash. Consequently, a crack habit is ultimately a very expensive one.

When an addict becomes successful and leaves the inner city, as is the case of high-paid athletes, for example, the drug of choice almost overnight becomes the more expensive higher-grade cocaine. It is also a common drug of choice for hard-driving, successful (at least until cocaine takes its toll) yuppies who need to always be at their peak of energy and performance. Cocaine is also the drug of choice for those suffering from chronic depression that began in childhood and results in an adult who consistently feels "wooden." These individuals state in treatment that cocaine made them feel alive. Finally, it may come as a surprise to you that cocaine is a common drug of choice for adults who in childhood were erroneously given Ritalin or other stimulant medications for misdiagnosed ADD or ADHD.

When you see a cocaine addict for the first time, you will find his talkativeness striking. In spite of their running chatter, coke addicts do not say much of importance. If pressed for the presenting problem, they readily blame the other guy for their troubles. The addicts who are snorting rather than shooting will have the telltale runny nose. But the primary thing to look for is the patient's sheer and absolute grandiosity. The expansiveness and bragging rolls off the patient's tongue without much restraint.

The opposite will be true if the patient is crashing. There will be a profound depression in which all the vegetative signs are of recent origin. It is as if the patient woke up one or two days ago, suddenly feeling depressed and suicidal. Real depression does not hit that suddenly; when you are confronted with lack of a genuine presenting problem, coupled with either grandiosity or sudden depression, cocaine addiction is likely.

The primary mechanism of *amphetamines* (*speed, uppers, meth, crystal, crank*; archaic: *reds, black beauties*) is to release newly synthesized monoamines (norepinephrine, dopamine, and serotonin) and then block their reuptake. The increase in NE enhances alertness and motor activity while decreasing fatigue. The increased dopamine (DA) in the system causes stereotypical behavior and is likely responsible for the psychosis and paranoia associated with amphetamine use. The increased serotonin (5-HT) in the system causes some stereotypical behavior and may also contribute to the psychosis and euphoria. Amphetamines are usually taken orally, but advanced users inject the drug, hastening the psychosis and paranoia. Some kind of paranoia, often leading to violent behavior, is the result of heavy, prolonged use.

Recently in Phoenix a man who had been on a methamphetamine binge for several weeks poured gasoline over his two-year-old daughter and burned her alive. He did not flee from the police, reporting that he had purged his daughter's soul of the bad spirits that had invaded her. He offered as proof of the evil spirits that the burning little girl crawled more than ten feet before she died, a fact confirmed by the police in their assessment of the physical evidence. The drug-induced paranoia told him that the malevolence was attempting to escape the burning body and accompany his daughter's soul to heaven. In jail awaiting trial for murder, the speedinduced paranoia cleared up; this father is not only remorseful but also aghast at his behavior. His remorse, however, did not constrain him from using drug-induced insanity as a defense.

Typical users of amphetamines are adolescent girl's and young women who wish to lose weight; they readily obtain prescriptions for amphetamines from so-called diet doctors and even from their primary- care physicians. It is easy to abuse this prescription drug, using it as an upper and going beyond the intended goal of losing weight. Many of these dieters graduate to street versions. As with cocaine, many chronic depressives self-medicate with the cheaper amphetamines. Ritalin, Cylert, and Dextroamphetamine are stimulants used to treat ADD and ADHD, and are also found on the street. Most of the street versions are found in our schools, as are Ritalin and Cylert, which, as mentioned earlier, are resold by the children for whom they were originally prescribed. A surprising number of children receiving these stimulants, and especially those who received them because of misdiagnosis, graduate to street versions of these drugs or even the stronger and cheaper crystal meth and other forms of speed that are "cooked" in underground laboratories throughout the nation. (These "cooking kitchens" are everywhere, but the neighbors seldom realize their proximity until one of the kitchens blows up. Unfortunately, the cookers too often partake heavily of their own products and become careless.)

Methamphetamine (crystal meth) is available only rarely by prescription, so almost all of this drug is obtained on the street. It is very popular among teens and even younger children, with the average age of first use being fourteen. Many working-class persons see this as the drug of choice because it is cheaper than cocaine, and the euphoria lasts much longer. Many accidents in plants and other bluecollar employment centers have been traced to amphetamine use and its accompanying carelessness. Amphetamines are frighteningly popular with truck drivers who need to stay up on long hauls.

Because of the euphoria and her decreased appetite for food, the amphetamine addict is quite thin, eventually to the point of emaciation, especially if she is injecting the drug. This kind of physique, in the absence of compulsive exercise or anorexia, should alert you to explore for other signs of amphetamine addiction. The mainliner will have needle marks, but most addicts use the drugs orally. Nervousness, inability to sleep, irritability, and eventually fleeting paranoia are all signs of speed use. Because of the often intense insomnia, many addicts will resort to alcohol or other downers at bedtime, and, interestingly, the patient is more likely to report this secondary use rather than the primary use of speed. It is important, therefore, to inquire about speed when the patient is thin, irritable, and insomniac. Girls and young women will manifest tweaking behavior-the picking of their face or the pulling of their hair.

Downers: Depressants and Opiates

There are two very distinct types of downers, and although they both have a sedating effect, they are so different in their action that we have listed them together only because they are lumped together in common parlance among addicts and, surprisingly, by some physicians.

The first group are the depressants, such as alcohol and benzodiazepines, that work on the gamma-aminobutyric acid (GABA) system; the second group are the opiates (narcotics), whose action is on the endorphin (and enkephalin) system. Although alcohol is the far most common drug in use, it is listed after the benzodiazepines and barbiturates for two reasons: (1) these are the drugs most commonly and regularly mixed with or substituted for alcohol, and (2) the pharmacological actions on the GABA system are very similar.

Central Nervous System (CNS) Depressants

Known in the medical profession as minor tranquilizers, almost all *benzodiazepines* (*benzos, downers, ropies*; *Valium, Librium, Xanax*, and *many others*) are obtained legally because physicians freely and sometimes too liberally prescribe them. Consequently, the street name of benzos (as differentiated from bennies, for the once very popular Benzedrine) is rare, as is the term "downer." The only common street name in this class is "ropy" for Rohypnol, a benzodiazepine that is known as the date-rape drug and is available only on the street. It is banned in the United States because it has been used by young men on dates in the very kind of sexual assault on women that its tag line suggests. However, it is legally available in Mexico, and because of demand it is smuggled into the United States.

The primary mechanism for benzodiazepines is the facilitation of GABA neurotransmission. GABA is the primary inhibitory neurotransmitter, and when it is stimulated, nerve transmission is reduced, and CNS depression results. This depression further blocks nervous system stimulation that originates in the reticular formation in the brain stem, and thus diminishes activity in the area of the brain associated with emotion (that is, the amygdala, hippocampus, and hypothalamus). The person is seeking a drug-induced "cool" with an absence of troubling emotions.

Typical users of benzodiazepines are the various kinds of patients to whom physicians freely hand out prescriptions. These include anyone complaining to the doctor of depression, anxiety, or even bereavement. Middle-class "nervous house-wives" who would never think of taking a street drug can and do obtain large quantities of Valium; they abuse the drug but rationalize their behavior because it is a doctor's prescription. They overlook the fact that they may have five different physicians prescribing, each unknown to the others.

Individuals with underlying phobias or mitral valve prolapse (MVP) who are prescribed Valium can overly rely on them to dissolve their phobias, and they thus rapidly become dependent. Alcoholics are often given Librium as part of their treatment for alcoholism, and a large number learn to prefer it to alcohol because it is longer lasting and does not show the telltale signs of inebriation. Even more frequently, alcoholics learn to use Librium in combination with alcohol to potentiate the effects.

Xanax has replaced both Librium and Valium as the benzodiazepine most prescribed by doctors. Librium was first introduced as a minor tranquilizer that was supposedly nonaddictive. When this proved to be wrong, Valium was heralded as a benzodiazepine that was more effective and not addictive. Because the half-life (the period in which the drug remains partially active after the initial effect) of Valium is nine to ten times that of Librium, it is no wonder that Valium was found to be far more addictive than Librium, as the user typically ingests more Valium long before the previous dose has reached its halflife. When heroin dries up on the street, hopheads (heroin addicts, also known as junkies) buy and swallow, and even shoot, large quantities of Valium to see them through.

The benzodiazepine abuser will present with a calmness that belies any need for the patient to be seen at all. The affect can be flat, or it will be displaced so that important problems are minimized, while trivial problems are exaggerated. There may be a history of traffic accidents but with no DUI charges because the benzo addict escapes the Breathalyzer test. The patient will complain that he just can't get it together. A housewife may not quite get to the grocery store or begin other errands. There may be sleeplessness at night accompanied by the patient's sleeping a good part of the day. The most telltale sign is a peculiar forgetfulness, such as forgetting to pick up the kids at school or the day-care center. If the patient has been off the drug, she will feel an incredible nervousness, often described as "jumping out of my skin."

The mechanism of *barbiturates* (*downers, barbs*; archaic: *yellow jackets, dolls*) is similar to that of the benzodiazepines in that they act on GABA, except that there are increased effects on the reticular system, with the greater likelihood of coma or death. Before the advent of benzodiazepines, these drugs were in widespread use, both legally and illegally. One of the most frequent reasons a mental health professional was called to the emergency room was for barbiturate overdose. The tolerance level between the sought-after "warm fuzzy" feeling and coma can be very small, and it may change from time to time.

Typical barbiturate abusers were exactly the same people who are now described as typical users of benzodiazepines; they have now been moved on to the use and abuse of the latest CNS depressant drug. At one time, physicians prescribed barbiturates as freely as they now give benzodiazepines. From the best-selling novel and subsequent movie *Valley of the Dolls*, which glamorized barbiturate use among middle-class housewives, through several other movies, to the recent movie *Copycat* in which Sigourney Weaver washed down pills with copious quantities of alcohol, the TV and motion picture industries do much to popularize the housewife's prescription drug abuse. There were a number of problems with barbiturates, and physicians were relieved to move on to benzodiazepines without having to change their prescribing patterns. Short-duration barbiturates are still used as anesthesia, and some of long duration are used as anticonvulsants. And there are still barbiturates on the street, but they are sought after by longtime users who never switched to the newer CNS depressants or by addicts who cannot obtain an immediate prescription for their preferred benzodiazepine because they are ingesting it much faster than the rate at which it is prescribed to them. To hide their addiction to benzodiazepines and not jeopardize a continued source from their physicians, these addicts supplement their prescriptions with illegally obtained barbiturates, as both drugs belong to the same class and are interchangeable.

The barbiturate abuser will present with a calmness, flat and displaced affect, and other symptoms and behaviors typical of the benzodiazepine addict. Do not be surprised to see the same history of sleep reversal, traffic accidents, and forgetfulness, along with the jumping-out-of-my-skin nervousness without the drug.

A number of CNS depressants once in wide use have fallen out of favor, because of either the problems associated with them or their propensity to be widely abused by patients who were prescribed these drugs. Again, most have been replaced by benzodiazepines, but they still linger, and you may have a patient who has remained addicted to the older medication. Again, with the exception that this will be an older addict, the symptoms and behaviors resemble those associated with benzodiazepine addiction.

Meprobamate (*Miltown*, MB-TAB, PMB, *Equagesic*, *Equinil*, *Meprospan*) was among the first of the new genre of "tranquilizers" to appear after World War II. It was freely prescribed because it was believed to be both safe and nonaddictive. Quickly it became the most widely abused drug in history, and frequently it was combined with alcohol. The "M&M" (Miltown and martini) was the rage, and it was chic to have a bowl of Miltowns on the coffee table during a party. In time it became apparent not only that the meprobamates were highly addictive but that withdrawal could result in grand mal seizures and death. Consequently, these drugs are rarely seen today.

Methaqualone (*Quaalude*, *sopors*, *ludes*) is a barbiturate-like drug that became popular as a sexual facilitator, especially for women who would take it at "swinger" parties or even with their boyfriends. It has a very high abuse potential, and the withdrawal is worse than that from barbiturates. It is characterized by delirium, convulsions, and even death. Its uses as an anticonvulsant, local anesthetic, or antitussive are better met by other medications, and the drug was banned in the 1980s. It continues to be sought after because of its reputation as a sexual facilitator, and it is available on the street as "ludes" or "soaps."

Before the advent of neuroleptic and antipsychotic medications, *chloral hydrate* was widely used in mental hospitals to quiet patients. It has many barbiturate-like effects. It is a short-term sleep aid, suitable for one to three nights for patients with agitation, but it causes respiratory depression thereafter, and from the outset causes severe gastrointestinal (GI) upset. For these reasons it is rarely seen today.

Paraldehyde is a barbiturate-like liquid that was used in the past to supposedly facilitate alcohol withdrawal. It was discontinued because patients quickly began to prefer it to alcohol in spite of the fact that it causes GI irritation and very bad breath. If alcoholics can get their hands on it, they will use it for a grand party, often ending up in the emergency room. Diagnosis of severe paraldehyde overdose is easily established from the pungently bad breath.

Finally, *glutethimide* (*Doriden*) and *methyprylon* (*Noludar*) are barbiturate-like in their action but are still prescribed for motion sickness. If these are abused it is because some kid has found it in the medicine cabinet at home and discovered that she can get high on it.

The symptoms and behaviors of users of these various "outmoded" CNS depressants will closely resemble those seen in benzodiazepine abusers. The difference will be that this is an older addict who has been addicted for a long time or who has recently resumed a previous addiction to barbiturates or these other less common drugs, thus accounting for the preference. Because physicians no longer prescribe these substances, the patient has learned to purchase them on the street. It is surprising how many of these addicts are still being seen and misdiagnosed in the first session with a psychotherapist.

The mechanisms of *alcohol* are essentially the same as those for benzodiazepines and barbiturates, so we will not repeat them. Measure for measure, however, alcohol is less potent and requires greater quantities to obtain the level known in the drug and alcohol world as "stoned." (For a person to seek that state is a certain sign of alcoholism, which raises alarms about binge drinking among college students.) More than with other substances, there is an early interference with certain motor functions such as walking and talking, making the ingestion of too much alcohol apparent to others, while the drinker is unaware of the reduction in motor function. Chronic alcoholics at some point reach the stage of the blackout, in which they walk and talk almost normally but recall none of the things they did or that happened during that period. These episodes can last from minutes to days, but mostly their duration is a matter of six to twelve hours.

Alcohol remains the most widely used and abused substance in the United States, as well as in most countries throughout the nonIslamic world. (Although it is forbidden by Islamic law in a number of countries, alcohol ingestion exists, but alcoholism is rare.) Within any culture are superimposed familial influences; sometimes family attitudes are counter to the culture in which the family is living. This can be especially true for immigrants whose mores of origin may clash with their new environment. Individuals raised in alcoholic families are predisposed to becoming alcoholics. But surprisingly, there is a similar predisposition for individuals who are raised in families that are strongly against any alcohol use. When the familial influences coincide with cultural and ethnic factors, there is less conflict leading to alcoholism. Many families of Italian or French descent would not think of eating dinner without wine, and many fathers of Irish extraction are proud of sons who can "hold their liquor" (engage in heavy drinking without losing control, although brawling seems to be an admired exception).

We have already discussed the slower-acting dehydrogenase enzyme as a well-known example of genetic predisposition to the overuse of alcohol. In contrast, the so-called Asian flush found among many Asians is an allergy to alcohol that mitigates against heavy drinking; for some individuals, the severity of the allergy makes any drinking whatsoever too unpleasant.

As we mentioned earlier, individuals who sustained prenatal exposure are especially predisposed to alcoholism, sometimes beginning at an early age. This is true of prenatal exposure to all drugs, but physicians are much more likely to address the pregnant woman's use of drugs other than alcohol, believing that small amounts of alcohol are harmless. In addition, the earlier in life (childhood, adolescence) alcohol use begins, the more likely the addiction will occur. Those children and adolescents who reveal the early signs of future Axis II disorders frequently become alcoholics in adulthood. Axis II children include those who, as children, are overly indulged, as well as those whose needs are inconsistently met by their parents.

As might be expected, those who are predisposed to anxiety or depression often begin to self-medicate with alcohol. One drink relieves the depression or dissolves the anxiety, but in time it takes more and more drinks, resulting in dependency. Furthermore, as a CNS depressant, alcohol only aggravates depression in the long run, and the rebound anxiety after drinking only aggravates the person's anxiety. Yet many depressives or anxiety neurotics self-medicate with alcohol and find themselves having to increase both frequency and amount because the temporary relief is followed by exacerbation. A dependency is created that escalates to addiction. It can be said that the more a person drinks medicinally, the more likely the addiction. Lifelong social drinkers have been shown to be those who use alcohol only convivially. College students under the stress of being away from home the first time and who lack the coping skills necessary for self-motivation are especially susceptible to seeking relief from homesickness through drinking. Of these individuals, the ones most likely to fall prey to alcoholism are those who seek popularity over academic success. Such persons, unfortunately, are the ones likely to become officers in the fraternity or sorority houses and set the pattern of initiation and other rites that involve binge drinking.

It surprises counselors and therapists when they learn that the most common alcoholic in the United States is the "beeraholic." There is a myth that a person cannot become an alcoholic on beer, yet people who drink one to two six-packs every night, or who are never without a beer can in hand all weekend long, abound. These are mostly men, but women are catching up, often preferring wine but more and more taking to the familiar beer can in the hand.

Let us look at the potencies. Whisky is generally eighty proof, or 40 percent alcohol. Beer is 4 percent alcohol, so ten ounces of beer (less than one can) is equivalent to a shot of whisky. Thus two sixpacks (at twelve ounces per can or bottle) is equivalent to fourteen shots of whisky, a hefty amount for one night. At 12 to 14 percent alcohol (by volume), a thirty-two-ounce bottle of wine is also the equivalent of twelve to fourteen shots of whisky; "wine people" characteristically drink most or all of one bottle each night after work.

Pure alcoholics (that is, those who abuse solely alcohol) are patients forty-five and older. We have not seen a patient in years who is under forty-five and an old-fashioned alcoholic. The current chemical dependency scene is one of polydrug abuse, with alcohol being the most common ingredient in cross-addiction. Your patient under forty-five will mix alcohol with uppers, downers, marijuana, and cocaine, at least occasionally; most prefer alcohol with just one of these other substances.

Alcohol is known among many addicts as "mother's milk." Heroin addicts who abandon heroin and are still alive after fifty are often very heavy drinkers, as are former heavy LSD users. Amusingly, Timothy Leary, known as the High Priest of LSD, in the few years preceding his death made the following pronouncement: "After that long journey through psychedelics, I have found that Ripple Wine is the best high."[5] Further, alcohol in combination with almost any drug will potentiate that drug's effects. Addicts mix it principally with cocaine, barbiturates, and benzodiazepines, but addicts may combine any drug with booze. Former heroin addicts being treated with methadone have found that mixing methadone with alcohol produces a high rivaling heroin, yet yields a drug-free urine test.

The alcoholic of long standing will have pasty skin, and those of very long standing will manifest some shakiness of the hands. There will be a history of blackouts. Most alcoholics will not be so advanced as to have developed a bulbous nose and large bags under the eyes, but it is surprising how often those are still seen in older patients. If the patient is mixing alcohol with other drugs, especially CNS depressants, the debilitating effects will be accelerated. Further, the patient can present any of the symptoms and behaviors listed for the drugs involved in the cross-addiction.

Alcoholics will present for problems other than their drinking. The most frequent will be marital stress, job stress, or both; if the patient has been referred by the court, it most likely will be for DUI, and sometimes for disorderly conduct.

Opiates (Narcotics)

Opiates and *opioids*, including *morphine* (*morph*), *codeine, demerol, methadone,* and *heroin* (*horse, smack, H, shit*) are known as *narcotic analgesics* because their action mimics the endogenous (that is, the brain's own) opioid system, which includes enkephalins, endorphins, and dynorphans.

Patients who are placed on self-administering doses of opiates-especially morphine, codeine, and demerol-for pain are likely to become addicted. Patients who are given these pain killers on a predetermined regimen or schedule are far less likely to become chemically dependent. The tendency to go beyond the pain-killing aspects and into euphoria is compelling and leads to addiction, whereas a schedule is constructed to keep the use of the opiate within treatment bounds.

About half of all heroin addicts in the United States reside in New York City, probably because of the availability of smack, but also probably because of the comfort that derives from being a part of a group so large as to be a subculture. Typical heroin users are graduates of lesser analgesics. For several years heroin use was declining, but in recent years there has been a significant resurgence. This has been attributed to the entertainment and fashion industries that have made the drug chic; in fact, the fashion magazines have gone so far as to tout "heroin chic." Their influence on teenagers and young adults who consequently took up the drug was so alarming that President Clinton invoked the powers of his office to warn both the fashion industry and Hollywood of possible sanctions if they continued to make heroin glamorous.

Nurses who have easy access to hospital supplies prefer morphine, and often falsify records to support their habit. Recently Demerol has become the abused drug of choice among health professionals in general, especially if they have access to the narcotics cabinet.

Long-time stimulant users (of cocaine, crystal meth) use heroin either to speedball or to calm the side effects of long-term stimulant abuse. These include insomnia, anxiety, and paranoia, all relieved by heroin, which then often ascends to becoming the primary addiction. Stimulant addiction is increasing; so is the trend to relieve its negative effects with heroin.

Narcotic addiction is severe addiction and involves the most consistent denial and deceit. Heroin addicts especially do not present for psychotherapy; if they do, there are compelling reasons. One would be because heroin has temporarily dried up on the street, which occurs whenever the police have made a very large supplier drug bust. In such instances the psychotherapist will see a patient who is fidgety and even tremulous. He will tend to pace, complaining of an 'anxiety attack' and requesting a prescription for lesser narcotics. Or finding that not forthcoming, for Valium or other benzodiazapines. If denied a prescription the patient may erupt in anger, berating the psychotherapist. This can alternate with an inappropriate breeziness, most often of the "Who needs you?" variety. As withdrawal progresses, the heroin addict is severely strung out, suffering from painful abdominal cramps, along with vomiting and diarrhea. At that moment, the addict will do anything for a fix, rendering late-night convenience stores and gas stations sitting targets. These are desperation robberies, for the patient is so strung out that caution is impossible. The strung-out narcotics addict will reveal the same desperation in your office. They will beg for a fix. Often they have been sent to you because they previously were begging the emergency-room physician or on-call doctor for the same fix they want from you. They know they cannot be prescribed heroin, but they name the lesser narcotics they know and want: percodan and dilaudid. These addicts resent codeine and darvon because these yield less of a high.

More likely you will see a patient because he or she is a health professional whose license is on the line for pilfering from the narcotics cabinet, a lawyer who is about to be disbarred, or some other professional who wants to escape the consequences of the opiate addiction. We have seen a number of athletes who had been suspended, and even more musicians who got caught. These patients will minimize the degree of addiction, but you can discern the severity from the needle marks, known as spider tracks. Do not just look in the usual places such as arm and leg veins: look between the toes. Long-standing heroin addicts have burned out most of their veins, leaving permanent spider tracks. Clever mainliners; will begin early to shoot in obscure places so as to hide their addiction. In the beginning, narcotics addicts snort the drug or take it orally, but they soon find that the quantities they need are too great without graduating to the needle.

An exception to this pattern of progression to the needle is the middle- or upper-class housewife who disdains the idea of using the needle. Instead, she ingests larger and larger quantities of pills, often mixing them with alcohol. It is difficult if not impossible, to truly engage a heroin addict who is well fixed, or high. They are the cleverest of liars and the most convincing of con artists, even when they are hip-deep in trouble. The drug makes them feel confident and invulnerable. The longer they are on the jitters, however, the more productive will be the interchange. For the most part, your task will be to motivate and refer the patient for the difficult detoxification and withdrawal ahead. However, if in the first session you completely miss the narcotics addiction, the subsequent treatment will be a nightmare of patient deceit: you will be drawn into a number of discrepancies, contradictions, and even traps.

Hallucinogens

The mechanisms of *psychedelic drugs* (*LSD, lysergic acid, acid*; *mescaline, mesc, peyote*; *psilocybin, sacred mushrooms, shrooms*) have not been sufficiently studied and therefore are not understood. It is believed that these chemicals involve stimulation of 5-HT2 (serotonin, type 2) receptors.

There are four types of typical users. The first of these includes those in college who are not great students, or the converse: bright individuals who should be in college but instead are going nowhere. Both of these types of young persons believe they are expanding their minds and have discovered internal truths that no one else knows. The second group is composed of persons who wish to drop out of society. For such individuals the psychedelic facilitates the illusion that the world is wrong or corrupt and that she is justified in not participating in society. The third group is an often transitory one. It is composed of prepsychotic individuals who want to blame drugs for their frightening and impending psychosis. Their involvement with psychedelics understandably terminates with their hospitalization, but for some who remain in the prepsychotic state for years, these drugs maintain the rationalization that "I am not really going crazy." The fourth group is almost quaint in today's drug scene. These are the army of "deadheads" who veritably worship the late Jerry Garcia and who follow the Grateful Dead from concert to concert. Hallucinogens are still readily available on the street, but their use and abuse is far below the level of the "psychedelic era" of the 1960s and 1970s.

At the first session, the user is likely to talk about anything except his hallucinogens. If he comes in because he has begun having bad trips, his expectation is that you will help him have only good trips. The deadheads are obvious in their appearance; in contrast, users who are in college but going nowhere do not always fit a stereotype. Occasionally they exhibit bizarre behavior in public while they are tripping out and, depending on the community and the level of tolerance, get picked up by the police.

Although *marijuana* (*cannabis*, *Mary Jane*, *pot*, *grass*, *weed*) may have mild hallucinogenic properties, it is not classified pharmacologically as a hallucinogenic drug. Actually, the exact nature of how this drug works remains unknown, because the federal government put a halt to all research with marijuana. We have included it in this section for the convenience of referring back to this material, because popularly it is usually lumped into this category.

Marijuana is second only to alcohol as the most abused drug in the United States. It is the entry point into drugs for almost everyone who progresses up the ladder of addiction, discrediting the once widely held notion that smoking pot does not lead to hard drugs. However, not everyone moves on to hard drugs, and there are many "potheads," many of whom are employed or marginally employed. There are also individuals who use marijuana only occasionally and never progress to extensive use.

Marijuana is used by persons of all socioeconomic levels and of almost all ages: children, adolescents, young adults, and middle-aged adults. However, most middle-aged users began in childhood, their teens, or as young adults. Marijuana is occasionally used by successful adults at parties, especially by those who had experimented with the drug in the "hippie era." But the majority of users are young persons, sometimes as young as eight years old. The younger the onset of usage of marijuana, the more likely it is that the individual will move on to harder drugs.

The chronic user, or pothead, is typically a person of low motivation who is attracted to a drug that allows her to lay back. However, the drug is known to produce amotivational syndrome, raising the chicken-or-egg question. Many potheads are found in small counterculture colonies in remote areas. Favorites are the coast and the deep forests of Northern California, but remote areas in New Mexico, Idaho, and Montana are also in vogue. Many potheads continue to live in the city and engage in some semblance of employment. Such jobs as gardening (yard work) are favorites because no one bothers the individual, who can remain stoned while working.

The most striking characteristic of the first session with pot users is that the interview does not seem to go in any productive direction. This is a reflection of the amotivational syndrome, in which the patient expresses a vague dissatisfaction, but with nothing specific. He may complain that he cannot keep a job, but is unable to explain why. These are generally easygoing patients who are affable and do not blame anyone. There is the general impression of a nice person, but one who is empty. She demonstrates a nominal interest in certain activities (music, movies, sports, literature), but the intensity or commitment is lacking. If you are not aware of the ramifications of the arnotivational syndrome, the interview can be perplexing.

Mixes of Other Drugs

There are numerous *designer drugs* (*Ecstasy*, *XTC*, *white China*, *synthetic heroin*, *nexus*, *eros*) with slight alterations of chemical structure, making it nonproductive to study their effects, as the chemical under study will disappear before the study is even undertaken. Cookers (underground chemists) work independently, so the product of one chemist is different than that of all others. This, too, makes study impossible. Nonetheless, the general mechanisms of these drugs are essentially known.

MDA (*Ecstasy*, *XTQ*) is now really a class of drugs, each with a slight variation in structure. These act on a small percentage of specialized serotonin neurons in the brain. The drug kills these cells in about twenty doses, thus requiring the cookers to come up with a slight variation that will act on a different small number of neurons. As the user switches from one variation to another, eventually there are none of these specialized neurons left. The immediate result is that this class of drugs no longer produces the desired effect and the user finds himself more and more abusing alcohol. This brain damage is permanent and the neuron deficit reveals itself as "a quart short" as the user reaches his older years. At present, it's almost exclusively young users.

Gamma-hydroxybutyrate (*GHB*) has a structure similar to GABA (see the discussion of the CNS depressants). The drug suppresses dopamine release, with a subsequent rebound and increase in dopamine as well as natural endogenous opioids. Relaxation and euphoria are the result. In 1990, GHB was widely distributed as a health food supplement that would promote weight loss and muscle development. It was banned the same year because of widespread reports of poisonings resulting in seizures and deaths.

Alpha methyl fentanyl (*white China, synthetic heroin*) is the most common of a group of fentanyl analogs deriving from a powerful synthetic opioid. It has an action very similar to real opioids, but tends to be more powerful than morphine and is sold on the street as white China or synthetic heroin.

A drug of deception, *2 C-B* (*4-bromo-2, 5-dimethoxyphenethylamine, Nexus, eros*) is sold as Ecstasy, but it actually has a far more intense hallucinogenic effect than Ecstasy. Users expecting the effects of Ecstasy are often terrified, and some suicides have resulted.

Although widely sold on the street, designer drugs have remained legal because cookers stay one step ahead of the authorities. By creating a new drug that has not yet been chemically identified and listed under the Controlled Substances Act, they avoid prosecution. Users are smug that they too can escape charges for possession of an illegal substance, inasmuch as the latest version has not yet been catalogued as such. The jeopardy, of course, is that the individual is risking unknown consequences by being the first to ingest the latest variation. If the local anonymous cooker is inept and the user becomes ill and even dies, there is no recourse under product liability laws. A frequent contaminant of designer drugs is MPTP, which causes Parkinsonism. Yet there is no end to those who volunteer to be the first. Who are these persons? As might be expected, many are underachievers doing little in life; others are seeking to go all the way and drop out of society. The surprising users are the yuppies who are bored with their lives, are pushing themselves beyond their limits in order to succeed, and perceive a need to "crash" periodically. These crashes tend to take the form of a monthly three-day weekend on designer drugs.

The most typical presentation will be the rather successful yuppies who will talk about being bored with life in spite of pushing themselves. They will not reveal the periodic crash into designer drugs unless you ask. When confronted with a patient in this age group who is ostensibly succeeding but is insecure about whether she can keep it up, you should be alerted to possible use of designer drugs. The patient is well into the successful world and cannot risk arrest for use of illicit drugs. The fact that designer drugs are elusive and "legal" makes them attractive to this person. Typically the use is occasional or periodic and does not present addictive features. Those who become addicted have moved on to other drugs, mixing designer drugs with other drugs for a bigger kick.

Although the mechanisrns are not entirely known, it is believed that *dissociative anesthetics* (*phencyclidine*, *PCP*, *angel dust*; *ketamine*, *Special K*, *Vitamin K*) bind to sigma receptors, which are possibly related to schizophrenia, or to glutamate (an excitatory amino acid neurotransmitter) receptors, or to both.

Developed mostly as anesthetics for animals, these substances are used in veterinary medicine and provide a cheap high. Therefore, the primary user is a younger person in the inner city or of lower socioeconomic status. It is also used by prepsychotic individuals who want to blame the drug for their psychotic symptoms. At times such persons are pushed over the edge into full-blown psychosis, with alarming results, such as attempts to fly off a tall building, or violent behavior toward others. Some individuals mix these drugs with other drugs to increase the high. With the emergence of designer drugs, which are also inexpensive, the use of dissociative anesthetics has greatly diminished.

You are unlikely to see these individuals unless the drug has resulted in bizarre behavior that led to their admission to the county hospital. This is most likely with angel dust. You may be asked to help with a differential diagnosis of a prepsychotic individual who was pushed into a full-blown psychosis. A history of indulging in cheap drugs and the sudden onset of the bizarre behavior are important clues in establishing the diagnosis.

Inhalants are legal substances that were never intended for ingestion. They include gasoline, airplane glue, organic solvents, antistick cooking spray (such as Pam), some marking pens, correction fluid and correction fluid thinner, nail polish remover, paints, industrial solutions, adhesives, butane in cigarette lighters, and aerosol propellants. It is estimated that the average household will have between fifty and one hundred commonly used substances that can be inhaled to attain a high.

Inhalants produce an intoxication in the brain but also result in damage to brain cells. With continued use, more and more brain cells are affected. It is difficult to assess to what extent the neuropsychological problems seen by behavioral care practitioners were preceded by abuse of inhalants. Before you diagnose ADD, ADHD, or other similar conditions, it is important to gain the child's or adolescent's confidence and obtain an accurate history in this regard.

Inhalant abuse is widespread among children, adolescents, and young adults of lower socioeconomic status. It is cheap, universally available, and legal. Use usually begins with one child in grammar or high school learning about it from an older sibling or friend and introducing it to his classmates. Because most inhalant abusers are boys, it seriously raises the question of how many of the problems seen in boys are due to brain damage from repeated inhalant abuse. In addition, it is surprising how many children, adolescents, and young adults who were placed on Ritalin or other stimulant medications following the misdiagnosis of ADD or ADHD become inhalant abusers once they achieve young adulthood. Some children start earlier, selling their Ritalin to their friends and classmates while substituting the free and plentiful inhalants.

Typically the child or adolescent has been brought in by the parents or has been referred by the school, because of poor grades and even worse attendance. The patient does not want to be there but may feign cooperation to get the matter over with. There are times when the child or adolescent has been caught in the act of inhaling, so the purpose of the visit is out in the open. Most of the time, however, the patient has been brought in because of the consequences of the abuse. When confronted with this age group and with a report of poor school performance and attendance, you should look for tremulousness, reports of severe mood swings, and soiled spots on clothing. More advanced abusers show severe motor problems due to the permanent damage to the motor cortex that inhalants eventually cause.

Inhalant abuse has gone beyond the former airplane glue-sniffing level. It is now the most frequent form of substance abuse among children and adolescents, with some schools reporting as many as 20 percent of their students involved. The complete availability of these inhalants makes them impossible to control, and latchkey kids have plenty of time to get high on the endless array. You should not be dissuaded by the youth of the patient, as the practice has become common among third graders.

The Ultimate Mix: Speedballing

It is important to give special attention to the growing practice of speedballing, the taking of an upper and a downer at the same time. This produces a virtual roller-coaster ride, inasmuch as the body does not shut down one system in favor of the other but attempts to accommodate both at the same time. The strain on the nervous and cardiovascular systems is enormous, and death is not infrequent. Although hundreds have died, the public hears about speedballing only when such celebrities as John Belushi or Kurt Cobain succumb.

Speedballing differs from the practice of taking a downer to relax after partaking of cocaine or another upper. It is a deliberate simultaneous intake for those who have become jaded or bored with the more usual high and who can afford to buy the costly cocaine and heroin. There is also lesser speedballing, and although it is not as disastrous to the body in the immediate term, with prolonged use it can be physically debilitating. Those with less money mix amphetamines with benzodiazepines, and the person who would never think of buying an illicit drug can experience low-grade speedballing all day long by taking large quantities of over-the-counter cold medications and reducing the sleepiness of the antihistamines (downers) with corresponding amounts of amphetamines (uppers). This person is a potential menace on the highway and can experience severe reactions in the evening when she joins spouse or friends in convivial before-dinner cocktails. This lesser form of speedballing is one of the most frequent reasons someone is inexplicably carried to the emergency room.

I'll Get High on Anything: A Therapist's Summary

The historical reassurance by NIDA that cocaine is not addictive is unfortunately matched by the Food and Drug Administration (FDA) in its repeated assurances that the latest mind-altering drug was not addictive. We saw how the first of these, Miltown, quickly became the largest-selling drug in America. Within a few years it was seen as having high addiction potential; it is almost never prescribed today. Librium followed, and was thought to be nonaddictive. When this was found to be untrue, Valium was heralded with assurances that it had none of the drawbacks of Librium and was nonaddictive. Soon Valium became the most prescribed drug in America.

We have already discussed the tendency of NIDA, the FDA, and other relevant agencies to presume the "innocence" of the latest mind-altering drug, only to discover later that the substance was addictive. When reports begin to come in regarding the drug's negative characteristics (for example, that it is addictive, potentially lethal when mixed with alcohol, hazardous for drivers), drug manufacturers tend to ignore them as long as they can. It sometimes is literally a matter of years before the information is distributed to physicians in "drug alerts." To us there was no reason to believe that Xanax, initially heralded as a nonaddictive benzodiazepine, would not now be regarded as addictive.

Since Xanax came on the market, more recent benzodiazepines such as Atavan and Serak are being regarded as "less addictive." Our prediction, because of the cellular changes and behavioral reinforcement that accompany benzodiazepines generally, these newer drugs will one day have their own physician drug alerts.

One of the problems is with the FDA approval system: once a drug is approved, there are no follow-up clinical trials. It takes time and considerable usage before the problems surface, and by that time the FDA is long gone. Meanwhile, the manufacturer is attempting to delay the dissemination of information until after the patents have expired on its "best-seller."

Practitioners who treat substance abuse must pragmatically accept the fact that someone who is determined to get high will find a chemical with which to do it. We saw a man who was consuming three boxes of Bromo-Seltzer a day just to get enough bromine from the small amounts found in that over-the-counter medication. We saw another a man who remained sober following his successful completion of a drug rehab program. However, his physicians were worried because his potassium level was low enough to endanger his metabolism. It was eventually discovered by an intern who pursued the cause of the patient's black mouth that this man was consuming two pounds of licorice per day. During his drinking days he used licorice to mask his alcohol breath; he apparently became addicted to licorice and quadrupled his intake after giving up alcohol. The large amounts of licorice were leeching his potassium. Impotent men will obtain Trazadone (Desyrel) in the hopes of getting the drug's infrequent but rather painful side effect of priapism. They take the drug in such large doses as to almost guarantee this result.

Two rather startling examples are illustrative of the abuser's determination.

Water, Water Everywhere

In the past, when the so-called chronic inebriate was subject to involuntary hospitalization, I (Nick) discovered emphatically what later became the truism that an addict can and will find something to get high on. In the state hospital where I was working, suddenly all the patients were behaving as if they were very drunk. They had moved their cots into the large men's and women's bathrooms that were characteristic of the state-run institutions of the time. We concluded that some kind of still had been hidden in the bathrooms and was churning out alcohol. Our maintenance crews all but tore apart the relevant parts of the building, but found nothing.

In a matter of two more days, during which time our patients were very, very drunk, we discovered that they were doing this on water. A recent admission was a biochemist who taught his fellow patients that if you drink eight gallons of water per day, the pH level of the blood is altered and you feel drunk. The patients tried it out and were delighted. For efficiency's sake, they moved their cots into the bathrooms so as to be near the water, as eight gallons is an enormous amount to drink in one day. Further, this put them near the toilets, an imperative brought on by their huge water intake. It was fortunate that we discovered the cause of their inebriation and put an end to it, for if the pH imbalance had continued for a couple more days, severe medical consequences and even death would have resulted.

Everything's Up-to-Date in Addict City

Within weeks following the introduction of Viagra, the drug was found on the street. Substance abusers incorporate it into their chemically dependent behavior in two ways. The first is to use Viagra in combination with nitroglycerin or other nitrate medications, which are used medically to lower blood pressure in patients suffering from angina or other forms of heart disease. Abusers mixing the two insist that there is an increase in both sexual performance and accompanying euphoria. This combination can drastically lower blood pressure and can prove fatal. Warnings have been issued by the FDA not to mix Viagra with blood pressure medication, but substance abusers are not known for their attention to such warnings.

The second method is to take Viagra in combination with amyl nitrate and amphetamine. This odd combination is thought to increase stamina on intercourse. However, the practice can lead to cardiac arrest. The combination speeds heart rate and respiration while decreasing blood pressure, creating extreme physical distress. In spite of these hazards, the combination is very tempting to men who are impotent as a result of prolonged substance abuse and seek yet another chemical solution, or to those who are "sex addicts" and wish to perform beyond normal physical limitations.

Special Considerations

No discussion of the specific properties of drugs and their effects on various populations can be complete without paying special attention to two exceptional instances: (1) substance abuse among older adults and (2) so-called foodaholism.

The first is of importance because more Americans are living longer, and psychotherapy under Medicare is the fastest-growing sector of our practice. Yet most psychotherapists know little about the treatment of older patients, and the prescribing physician forgets that medication trials did not include the elderly. Much of this oversight is in the process of being rectified, and the field of geropsychology is new, exciting, and growing. Yet even geropsychologists know little about chemical dependency among older adults and are unaware that it is largely iatrogenic-that is, induced by doctors. For these and other compelling reasons, we have added this section.

Foodaholism is important to addictionology because the physiology, cravings, and treatment of food addiction not only closely parallel what occurs in substance abuse but also may well be the prototype for it. This provocative notion encompasses the fact that overeating can both excite and sedate. To many physiologists, the original addiction in childhood is to sugar, and this addiction is carried forward into adulthood in forms that predispose many to substance abuse[6]. The increasing use of sugar among infants and young children may be an overlooked factor in subsequent chemical dependency. To the small child, sugar is the ultimate high.

Substance Abuse Among Older Adults

Most active substance abusers do not carry their behavior into old age, as the health consequences of drug addiction mitigate against longevity, although a few substance abusers do make it to their sixties and even beyond. Most chemical dependency among older adults is iatrogenic, however. This is a growing and important area for counselors and therapists inasmuch as the federal government is including us in Medicare networks. We shall be seeing more of the elderly. It is important to realize that the confusion and befuddlement of an older adult who is suspected of Alzheimer's or other dementia often clear up in a few days to two weeks when the chemical reason for the patient's mental state is discovered and corrected. The following are considerations all practitioners should note.

- Physicians do not consistently warn patients not to use alcohol in combination with their prescription medications. Many persons who have been moderate, social drinkers all of their lives suddenly find that their usual one drink before dinner or wine with dinner is potentiated by another CNS depressant (such as a benzodiazepine). Unfortunately, the older person may not be aware of the effect.
- As a person grows older, she has less tolerance for alcohol. The moderate degree of social drinking she has engaged in all her life may now result in intoxication. Again, the older person is not likely to be

aware of the change in effect. Again, physicians do not warn the patient, often reassuring her that her amount of alcohol consumption is reasonable.

- The elderly forget they have taken a medication and frequently take extra doses unknowingly. Practitioners need to involve a family member as monitor and make use of the easily available mnemonic devices that dispense the pills on a schedule.

- The elderly are a very overly medicated group. Physicians characteristically dismiss the elderly with a patronizing "You're not as young as you used to be" and send them out with yet another pill. Some of these medications are antagonistic to each other, or they overly potentiate each other; still others should be prescribed with care. The National Institute for Aging publishes a list of over seventy common medications that should not be prescribed for older adults or should be dispensed with great care and extreme caution[7]. Although this list is readily available and widely acknowledged, most physicians have never seen it. These include CNS depressants, antidepressants, and narcotic analgesics, all of which should be pre scribed with caution and in smaller doses.

- More than for younger patients, physicians are too quick to inappropriately medicate the elderly for grief or other psychological conditions. The pervasive attitude is that "I can't really do very much for this old person."

- Pharmokinetic changes in older adults may cause them to react differently to medications. Briefly, these reactions include the following:
  - The rate of absorption of drugs is slowed down, so there may be an unexpected delayed reaction.
  - All psychotropic medications (other than lithium carbonate) bind with proteins; because the levels of these proteins decrease with age, older patients are susceptible to toxic responses and require lower dosages.
  - Hepatic (liver) metabolism declines with age, increasing the amount of unmetabolized medications, thus enhancing the potential for toxicity.
  - Most drugs are excreted primarily through the kidneys; because older adults have decreased kidney function, excretion may be delayed, leading to toxicity.

The drugs with the highest abuse potential are CNS depressants, such as benzodiazepines and barbiturates. Given for their sedating effect, they can often cause oversedation and even coma in the elderly. This oversedation is often accompanied by a sense of helplessness, withdrawal, and disordered behavior, and can be misdiagnosed as depression. Other drugs that can produce oversedation in older adults are sedating tricyclics, sedating antipsychotics, and inappropriate combinations of common medications.

Confusion is a common reaction to medication in the elderly and can result from oversedation, anticholinergic side effects, or the toxic effects of lithium carbonate. Older adults with early or subclinical brain dysfunction or dementia are especially susceptible to confusion, which may appear as disorientation, irritability, agitation, sundowner's syndrome, assaultive behavior, hallucinations, or a combination of these. Their condition is then most often misdiagnosed as full-blown dementia.

Tremors and shaking can be severe in older adults, probably because of lowered dopamine levels. Patients who have been prescribed phenothiazines and other drugs over many years may develop uncontrollable shaking when they are older, which can be treated only by increased dosages of the offending drug. This sets up the next level of uncontrolled shaking, with the need to once again increase the dosage. Eventually there is a point where nothing will work.

The Foodaholic: Special Comments on Food Addiction

Although definitely demonstrating many of the physical and psychological characteristics of substance abuse, calorie dependency differs in a number of ways and requires special consideration. The foodaholic is not everyone or even most of those who overeat and are obese. Genetic factors, such as "slow metabolism" and general body structure, contribute to obesity; they do not necessarily contribute to food addiction, however. But the persons born with unlucky genetics make up only a small percentage of the existing obese population. Most obese persons have developed poor nutritional and exercise habits, but they do not use food addictively. The food addict is specifically defined as that person who eats because he is depressed, lonely, or anxious, or experiences a combination of these. Compulsive eating relieves or dulls these emotions; if the person does not resort to overeating, his anxiety mounts to an intolerable level. In addition, the foodaholic is fearful of commitment in relationships, uses scarfing as a way of blunting the loneliness that results, and then feels safe because seldom is a potential lover attracted by obesity.

Every foodaholic has a list of "nemesis foods." These can include ice cream (by the quart), peanut butter (by the jar), chocolate (by the box), and the surprisingly ubiquitous white bread (by the loaf), usually with copious amounts of butter. The nemesis varies, but whatever it is (defined as the food of which one taste triggers scarfing), it is always high in calories. Quantity is important, but no amount of carrots, spinach, or other such healthful food can quell the craving for fats and sugars.

Satiety helps shift the nervous system from sympathetic activity to parasympathetic activity, which is most involved in digestion. This shift also signals to the person, "I have had enough." Overeating makes the shift even more dramatic, with an abrupt reduction of the hormones and neurotransmitters associated with stress.

Therefore, scarfing has a direct effect on the limbic system, reducing its ability to generate strong emotions. The foodaholic experiences freedom from anxiety, loneliness, and depression, and if not, will continue to overeat until that relief is forthcoming. It is possible that enkephalins and endorphins, and perhaps even serotonin, are associated with oversatiation. Thus, along with the psychological reinforcement of relief from nervous tension, the foodaholic may also become dependent on the chemicals her body produces when she overeats.

Women are more likely to become foodaholics than are men, who have fewer inhibitions with regard to using alcohol and illicit drugs. Individuals who were "sugar addicts" in childhood are at high risk for any addictive behavior in adulthood, but the link is most clear with food addiction. Individuals raised in families where food was the medium of communication are particularly susceptible. These families are of two types. In the first, food is used as both reward and punishment. (For example, "You had a great report card; have a cookie," or "Your report card is bad; go to bed without supper.") In the second, the parents purvey food rather than convey affection. Food becomes the primary means of comforting the child, who in turn fails to learn other means of comforting herself. Individuals who were raised in substance abusing families and were hurt by it often vow never to abuse drugs when they attain their own adulthood. However, they have been indoctrinated with addictive behavior by their parents, and not surprisingly, food addiction is the compromise. It is addictive behavior that can be rationalized by telling oneself, "I am not abusing drugs or alcohol." Finally, individuals whose early dependency needs were never met or were inconsistently met often learn to depend on food for their solace.

It must be emphasized that foodaholics are no less adept at denial than those with outright chemical dependencies. However, the foodaholic's denial understandably differs in content and often in form, so this will be specifically addressed in our discussion of the denial expected from addicts in general on the first interview. The foodaholic's denials are often exceptionally adept, as body weight of three hundred to four hundred pounds is not easily hidden or dismissed.

The concept of *abstinence* for the compulsive eater poses a dilemma inasmuch as the person still has to eat. But this is a contradiction only for the normal eater. The foodaholic, when not in denial, knows and understands that abstinence means refraining from scarfing, nemesis foods, and eating when lonely, anxious, or depressed.

Footnotes

1 . Murray, R. M., & Stabenau, J. R. (1992). Genetic factors in alcoholism predisposition. In E. Pattison & E. Kaupman (Eds.), *Encyclopedic handbook of alcoholism*. New York: Gardner.

2. Wallace, J. (1982). Alcoholism from the inside out: A phenomenological analysis. In N. Estes & M. Heineman (Eds.), *Alcoholism: Development, consequences, and interventions*. New York: Mosby.

3. Brokaw, T. (1999). *"NBC Nightly News"* (January 2 1).
4. Carlson, N. R. (1986). *Physiology of behavior* (3rd ed.). Boston: Allyn & Bacon; Bloom, E E., Lazerson, A., & Hofstadter, L. (1985). *Brain, mind, and behavior.* New York: W. H. Freeman; Carnes, P.(1992). *Out of the shadows* (2nd ed.). Center City, MN: Hazelden.
5. Personal communication, October 1985.
6. Cummings, N. A. (1982). *Biodyne training manual* (2nd ed.). South San Francisco: Foundation for Behavioral Health; Feingold, B. E. (1974). *Why your child is hyperactive.* New York: Random House.
7. Hartman-Stein, P. E. (1998). *Innovative behavioral healthcare for older adults.* San Francisco: jossey-Bass.

Substance Abuse Treatment within Primary Care: Frontline Detection and Intervention

Nicholas A. Cummings, Ph.D., Sc.D.
Janet L. Cummings, Psy.D.
University of Nevada, Reno and the
Cummings Foundation for Behavioral Health

All of his physicians considered 41 year-old Rodney a model diabetic patient, as his compliance with his medical regimen was extraordinary. He not only judiciously monitored his blood sugar and consistently stayed on his diet, he vigorously exercised regularly. The only problem was that Rodney had to be admitted to the emergency room in a coma about every three or four months, seven times in the past two years. His primary care physician in a hallway conversation asked the co-located psychologist if there could be a stress or other psychological reason for Rodney's baffling behavior. In seeing the patient in a 15 minute interview, the psychologist quickly determined that the patient was a secret binge drinker. About every three or four months he would succumb to his urge to drink, and after several days of very heavy drinking he would go into a coma. Rodney was very ashamed of his behavior, and each time he determined and believed this binge relapse would be his last. He deceitfully kept the information from his physician.

As unique as this case may seem, similar cases are not infrequent and they can be even more dramatic. Routine surgery on a 53 year-old stevedore resulted in severe post-surgical paranoid hallucinations during which the patient assaulted the staff and tried to jump out the hospital window. His severe alcoholism had been missed, and the combination of withdrawal plus the anesthesia resulted in both a violent and suicidal reaction so severe that full restraint and transfer to a psychiatric hospital were required. Missed diagnosis of substance abuse is a significant drain and strain on the primary care system, but as these two illustrations indicate, they can be life threatening as well.

In this chapter the authors will demonstrate not only the feasibility, but also the advantages of having frontline detection and treatment of substance abuse within an integrated primary care setting. Even as healthcare is moving toward the integration of behavioral health in primary care, most planners continue to think of substance abuse treatment as a specialty and are not preparing to address chemical dependency (CD) as it impacts upon and complicates primary care. As a previous article by one of the present authors indicated (J. Cummings, 2003), this omission could be costly and unfortunately antithetical to seamless care.

Prevalence of CD in Primary Care

Surprisingly, a recent Substance Abuse and Mental Health Services Administration (SAMHSA) survey reveals that 26% of patients seen in primary care have substance abuse related physical illnesses, yet less than one tenth of these are identified by their primary care physicians (PCPs) who are focusing on the patients' physical illnesses.

Inquiry into their alcohol or drug habits is rarely conducted, and when asked to list the medications they take, patients invariably limit their responses to those prescribed by their physicians (Gentiello, 1999). They do not report use of illegal drugs, overuse of alcohol or inappropriate use of prescription medications. Furthermore, 50% of patients seen in trauma centers have intoxication related accidents, but less than 1% are tested for intoxication. Similarly, seldom do emergency rooms (ERs) test for intoxication (Zimmerman, 2003).

The National Institute of Alcohol and Alcohol Abuse (NIAAA) and the National Institute of Drug Abuse (NIDA) report that 20% of Americans are substance abusers (Cummings & Cummings, 2000) in the following numbers, with considerable overlap since polydrug abuse is the order of the day:

Alcohol abuse	30 million Americans
Marijuana abuse	17 million
Heroin addicts	3 million
Cocaine (and crack)	4 million
Barbiturate abuse	11 million (includes benzodiazepines)

Yet 73% of substance abusers are employed, and therefore most of these have employer sponsored health insurance that makes them direct consumers of mainstream healthcare. With the increased incidence of poor health associated with substance abuse, it is no wonder that 26% of patients seen in primary care have substance abuse related physical illnesses.

According to SAMHSA, abuse of prescription drugs has risen dramatically in the past decade (Clark, 2003). Physician prescribed opiates, stimulants, benzodiazepines and antidepressants are the most often abused legal drugs, with a rise of 19% in adults over 25. Startling is the 12% increase in 18 to 25 year olds, and the 8% rise in 12 to 17 year olds. With drug costs skyrocketing during this same decade, the inappropriate use of prescription drugs is an important cost, as well as a serious health problem.

Even more dramatic is the increase from 1994 to 2001 in specific drug requests, very often the most telling indicator of substance abuse and addiction. Again according to SAMHSA, hospital ERs and outpatient emergent care services report a 352% increase in the requests for oxycodone, a 230% increase in the specific request for methadone, and 210% and 130% increases, respectively, for morphine and hydrocodone. When coupled with the prevalent, but difficult to measure incidence of patients deriving prescriptions from more than one physician, clearly, our healthcare system has become a source of drugs for abuse. The present writers have had addicted patients confide that they were obtaining prescriptions for their drugs of abuse from as many as eight and ten different physicians without the various physicians' knowledge they were being manipulated.

The Cost Factor

In a landmark five-year study that increased the address of substance abuse within its own primary care system, the Kaiser Permanente Health Plan discovered that medical and surgical hospitalizations of substance abusers cost two-and-one-half times that of patients without substance abuse. The substance abuse patients exhibited complications that resulted in longer lengths of stay, and required more procedures and interventions. Similarly, post-hospitalization costs were considerably higher for the substance-abusing patients because they were notoriously non-compliant. In the post-hospitalization period, their continued substance abuse behavior retarded the healing process and often created additional medical problems (KPHP, 1981). Among behaviors discovered was the not uncommon injection of heroin by visitors (usually fellow addicts) into the bag containing the patient's intravenous solution. Unfortunately, our medical system is not created to be a garrison, but rather a trusting eleemosynary institution.

A three-year federally funded study at Harborview (Seattle) Medical Center demonstrated that thirty minutes of counseling of trauma patients resulted in a 47% reduction in serious injuries in the next three years, and a 48% reduction in less serious injuries during the same period (Zimmerman, 2003). The researchers projected that a 50% reduction in repeat trauma care nationally would translate into billions of dollars, and all for just thirty minutes of counseling.

The seven year Health Care Financing Administration (HCFA)-Hawaii Project involving 36,000 Medicaid recipients and 92,000 federal employees, using brief, targeted behavioral interventions for substance abusers in a collaborative primary care system, resulted in a $970 saving per patient per year, while traditional services *increased* medical/surgical costs by over $1,020 per year per patient (Cummings, Dorken, Pallak, & Henke, 1991; 1993). This $2,000 spread per patient between targeted care versus traditional care among the substance abusing population was substantially greater than even the impressive savings among both the somatizing and the chronically ill populations who received brief, targeted behavioral interventions for their respective conditions.

Impediments

There are a number of impediments to the frontline detection and treatment of substance abuse within primary care, the perennial problem of provider reimbursement for the behavioral interventions within the primary care system being foremost. The new 9615x CPT codes, yet to be fully tested as to applicability, hold promise. But a significant number of integrated primary care settings have successfully billed using the medical diagnosis. For example, the services provided the binge drinking alcoholic/diabetic as described above were for behavior complicating his diabetes, placing his life in jeopardy, and running up inordinate costs in periodic emergency care. There was no attempt at subterfuge, and a straightforward billing for diabetes treatment was reimbursed by the payor, as were frequent similar billings with other patients for different medical conditions being complicated by substance abuse.

The almost universal avoidance of testing for substance abuse in trauma centers, hospital emergency rooms, and outpatient emergent care clinics is a unique impediment to the frontline detection and treatment of substance abuse. It derives from the circa 1947 Uniform Individual Accident and Sickness Provision Laws (UPPL) and continues to perpetuate the missed diagnosis of substance abuse. The UPPLs, found in almost every state, allow insurers to disallow payment for any condition directly resulting from intoxication. Providers, playing it safe, avoid making the diagnosis of intoxication (or even substance abuse) lest they not be reimbursed for costly services. Paradoxically, the Health Insurance Association of America (HIAA), which was behind the enactment of the UPPLs more than half a century ago, accuses providers of being dishonest. In turn, the providers accuse the HIAA of financially stifling appropriate care. The record of identification and referral of substance abuse is appalling: less than 10% from primary care settings, about 5% from outpatient emergent care, less than 4% from hospital emergency rooms, and only 1% from trauma centers (Zimmerman, 2003). To make it worse, those who are identified and referred are most often patients who themselves bring up their problem of substance abuse. The successful challenge by Harborview Hospital of the UPPL problem may suggest that these are now virtually outmoded, or "blue laws" that are seldom, if ever enforced. The status and requirements of healthcare delivery in the 21st Century are considerably different than the reimbursement climate of 1947, and it is doubtful the HIAA would wish to litigate a test case. The pervasive impediment is the physician's own time constraints, and the belief that pursuing the matter of substance abuse is opening a Pandora's box with the patient.

Screening Devices

There are a number of screening devices for substance abuse, and these have been summarized (J. Cummings, 2003). None is wholly satisfactory, and they are:

CAGE (Ewing, 1984)	4 items
Michigan Alcohol Screening Test	25
Alcohol Use Disorders Inventory (AUDIT)	10
Substance Abuse Subtle Screening Inventory (SASSI)	93

The problem is that while physicians find any screening device with more than eleven items cumbersome, those with less are unreliable. In large scale integrated systems such as at Kaiser Permanente, indicators voiced advertently or inadvertently by the patient during the primary care visit are the most helpful and reliable. In addition, they provide an acceptable entry point to pursue the probability of substance abuse. These will be described below, along with historical signs and observable behaviors.

Behavioral Alerts (from Cummings and Cummings, 2000)

There are a number of indicators found in either the patient's history, or their observable behavior during the primary care visit, that constitute alerts. They are so-called because even though each alone is not conclusive of chemical dependency, they are a "heads-up" for the PCP that the patient may have significant CD issues that will exacerbate the physical condition, or complicate medical treatment. Two or more constitute an escalation of the alert.

Historical behaviors or signposts may emerge during the interview, either because they have been memorialized in the patient's chart, or because the patient or a family member is voicing concern.

1. Two or more bone fractures in a 3 to 5 year period (a falling down drunk?).
2. Frequent automobile accidents.
3. Frequent traffic violations, especially for reckless driving.
4. Even one DUI, but especially more than one.
5. Spousal battery, abuse of children, or both (usually intoxicated behavior).

Observable Behaviors during the visit itself. Physicians for the most part know these behaviors, but in an effort to adhere to an unrelenting schedule, or to avoid the Pandora's box, they are far from the forefront of their examination.

1. Unusual physique (as in the emaciation of heavy amphetamine use).
2. Tweaking, especially females.
3. Tremulousness, irritability, puffy eyes and face, small or large pupils.
4. Skin sores and infections suggesting injections (arms, toes, etc.)
5. Paranoia that is non-schizophrenic (heavy amphetamine use).
6. Demanding a specific drug, and anger when it is not prescribed.
7. Ingratiating behavior, followed by a sad story, and a request for a specific drug.
8. Immature behavior reminiscent of "missed adolescence" because of drug use.
9. Dramatic exclamation, "I've lost everything," with need for sedatives, etc. The exclamation, "I've lost everything," is very typical of chronic drug users.
10. The complaint, "My children don't respect me," may be because he/she is drunk.
11. Alcohol on breath is often ignored, as are the cover-ups: breath mints, licorice.

12. A vague, unspecified and reoccurring anxiety for which a patient asks for a benzodiazepine by name may connote the patient's favorite drug for getting off a binge, getting through the day at work after drinking heavily the night before, or marking time when opiates (and particularly heroin) are scarce.
13. In children and adolescents, stains on clothing, red eyes/nose, sores around the the mouth, poor muscle control and loss of appetite indicate inhalant abuse.

The Best Indicators: Watch for Them!

Every substance abuser is inwardly concerned that he or she has become chemically dependent and seeks reassurance that the behavior is really under control. The most likely place to find reassurance is from the physician, and this is sought during visits to the PCP. However, since denial and its companion self-deceit are very much operative, this leads to seeking reassurance by invoking the desired response. This propensity is almost universal among substance abusers, and leads to making an aside or seemingly inconsequential comment to the unsuspecting physician. These are surprisingly similar and with little variation, so it is important to alert the PCP to the most common of these.

Beware of the aside. This type of indicator of substance abuse is thrown out casually, but cleverly crafted to invoke the desired response. The following are typical examples, along with their true meaning and the desired response. The patient can then go home satisfied, "I told the doctor how much I imbibe and the doctor said it is okay." It is important that patients who are really imbibing as little as the aside suggests would never think of bringing it up.

Patient: By the way, doctor, sometimes I have trouble sleeping so I have a shot of whisky before going to bed.
Desired response: That's fine, and it is probably better than a sleeping pill.
The truth: The patient is drinking himself into a stupor, and may be even "sucking on a lemon" (alcoholic's vernacular for going to bed with a bottle).
Patient: I like a little glass of wine with dinner.
Desired response: A glass of wine every night has been shown to be beneficial.
The truth: The patient is drinking an entire bottle and perhaps even more.
Patient: My only vice is that I smoke a little grass once in a while.
Desired response: That is not unusual these days
The truth: The patient is smoking several joints a day.
Patient: By the way, doc, I like a couple of beers on weekends.
Desired response: That's fine. It is important to relax on weekends.
The truth: The patient is putting away a case of beer or more per weekend.
Patient: I've tried coke a couple of times to see what it is like.
Desired response: Well, I don't recommend it, but if that is all it is, okay.

The truth: The patient is snorting more and more at parties, and has done it at home.

Patient: Gee, I sometimes forget that I've taken my medicine and I take it again.

Desired response: Try to keep tabs on what you've taken.

The truth: Patient is using prescribed medication recreationally.

Patient: A Valium once in a while is the only thing that helps when I'm tense.

Desired response: That is what they are for, to use it when your tense.

The truth: The patient is popping pills all day long.

Statements designed to get more medications, typically presented seemingly with alacrity and utmost apology. The tip-off is the anger of the patient if the physician expresses skepticism. Most of the time the patient succeeds in getting another prescription as a conscientious PCP is prone to give the patient the benefit of the doubt. It must be remembered that substance abusers look like everyone else, and may even be a sweet grandmother.

1. The airlines lost my luggage and my pills were in my suitcase.
2. My houseguest forgot her medications and she used up all of mine.
3. I accidentally dropped my pills down the toilet.
4. I use so few of my pills, I thought I was throwing away the expired medication.
5. I'm so forgetful that I keep losing my pills.
6. My cat scattered my medications all over the dirty floor, so I threw them away.
7. I'm so ashamed, on the way home from the drug store I left my new prescriptions on the bus.
8. I think the cleaning woman stole my pills.

Frequently Missed Diagnoses of Substance Abuse

Amotivational syndrome accompanying heavy marijuana use is often misdiagnosed as depression, and antidepressants are prescribed, with no improvement. These patients are vague about their symptoms, complaining only that they can't seem to "get it together" or to complete a task at home or at work. They are not hiding their cannabis use, but do not think of "pot" as being the root of the problem. When confronted they readily admit using marijuana, and this should not be lightly dismissed. The pot of today is seven to ten times more potent than that of the 1970s, with "Winnipeg wheelchair" from Canada guaranteed by potheads to "knock you on your butt."

Patients complaining of severe overwork and inability to sleep are often given the inexact and dubious label of *exhaustion syndrome.* These patients have a plausible story of ever-increasing work, leading to loss of sleep because of worry and long work hours. They may even earn the appellation of obsessive-compulsive disorder (OCD) because of their seeming over-devotion to work. The problem in a surprising number of these cases is regularly drinking all night or the next day crashes following frequent all night amphetamine and cocaine abuse.

The irritability often accompanying chronic alcohol or amphetamine abuse is frequently misdiagnosed as *anxiety disorder*. This can be complicated in cases of actual agoraphobia or panic and anxiety attacks in which the patient has relied more and more on medication and has now become addicted. In these cases withdrawal from medication and the original panic disorder become indistinguishable, and most often the addiction part is overlooked.

Depressed substance abusers are at high risk for suicide, especially if their drug of abuse is a CNS depressant. Their depression is often masked by their chemical dependency, and when they complain of tremulousness and other complications of heavy drinking, etc. they are given benzodiazepines which can markedly accelerate their depression, and further increase the risk of suicide.

Chronic sinusitis can be a roadmap pointing to cocaine snorting, but the chemical dependency is often missed and the patient is treated for the physical symptoms. Chronic constipation can be an indication of opiate abuse, especially heroin. A sudden, severe emergence of hypertension may indicate heavy amphetamine abuse, especially in a person age 35 or under. This becomes even a stronger indicator if the patient also manifests severe insomnia for which he or she is self-medicating with large amounts of alcohol (i.e., in attempt to "come down"). An overdose (and especially if more than one) of prescribed medication can be a signal that the patient is abusing the medication. Addiction can perpetuate the pain for which the pain-killer was originally prescribed. It is axiomatic in addictionology that when taking medication for pain, once addicted, the body will perpetuate the pain long after healing has occurred so as to keep obtaining the pain-killer.

A Special Heads-up: Guard Your Prescription Pad!

After many years of conducting addiction group therapy, we are amazed at the frequency with which patients openly discuss how they have perpetuated their addiction for years by stealing prescription pads from one or more physicians and then forging the doctor's signature by copying it from a legitimately obtained prescription. We are even more amazed how even after we have alerted the well-meaning, trusting physicians whose prescription pads had been pilfered, the same physicians' names keep emerging as "patsies" among addicts. Given that addicts like to brag how they conned the system, it is still apparent that the problem exists and vigilance is appropriate.

An Integrated Primary Care Model for Substance Abuse Detection and Treatment

Chemical dependency first manifests itself in the primary care setting, and long before the severe complications of addiction, but these are most often missed because the primary care setting is not constructed in such a way as to detect most of these problems.

Even when they are detected and referred out to specialty substance abuse care, only a small fraction of those referred follow through. A close collaborative relationship with specialty care can increase the number of successfully referred cases, but it still falls far short of what occurs within an integrated system. When the primary care system itself is structured so it can detect and intervene in cases of chemical dependency, the majority of those identified will follow through with sessions with the co-located behavioral care provider (BCP) whom the PCP has brought into the case (J. Cummings, 2003). The co-location of BCPs in primary care has been extensively discussed (Blount, 1998; Cummings, Cummings, & Johnson, 1997; Cummings, O'Donohue, Hayes, & Follette, 2001; Cummings, O'Donohue, & Ferguson, 2002) and will not be repeated here. It is, however, important to note the differences and additions that have to be made to the usual behavioral health/primary care integration model in order to adequately address the significant, and most importantly the early substance abuse problems that so often are undetected in the primary care setting.

There are a number of large-scale programs integrating behavioral and primary care (e.g., Kaiser Permanente, U.S. Air Force, Veterans Administration, several community health centers, and several smaller HMOs), but none have encompassed the deliberate and comprehensive address of chemical dependency that has been proffered by J. Cummings (2003). Her recommendations for including frontline detection and treatment for chemical dependency is in the direction of the Biodyne Model, which extends behavior interventions in primary care beyond the model found in the aforementioned programs (Strosahl, 1997; 2001). In this model as seen in the original Kaiser program of the 1960s (Cummings, 1979; Cummings, Cummings, & Johnson, 1997), as well as in the Hawaii Project I (Cummings, Dorken, Pallak, & Henke, 1993) and Hawaii Project II (Laygo et al., 2003), 60% or more of behavioral health problems are treated within the primary care setting, with often as little as 20 to 40% being referred to specialty psychiatric care. J. Cummings (2003) projects this extended primary care model even further to include frontline detection and treatment of substance abuse, a condition that is almost invariably referred to specialty addictionology even in highly integrated settings.

Not only will PCPs need reorientation to implement the inclusion of chemical dependency within primary care, stressing the foregoing indicators, but the co-located BCPs will need additional training as well. Psychologists and social workers who have not been appropriately trained are only slightly better at identifying substance abuse.

Even when they are aware the patient being treated is a severe substance abuser, psychotherapists get sidetracked into addressing the (to them) more interesting and familiar "psychological" problems. Every addict will demonstrate co-morbidity as well as varying underlying problems. Beneath the addiction will be a basic personality, with some being depressed or anxious and who self-medicate, to the more personality disordered and even sociopathic patients for whom addiction is just one of many asocial behaviors. Getting sidetracked with those issues, to the neglect of the substance abuse as the major initial concern, is to forget that all insight and understanding are soluble in alcohol and drugs. Not surprisingly, psychotherapists are trained primarily in the treatment of neuroses and, therefore, exacerbate characterological problems by treating them as in the same manner they treat neuroses.

The Medical, Psychological and Abstinence Models versus an Integrated Model

The so-called medical model has two forms of treatment: withdrawal by substituting another drug, and slow withdrawal by titration. Because the addict is addicted to a class of drugs rather than to just one member of the class, the substitution approach may relieve the pain and distress of physical withdrawal, but it fails to treat the addiction. Although the abrupt withdrawal of CNS depressants can result in seizures and other medical complications and must be titrated, the concept has been extended to withdrawal from drugs in which seizures or other complications are not a threat. Making withdrawal comfortable only encourages addiction, and contributes to a culture that believes a solution to any problem is found in a pill or a potion.

The psychological approach to treatment regards addictive behavior as a learned response (Wallace, 1982), and employs cognitive behaviorism and other approaches to change a set of learned behaviors (or habit patterns) that are regarded as the addiction. Although addictive behavior is a learned response and the comprehensive treatment of addiction relies heavily on behavior therapy, the model disregards the permanent tissue and enzyme changes brought about by the addiction, and which tend to heighten the craving and the dependency, most often permanently. Psychologist adherents ignore the most recent findings of cellular biology and genetics, and their militancy results in what unfortunately may resemble the tenets of a faith. The cornerstone is the need to demonstrate that following severe addiction, the abuser can become a social user. This approach is welcomed by every addict, as the basic psychological denial of addiction nurtures the belief that "I can beat all the odds and become a controlled user."

Even more militant are the adherents to the abstinence model whose enthusiasm may lead to exaggerated claims, and hostility toward all other approaches. This approach takes real cognizance of physiological concomitants of addiction, posits that addiction can never be "cured," and that the addict must be in recovery for life, staying clean and sober "one day at a time." Another name for the abstinence approach is the 12-step model, named for the principles enunciated by Alcoholics Anonymous (AA) founder Bill Wilson (1935). Many, if not most of the 12-step addiction counselors are themselves in recovery, and AA has grown into Narcotics Anonymous (NA), Gamblers Anonymous (GA), and a host of others, all adhering to the 12-step approach. The strength of the abstinence approach is seen in its many adherents worldwide, and one cannot go to any resort, cruise, or vacation destination without seeing the time and place of a spontaneous local AA meeting posted in someone's handwriting on the bulletin board. Persons in recovery look for these postings when traveling, as regular attendance is an important part of recovery and avoidance of relapse.

Research has shown that behavioral and abstinence models are about equally effective for up to two years post-treatment. However, through the third and fourth years the abstinence model clearly prevails over the behavioral model (Cummings & Cummings, 2000; Quimette, Finney, & Moos, 1997). Relapse is an expected part of recovery, but the senior author has followed hundreds of patients who attained three and four decades of sobriety. Once past the twenty-year mark, relapses become increasingly rare.

An integrated model within primary care employs all three modalities, medical, behavioral and abstinence, using each as appropriate and avoiding indiscriminate use of drugs during the withdrawal phase. A drug free life style for the addicted patient is the desired goal.

Treatment Strategies That Work

The kinds of interventions following frontline detection within the primary care setting have been described (J. Cummings, 2003; Cummings & Cummings, 2000) and will only be delineated here.

Inpatient versus Outpatient Care. The research overwhelmingly indicates that inpatient (hospitalized) treatment of substance abuse is not significantly more effective than outpatient treatment (Saxe & Goodman, 1988; Saxe, Dougherty, Esty, & Fine, 1983; N. Cummings, 1991, 1993; Pallak & Cummings, 1992). Further, the number of patients needing to detoxify in a hospital setting is smaller than previously believed. In the past twenty years there has been created a multibillion dollar for-profit inpatient addiction treatment industry described by those who have had several of these 28-day "rehabs" as "two weeks of being drugged followed by two weeks of being brainwashed" (Grisham, 1999). Anecdotes abound about patients who underwent several inpatient rehabilitation programs with no avail and finally achieved long term sobriety after the first outpatient program, and vice versa. A summary of the evidence, however, indicates that there are only three indicators for inpatient over outpatient care: (1) Medical, not psychological necessity. This does not include anyone addicted to a drug that needs titrating, as a skilled physician can accomplish this on an outpatient basis. Further, by use of a support system a skilled psychotherapist can even detox heroin addiction, as grueling as this is. (2) Severely addicted patients who are socially unstable and have no social support system may do better in hospitalized care. (3) Patients who have failed two or more outpatient programs, yet do not manifest either of the preceding two indicators.

Heroin and Opiate Outpatient Treatment. Late in 2002 The Food and Drug Administration (FDA) approved two new sublingual (under the tongue) formulations of buprenorphine for the treatment of opiate addiction, including addictions to heroin and prescription narcotic medications. Subutex (buprenorphine) and Suboxone (buprenorphine plus nalaxone, an opioid receptor blocker that guards against intravenous abuse of the medication) are the first narcotics approved for office-based administration under the federal Drug Addiction Treatment Act of

2000 (Brown University, 2002; Swift, 2001). Previously, narcotic treatment of opioid dependence (i.e., methadone maintenance) could be accomplished only in specialized clinics. Physicians can issue prescriptions for buprenorphine and allow patients to monitor their own medication rather than having to report to a specialized clinic on a daily basis. Also in late 2002, SAMHSA launched an initiative to encourage the treatment of opioid addictions in a primary care setting rather than in methadone clinics or other specialized centers, and is funding training session through the medical societies (Clay, 2003).

Pre-addictive Program. Much has been made of the concept of "bottom," meaning that addicts seldom clean up unless they have reached the point in which they want no more of the painful consequences of addiction. The bottom may vary, with most addicts quickly forgetting the latest tragedy as they slide to the next and even greater tragedy. There are addicts who do not seem to have a bottom, and they simply die in the streets after a period of homelessness. Until a patient has reached his or her bottom, denial prevails as they continue their deceit and resistance to treatment. For a psychotherapist to treat the person before reaching bottom is generally futile, but to wait until bottom has been reached may take a long time and may never occur. The authors believe that it is the obligation of the BCPs to hone their skills so as to be able to motivate for treatment a significant number of patients. Techniques have been developed and tested in large scale delivery systems over the past thirty years, and these are available, although hands on training is desirable to achieve the level of skill required (N. Cummings, 1979; Cummings & Sayama, 1995; N. Cummings, 1993; Cummings & Cummings, 2000; J. Cummings, 2003). These interventions are difficult, and require the skillful challenge of the addict's obstinate behavior through paradoxical and other treatment methods.

One relatively easy intervention is to challenge the patient to attend a five-session group program to ascertain whether he or she is addicted, assuring the patient that the patient will be the sole determiner. Research over many years indicates that attendance in the pre-addictive group triples the number of patients who will go on to a 20-session addictions group. The reason for this success is that a group milieu is created toward an abstinent lifestyle, and one by one the group members convince each other that they need to go into an outpatient rehabilitation. Addicts tend to be quite direct with each other and accept this directness from a fellow addict when they would never tolerate it from the therapist.

A pre-addictive program can be offered on site, especially after work hours that are not only more convenient for the participants, but is a time when office space is more available. The pre-addictive group meets for two hours daily, for five consecutive days. It is essentially a psychoeducational program that satisfies for most of the participants their objection that by going into an addictive program they are being erroneously labeled. The program is designed to soften the resistance (denial) of addicts who are far from hitting bottom and who object to abstinence-based programs. The group leader guides the atmosphere, but it is the addicts themselves who convince each other they need treatment.

For a more comprehensive description of the program, see J. Cummings (2003) and Cummings & Cummings (2000).

Group versus Individual Therapy

Group treatment for substance abuse is overwhelmingly more effective than individual treatment mainly because the direct, denial-piercing interventions come from the patients themselves (N. Cummings, 1991; Cummings & Cummings, 2000). Not only are addicts more able to recognize in their fellow patients the denial (called "the con"), once addicts are clean and sober they resent any fellow group member that might violate the group imposed code of abstinence and try to lie about it. The bluntness with which they attack "the con" is far beyond what any therapist could do and get away with. The behavior of substance abusers in denial is anti-authority (anti-parental, thus anti-physician and anti-psychotherapist) and is more influenced by peers (fellow adolescent-like addicts). The therapist who attempts to treat addiction in individual sessions is at the mercy of the inevitable and unrelenting con, so much so that the therapist is tempted to stray into safer but irrelevant areas of investigation (etiology, frustration, childhood traumas and neglect, the stresses of the job, and so forth), all of which play into the patient's resistance.

The Addictive Group

The protocol for the substance abuse (addictive) group designed to be conducted in the primary care setting has been extensively published (J. Cummings, 2003; N. Cummings, 1979, 1982, 1991; Cummings & Cummings, 2000) and will be only summarized here. The typical outpatient addictive group is composed of ten to twelve patients who have all undergone withdrawal and are abstinent. Many of these have gone through the pre-addictive group, while others had responded positively to the challenge as given in preliminary individual sessions. The patients are addicted to various substances, including gambling, which, of course is not a substance but replicates the behavioral and neurotransmitter changes that occur with substance abuse and often substitutes for substance abuse. This variety helps to emphasize the nature of addiction: an addict is not defined by what he/she ingests, shoots, or inhales but by his/her lifestyle. This type of mixed group is particularly eye opening for the patient addicted to prescription medications. Such a patient self-righteously believes he/she is not a real addict, and finding him/herself in a group program alongside patients addicted to hardcore street drugs can cut through this patient's strong denial.

The group meets once a week for twenty weeks, and for two hours, usually in the evening because it is a requirement that patients return to work as soon as possible. This also is a time when space is available within the primary care setting. All group members start on the same first session, and once the group begins, no one else can join. During the twenty weeks the patient has recourse to five individual sessions, but only in response to need. Thus, the approach allows for individual attention in a severe crisis, but without detracting from the group process. Attendance and abstinence are both required. At the beginning of each session, each patient is asked whether he/she has remained clean and sober since the last session. Any patient who has not remained clean and sober is assigned a "fall." A fall is also assigned to a patient who was absent the previous session, and whose absence the group deems to be unexcused. Patients receiving a fall for failing to maintain sobriety are dismissed, as they forfeit the remainder of the session. Each patient is allowed three falls, and on the fourth fall is excluded from the group. The group members are active in determining if any patient is lying, a scrutiny that is far more adept and accurate than that of the therapist. Longitudinal research indicates that such a program generally graduates about 60% of those who begin (N. Cummings. 1979, 1982; Cummings & Cummings, 2000), regarded as a high figure in the light of the abysmal record of substance abuse treatment.

After Care

Addiction may not be "cured," although "recovery" is possible. Therefore, most addicts who complete the addiction group program need to continue in some type of aftercare in order to maintain sobriety (i.e., prevent relapse). "Graduates" are strongly encouraged to participate in relevant 12-step programs (AA, NA, CA, GA, OA, etc.), and most have begun this participation before or during the group therapy program itself. One of the advantages of such programs is that they are available in every community of the United States, if not most of the world, and they are affordable. In our own programs we have greatly encouraged such participation by making meeting space available in our primary care setting, ensuring close coopera-tion between therapy and aftercare. Graduates also have access to the BCP when needed, and are encouraged to seek an appointment whenever the patient senses his/her addiction "closing in."

Motivating the Patient Through the Challenge

The training of the BCP to detect and treat substance abuse long before the patient may have struck "bottom" requires a skill in motivating the unmotivated patient that can only be learned through extensive training, supervision and experience. Early substance abusers are so steeped in denial that frontline treatment is rejected or sabotaged by these patients. Yet the skillful therapist can demonstrate exceptional, gratifying results. It is beyond the scope of this chapter to fully describe the skillful treatment of substance abuse within the primary care setting, and extensive reading is available in the methodology (J. Cummings, 2003; N. Cummings, 1979, 1982, 1991; Cummings & Cummings, 2000; Cummings & Sayama, 1995). The reader is referred to these sources, with the caveat there is no substitute for hands-on training and experience.

Conclusions

The inclusion of frontline detection and treatment of substance abuse problems in an integrated primary/behavioral care setting is necessitated by the increasing number of patients whose physical illnesses are being exacerbated and even caused by chemical dependency. In such an integrated setting that employs what has been termed the "extended model" (requiring only 20 to 30% referral to specialty psychiatry), it is relatively simple to augment the BCPs' behavioral skills with CD treatment skills, and to train PCPs in the early detection and address of substance abuse in their patients. The oft-cited Pandora's Box potential in these cases is eliminated by the immediate access to co-located BCPs whose skills include not only the frontline treatment of chemical dependency, but the ability to motivate the unmotivated substance abuser. Treatment within the extended model of integrated primary/behavioral care avoids the failure of the referral process to outside substance abuse care in a population that is notorious for not following through on such referrals. The inclusion of frontline detection and treatment of substance abuse within an integrated primary/behavioral care system is not only good patient care, but is also cost-effective.

References

Blount, A. (Ed.). (1998). *Integrated primary care: The future of medical and mental health collaboration*. New York, NY: W.W. Norton.

Brown University (2002). FDA approves buprenorphine for opioid dependence. *Psychopharmacology Update, 13*(11).

Clark, H. W. (2003). Prescription drug abuse rises. *SAMHSA News, 11(1)*, p. 2.

Clay, R. A. (2003). SAMHSA launches buprenorphine education initiative. *SAMHSA News, 11(1)*, p. 3.

Cummings, J. L. (2003). Identification and treatment of substance abuse in primary care settings. In W. T. O'Donohue, N. A. Cummings, D. Henderson, & M. Byrd (Eds.), *Behavioral integrated care: Treatments that work in the primary care setting*. Needham Heights, MA: Allyn and Bacon.

Cummings, N. A. (1979). Turning bread into stones: Our modern anti-miracle. *American Psychologist, 34(12)*, 1119-1129.

Cummings, N.A. (1991). Inpatient versus outpatient treatment of substance abuse: Recent developments in the controversy. *Contemporary Family Therapy, 13(5)*, 507-520.

Cummings, N. A. (1982). Exclusion therapy with addicts. In J. H. Masserman (Eds.), *Current psychiatric therapies, Volume 21*. New York, NY: Grune & Stratton.

Cummings, N. A. (1993). Psychotherapy with substance abusers. In G. Stricker & J. S. Gold (Eds.), *Comprehensive handbook of psychotherapy integration*. New York, NY: Plenum Press.

Cummings, N. A. & Cummings, J. L. (2000). *The first session with substance abusers: A step-by-step guide*. San Francisco, CA: Jossey-Bass (A Wiley Company).

Cummings, N. A., Cummings, J. L., & Johnson, J. N. (Eds.), (1997). *Behavioral health in primary care: A guide for clinical integration*. Madison, CT: Psychosocial Press (International Universities Press).

Cummings, N. A., O'Donohue, W., Hayes, S. C., & Follette, V. (Eds.), (2001). *Integrated behavioral healthcare: Positioning mental health practice with medical/ surgical practice*. San Diego, CA: Academic Press.

Cummings, N. A., O'Donohue, W. T., & K. E. Ferguson, (Eds.), (2002). *The impact of medical cost offset in practice and research: Making it work for you.* Foundation for Behavioral Health: Healthcare Utilization and Cost series, Vol. 5. Reno, NV: Context Press.

Cummings, N. A., Dorken, H., Pallak, M. S., & Henke, C. J. (1991). The impact of psychological intervention on health care costs and utilization. The Hawaii Medicaid Project. *HCFA Contract Report #11-C-983344/9.*

Cummings, N.A., Dorken, H., Pallak, M. S., & Henke, C. J. (1993). The impact of psychological intervention on health care costs and utilization: The Hawaii Medicaid Project. In N. A. Cummings & M. S. Pallak (Eds.), *Medicaid, managed behavioral health and implications for public policy, Vol. 2: Healthcare Utilization and cost series* (pp. 3-23). South San Francisco, CA: Foundation for Behavioral Health.

Cummings, N. & Sayama, M. (1995). *Focused psychotherapy: A casebook of brief, intermittent psychotherapy throughout the life cycle.* New York, NY: Brunner/Mazel (now Brunner/Routledge).

Curie, C. G. (2003). Prescription drug abuse rises: SAMHSA and FDA educate public. *SAMHSA News, 11(1),* p. 2.

Gatchel, R. J. & Oordt, M. S. (2003). *Clinical health psychology and primary care.* Washington, DC: APA Books.

Gentilello, L., Rivara, F. P., Donovan, D. M., Jurkovich, G. J., Daranciang, E., Dunn, C. W., Villaveces, A., Copass, M., & Ries, R. R. (1999). Alcohol interventions in a trauma center as a means of reducing the risk of injury recurrence. *Annals of Surgery, 230,* 473-484.

Grisham, J. (1999). *The testament.* New York, NY: Random House (Dell Books).

Kaiser Permanente Health Plan (1981). Relative costs of medical/surgical hospitalization of alcoholic versus non-alcoholic patients. *In-house Report.*

Laygo, R., O'Donohue, W., Hall, S., Kaplan, A., Wood, R., Cummings, J., Cummings, N.A., & Shaffer, I. (2003). Preliminary results from the Hawaii Integrated Care Project II. In N. A. Cummings, W. T. O'Donohue, & K.E. Ferguson, (Eds.), *Behavioral health as primary care: Beyond efficacy to effectiveness.* Cummings Foundation for Behavioral Health: Healthcare Utilization and Cost Series, Vol. 6. Reno, NV: Context Press.

Pallak, M. S. & Cummings, N. A. (1992). Inpatient and outpatient psychiatric treatment: The effect of matching patients to appropriate level of treatment on psychiatric and medical-surgical hospital days. *Applied and Preventive Psychology, 1,* 83-87.

Saxe, L., Dougherty, D., Esty, K. & Fine, M. (1983). The effectiveness and costs of alcoholism treatment. *Health Technology Study 22.* Washington, DC: Office of Technology Assessment.

Saxe, L. & Goodman, L. (1988). The effectiveness of outpatient versus inpatient treatment: Updating the OTA Report. *Health Technology Study 22 Update.* Washington, DC: Office of Technology Assessment.

Strosahl, K. (1997). Building primary care and behavioral health systems that work: A compass and a horizon. In N. A. Cummings, J. L. Cummings & J. N. Johnson (Eds.), *Behavioral health in primary care: A guide for clinical integration*. Madison, CT: Psychosocial Press (International Universities Press).

Strosahl, K. (2001). The integration of primary care and behavioral health: Type II changes in the era of managed care. In N. A. Cummings, W. O'Donohue, S. C. Hayes, & V. Follette (Eds.), *Integrated behavioral healthcare: Positioning mental health practice with medical/surgical practice*. San Diego, CA: Academic Press.

Swift, R. M. (2001). Can medication successfully treat substance addiction? *Psychopharmacology Update, 12(11)*.

Wallace, J. (1982). Alcoholism from the inside out: A phenomenological analysis. In N. Estes & M. Heineman (Eds.), *Alcoholism: Development, consequences and interventions*. New York, NY: Mosby.

Wilson, B. (1935). *Twelve steps to sobriety*. New York, NY: W.W. Norton.

Zimmerman, R. (2003). Why trauma units seldom test for alcohol, drugs. *Wall Street Journal, February 26*, pp. B1 and B3.

Issues in Addressing Substance Abuse in Primary Care

Ian Shaffer, M.D., M.M.M.
University Alliance for Behavioral Care

Substance abuse is an extremely important issue in health care. Twenty five percent of adults report that they have drinking problems that put them at risk in their lives. Many of those reporting substance abuse acknowledge that they have external problems related to their abuse and dependence. According to the National Institute on Alcohol Abuse and Addition, 7 percent of U.S. population met criteria for alcohol abuse and dependence. Many of these people regularly attend appointments with their primary care physician. These appointments are often for issues that are indirectly related to their alcohol abuse. Frequently, unfortunately many of these medical visits focus only on the complaint that led to their coming for the appointment and do not address the underlying substance abuse problem.

Alcohol impacts people in a variety of ways. There are specific illnesses that directly result from alcohol abuse and dependence. These include liver cirrhosis, ulcers, and esophageal bleeding. These illnesses often require frequent and intensive medical treatment. Even though at the point in medical care alcohol abuse is highly suspected the focus of treatment is sometimes limited to the presenting medical condition and not on the underlying alcohol or other substance abuse. Fetal alcohol syndrome can result when pregnant women continue to drink through their pregnancy. This creates significant to problems for the newborn child. Finally, there are a number of secondary medical conditions resulting from alcohol abuse. These include injuries related to accidents and falls. Some of these include various broken bones, as well as serious decrease in general nutritional and health status. It is important that we begin to address substance abuse with the same intensity that the secondary illnesses are addressed.

The abuse of alcohol and other substances interferes with the treatment of many medical conditions. People under the influence of substances often will not follow through with required treatment regimens. Moreover, the substances may interfere with the effects of prescribed medication. Substance abuse also complicates treatment of other primary illnesses when the substance abuse reaches the magnitude that it must be treated as a co-morbid condition. Often primary care physicians feel ill equipped to identify substance abuse and effectively develop treatment plans to address the issue. They are also concerned about the impact that confronting patient's substance abuse may have on their relationship with the individual.

In order to clarify issues of substance abuse it is important to have clear definitions. Moderate drinking is defined as men having no more than two drinks per day while women and those over 65 have no more than one drink per day. At risk drinking is defined as 14 drinks per week or four drinks per occasion for men. In women at risk drinking is defined as seven drinks per week or three drinks per occasion. These numbers are important, as it is easier for primary care physicians to ask specific questions about the number of drinks rather than getting into discussions about whether an individual believes they are drinking a large, moderate or small amount. Being able to ask about specific drinking habits and applying a series of standards to the responses allows a primary care physician to begin to consider whether a strategy needs to be developed to address substance use and abuse.

Importance of Primary Care in Approaches to Substance Abuse

The importance of primary care for those abusing substances comes first and foremost from the fact that for many people primary care is their entry into the health-care system. These individuals will start with their primary care physician requesting treatment or that the primary care physician determine what type of specialty care might be necessary if treatment is not being provided within the primary care office. Moreover, a number of health plans require a visit to a primary care physician prior to attendance at specialty care. It is therefore important that primary care physicians feel comfortable with substance abuse assessment. These physicians must also develop strategies to approach those patients they deem to be at risk with substance abuse problems and those requiring treatment for their substance abuse.

Primary care physicians tend to look at the overall health of the individual. Specialty physicians often look at a single narrow aspect of the individual. The specialists are answering a specific concern raised by the primary care physician. It is the primary care physician who must look at the overall picture and make a determination about what areas need to be addressed.

For some physicians in primary care, the treatment of substance abuse is an area that they prefer to address themselves. Others will make referrals to addiction medicine specialists and programs. This latter group of primary care physicians requires training and skills in bringing substance abuse issues to the surface and completing an interaction with the patient such that the referral to addiction medicine treatment is effective. Because the primary care physicians tend to view individuals in their entirety, it is this professional that is likely to see each patient more often than any other professional in the health-care system. As a result primary care physicians have the greatest opportunity to identify and begin to address substance abuse.

Addressing Substance Abuse in Primary Care

There are three key elements in beginning the treatment of substance abuse. The first involves the recognition of the substance abuse by the primary care physician. Many screening tools have been developed. There is no one specific tool that every primary care physician feels comfortable using. One example of a screening tool is called the **CAGE**. It involves asking four questions.

These questions are:

1. Have you felt you should *Cut* down on your drinking?
2. Have people *Annoyed* you by criticizing your drinking?
3. Have you felt bad or *Guilty* about your drinking?
4. Have you ever had a drink first thing in the morning to steady mirrors or get rid of the hangover (*Eye-opener*)?

In asking these questions the primary care physician or staff member can determine whether there is an at risk issue that needs to be addressed. If any one of these four questions gets answered in the positive the physician should begin to consider that this individual is possibly abusing alcohol and the physician should have a strategy ready to address this concern.

The second component of a primary care intervention is for the physician to talk with the patient in a way that begins the process of patient acceptance of substance abuse as an issue. Denial is a *sine qua non* of substance abuse. Physicians need to assume that patients will often deny the presence of problems in substance abuse when asked. It is important that physicians have a strategy to address this denial in a way that avoids the nonproductive discussions that can occur. If physicians take a very traditional medical posture of announcing the diagnosis without laying groundwork for its acceptance, they are likely to be met with a great deal of denial and anger. It is more useful for the physician to engage the patient in a discussion of specific concerns designed to decrease the denial that interferes with acceptance of the disease and entry into treatment. The physician must also recognize that the discussion regarding alcohol and other substance abuse may occur a number of times before the individual is willing to acknowledge that treatment is needed. If the physician is uncomfortable addressing substance abuse he might want to reach out to addiction medicine professionals who can assist the physician in having the individual recognize substance abuse as well as the risks, need for treatment and how to obtain the treatment.

When the individual has accepted the need for treatment the primary care physician must be prepared to make recommendations with respect to interventions. It is important for the physician to understand that interventions for substance abuse usually utilize a teamwork approach. The goal of the primary care physician must be to complete an initial referral and revisit the issue with the patient when there is a concern about the patient following through and entering treatment or working to ensure that the individual remains in treatment. Primary care must be aware as addiction medicine specialists are, of the fact that people frequently leave treatment prematurely. There must be efforts to continually reinforce acceptance of their substance abuse as a problem as well reinforcing the need to stay in treatment. Follow-up is extremely important in the long-term success of substance abuse treatment for each individual.

There is a great deal of conflict within primary care regarding the diagnosis and treatment of a substance abuse. Often times there is a concern that confronting an individual with their substance abuse can lead to that individual leaving the physician and not getting their substance abuse treated. It is important that the physician be comfortable in the recognition of substance abuse, its diagnosis, methods of intervention and treatment recommendations. The intervention methods are particularly important in order that the patient follow through with treatment recommendations.

An important adage in medicine is that one must look for a diagnosis and keep it in mind in order to make that diagnosis. Shutting one's eyes to the possibility of a disorder can readily happen with substance abuse. At the same time there are a number of ways that physicians can begin to carefully determine whether intervention is necessary. We have already discussed the CAGE as a screening test that can be used. This screening test can immediately raise suspicion to the primary care physicians. There are other complaints presented by patients that should raise suspicion about the possibility of substance abuse. Recurrent abdominal pain, recurrent trauma and any history of blackouts are some examples. If a patient has frequent visits to an emergency room or has more than one fracture in one year suspicion should be raised with respect to the abuse of substances. There are also several medical disorders that will raise the likelihood of substance abuse. Bleeding from the esophagus and certain types of liver disease such as cirrhosis are strongly suggestive of alcohol abuse.

Therefore, the first step for primary care physicians in the treatment of substance abuse is to have a strong knowledge of how to recognize the disorder. Each physician should decide what screening tests they are most comfortable with and utilize them on a regular basis. A number of tests are available and may be given by a physician assistant with the results being reviewed with the patient by a physician.

The next step in working with an individual is to get the person to accept the disorder. This raises a number of issues in physician's offices where visits are highly limited in time. The physician must clarify that in fact this is an individual in whom substance abuse is quite likely and schedule a second appointment that will be designed exclusively, for the purpose of addressing the potential substance abuse issue. The physician will need to decide whether it is appropriate to have members of the family present or whether this is to be done on an individual basis. Most likely there will be a strong degree of denial of substance abuse from the patient. Therefore, physicians may choose to utilize and prepare members of the family to assist in addressing the substance abuse. This may be done utilizing a technique that is known as an intervention where the members of the family express their support as well as their concern for the individual with a strong emphasis on that individual's entry into treatment.

A more common approach for the physician is to talk with the individual and in a nonjudgmental way present the data and the issues. The physician must present all of the medical data with respect to substance abuse. This should be done with the understanding that the physician is attempting to help the individual understand the disorder and how the disorder is negatively affecting him or her. Having a plan for entry into treatment is as important as methods to address acceptance of substance abuse. All of this must be done using a supportive nonjudgmental approach. In this way the physician is addressing the issue of a medical disorder that requires treatment and not making any form of social or personal judgment about the patient.

Finally, the physician should be prepared with and present specific treatment options that are available and ways in which the individual can obtain the needed treatment. In the meeting presenting these concerns the physician needs to be firm and non-judgmental in his approach presenting the options and specifically working through with the patient a treatment approach. The plan should be put in place including who the individual will be seeing, who will make the initial contact with the group or treatment center and how the physician will be advised of the result of that contact. These concrete steps are extremely important, as it is easy for the patient not to follow through if there are no direct specific plans made with the patient.

The next step in the process follows the initial acceptance that a problem exists. What the physician needs to understand is that a great deal of ambivalence exists even with the acceptance of the substance abuse disorder. While with the physician and in the face of overwhelming data, the individual may openly acknowledge the presence of the disorder. However, having left the physician's office and now left with their own thoughts they may begin to rapidly shift back to a high level of denial. This denial makes it easy for the patient not to follow through with the recommendations. This is why it is important that the physician ensure that the patient leaves with a very specific treatment plan. The physician should not allow the patient to go home and then decide what treatment program they might call. In the latter situation it is likely that the vagueness of the treatment plan will lead to a lack of follow through. Optimally the person will have the name of the treatment program, when to be there and who to ask for. It is also important for the physician to recognize that acceptance may not lead to follow through. The physician may need to repeat the intervention a number of times, having the patient each time accept the statements about substance abuse, understand the treatment plan and yet not follow through. Not understanding the power of the denial may lead the physician to become frustrated and decide that the patient is being manipulative with the physician discontinuing his efforts to address the substance abuse.

Monitoring of a treatment plan is another key component for the primary care physician. The treatment plan for example might involve contacting a specific agency for a more formal and detailed substance abuse assessment. The physician can assist this process by letting the treatment program know that the patient is coming and ask that he be included in the formulation of the treatment plan. This will assist by having the physician and the treatment center on the same page and avoid miscommunications that can be used by the patient not to follow through in the treatment being recommended.

The physician needs to recognize the relapsing nature of substance abuse. A significant percentage of patients will relapse after treatment. Recognizing relapse as a part of the disorder helps the physician avoid feeling that his efforts have failed or in some way feel that the patient is not doing what is necessary. This allows the physician to address any slips or relapses that occur in a non-judgmental way. The physician is then in a position understand with the individual that this happens and that they must move along to re-establish abstinence and understand what led to the slip. By effectively addressing relapses and slips with patients primary care physicians can assist in developing relapse prevention strategies. This includes the identification of relapse triggers and working with the patient to develop strategies to counteract the relapse pressures when they occur.

In looking at the treatment of substance abuse it is important that the physician present several options to the patient with confidence that the patient is able to utilize them and be successful. If there is any sense of uncertainty on behalf of the physician or a judgmental approach is evident, it will strengthen the denial that is already strongly present in almost all individuals abusing substances.

It is important for the physician to be available to the patient as needed. This is clearly a challenge in primary care offices where physician time is at a premium. One method to resolve this is to designate an individual within the practice who will be available on short notice to the patient. That individual can be introduced to the patient at the initiation of the intervention and ensures the patient has knowledge of whom they may call should the denial begin to increase or later if a slip or relapse occurs. It is this person that one hopes the patient would call when the patient has thoughts of leaving treatment for any reason. Many people with substance abuse leave the physician's office with every good intention of following through on the recommendations and the treatment plan. They then go about doing what they normally do in their day including possibly abusing substances and do not follow through with the treatment. The physician or a member of the physician's staff need to recognize that they may repeat the intervention and experience the acceptance by the patient on a number of occasions before there is actual follow through. It is important to continue to encourage the patient and support the need for treatment. While there is a waxing and waning of the patient's acceptance of the disorder and their willingness to enter treatment, the physician must continually reinforce the need to enter treatment and to follow it through. This continual encouragement is very important in order that the patient remain on the track toward treatment and abstinence.

Challenges for Primary Care Physicians

In focusing on the issues we have talked about in substance abuse it is clear that their number of challenges that present themselves in primary care. These are both of a medical and psychosocial nature. From the medical perspective, some physicians tend to be uncomfortable with substance abuse as an illness. For many people substance abuse continues to be seen as a social weakness and thus it is difficult for these physicians to approach this as they would any other disease. With limited office visit time it is very difficult for interventions to take place even when the substance abuse is recognized or when it is suspected and the physician wants to bring the problem forward. Also, physicians tend to want to treat illnesses as acute, have them resolve and move on. Some physicians have a difficult time when they must repeatedly address an illness such as substance abuse where relapses are a component of the disorder.

The psychosocial issues related to substance abuse begin with the methods of addressing potential substance abuse. Physicians generally tend to take the lead in determining the treatment of many illnesses. The physician is seen as the expert and is expected to present a treatment plan that the patient will follow. In substance abuse the patient must be a collaborator in the diagnosis, accept the need for treatment and follow through in the treatment plan. For a number of primary care physicians this type of collaboration can be very difficult.

Some physicians are concerned that raising the presence of substance abuse may result in the patient leaving the practice. The patient may leave the physician as the patient has difficulty getting past the denial and/or feels judged by the physician. Combining denial and guilt can lead to a shift in emotion and rather than dealing with the issue of substance abuse the person accuses the physician of not being understanding with the patient who then indignantly walks out.

Further, the physician has to face his own responses to the relapsing nature of the illness. Some physicians will feel as if they have been a failure if a relapse occurs. Such a feeling can lead to the physician avoiding discussion of critical issues. Physicians then ignore raising issues that are more problematic for the individual in order that the physician not have to face the frustration of failure to improve. This leads a patient/physician collaboration where no one faces the illness or relapses and an unspoken collaboration means a key issue is not addressed.

Training

Training in the recognition, diagnosis and initial treatment planning of substance abuse is very important for primary care physicians and their assistants. Understanding the variety of screening tests that are available and the decision on which ones would be effective in a given office must be made. Physicians must also understand the medical indicators that are suggestive of substance abuse and address them in a medical workup as part of the preparation for presenting the evidence of substance abuse and the need for treatment. The physician must always keep in mind the potential for substance abuse as a component of any problem. The absence of recognizing substance abuse as a potential diagnosis means the diagnosis is not likely to be made and as a result the problem will continue unabated.

Physicians and their staffs must obtain training in methods of intervention. They need to understand how to approach the patient with concern in a nonjudgmental way. They must very clearly present the medical evidence for what they are saying and why they believe it is extremely important that the patient for the follow through with treatment. Within the training and the preparations for the patients, primary care offices must decide how they plan to structure their visits when substance abuse is suspected. Specifically, they need to decide whether a follow appointment will be used for intervention, whom they would like at that second appointment and how they plan to address denial and ultimately the plan for treatment. It is important for the physician not only to become comfortable with the relapsing nature of this disorder but also to develop a methodology to present the potential for relapse to the patient. The patient needs to understand the importance of monitoring himself as well as recognizing the potential to study relapses if they occur and learn from them. One danger the physician must recognize is the possibility that relapse leads to the patient feeling rebuked by the physician or his staff. This can lead to premature treatment termination as well as destroying the relationship between the patient and the physician.

Office Operations

In developing a method to address substance abuse each physician and his or her staff must decide how this will fit into the overall operation of the office and the delivery of medical care. What screening test will be done? How will be screening tests be done and by whom? Once the screening tests have been done and interpreted and there is a need for intervention, a decision needs to be made as to how and when that intervention will be done. Time must be specifically allotted for that intervention and it will be important to determine who will be present at that meeting, that is which family members and who from the physician's staff. Moreover, it is important to have an individual member of the staff available to these patients as they need them, that is, who will be available for urgent phone calls and office visits if urgently needed.

Further, each office must determine the degree to which substance abuse will be addressed within that office. Each office must be prepared to intervene to the point that the patient accepts the need for treatment or the patient ends discussion in this area. Thereafter, the office may only choose to develop the referral. Other offices may choose to follow more closely each patient while in substance abuse treatment. All primary care physicians should be aware of the treatment being provided and understand as much as possible the relapse risks. This will allow relapse monitoring to take place not only within the treatment program but also within the primary care physicians office.

Behavioral Health Consultants

The presence of a behavioral health consultant can be very helpful in these cases. The consultant is a member of the primary care treatment team that focuses on the psychological and psychosocial aspects of each person's situation. They are in a position to expand the substance abuse assessment beyond the screening into a number of areas of behavior and living that are impractical in a typical primary care visit. This consultant has more time to work with the patient on acceptance of the substance abuse problem and have a more in depth discussion of treatment options. If the consultant is present in the office it is important that he follow up with the accepted treatment program to increase the likelihood of the patient following through with the referral. They should monitor and determine that the patient has entered and is continuing in treatment. When they notice some wavering about treatment, they should intervene in an attempt to get the patient back on track. Consultants are also available to assist in handling slips and relapses. Their role in slips and relapses is to address with the patient the slip or the relapse in a very matter-of-fact clinical fashion. The nature of the slip or relapse must be addressed, the triggers that caused the relapse must be identified and then interventions need to be developed to address each relapse trigger when they begin to exert their influence.

Summary

Individuals with substance abuse issues are highly prevalent in physician's offices. Given the high prevalence and the many concomitant medical illnesses that can occur it is clear that a large number of patients entering primary care offices are likely to suffer from substance abuse. The physician and their treatment staff must be comfortable looking for and addressing substance abuse. They need to recognize that substance abuse can be a frustrating illness to treat and that they're going to be forced to attend to relapses and provide interventions to get patients back on track. Even prior to relapses the physician will need to deal with many initial starts and stops before treatment fully gets underway. Physicians and their staff must develop methods to cope with their own frustrations when patients relapse. They cannot allow their frustrations to interfere with their ability to effectively manage the recurrences of illness that are likely to occur in many substance abusing individuals.

Behavioral health consultants can provide an expanded ability to intervene and treat these patients as well as provide support for the physician's staff. Consultants can take the time to further the assessment and address the denial that is present within many of these individuals. They will also maintain direct contact with the substance abuse treatment centers and develop a method to enhance the probability that patients referred make connections with those centers. When patients are not seen by those centers behavioral health consultants can follow up with the patient to learn what happened and what needs to be done in order to get treatment back on track. Having more time to deal with these behavioral issues, the consultant can enhance the treatment team's knowledge of the impact of the patient's substance abuse their life and ways that they can address the impact. Moreover, behavioral health consultants are readily available as needed and therefore do not face the sometime constraints that are experienced by primary care physicians. They have the ability to take the time to deliver more specific interventions and can engage more family members if needed, in an attempt to get the patient to enter treatment.

Finally, is very important for us to remember that substance abuse causes physical, emotional, social, and economic damage. Therefore, it is extremely important that this disorder be carefully addressed.

Early Detection and Treatment of Alcoholism in Primary Care

Peter E. Nathan, Ph.D.
University of Iowa

Alcohol Problems among U.S. Primary Care Patients

It has been estimated that one in five men and one in 10 women who visit primary health care providers in the U.S. meet criteria for at-risk drinking, problem drinking, or alcohol dependence (NIAAA, 2000). This translates into about 30 million men and 14 million women. Because most of these patients choose not to consult alcohol treatment specialists, their primary health care providers have the opportunity – and responsibility - to identify, treat, or refer for treatment a disproportionate share of the nation's citizens with potential or existing alcohol problems. Unhappily, however, as we will shortly observe, primary care providers are often unwilling or unable to take care of these problems in these persons.

Data from the multisite PRIME MD-1000 study (Johnson et al., 1995) revealed a gender distribution somewhat different from that reported by NIAAA (2000): 10% of the male patients and 2% of the female patients seen in the PRIME MD-1000 study met diagnostic criteria for alcohol abuse or alcohol dependence, for an overall prevalence figure of 5%. This lower prevalence rate likely reflects a definition of alcohol problems restricted to abuse and dependence, whereas the NIAAA data included persons demonstrating evidence of at-risk drinking.

Forty percent of individuals treated for head injuries in a group of U.S. emergency rooms had previously been treated for alcohol problems (Rose, Zweben, & Stoffel, 1999), 50 percent of persons admitted to a number of Level 1 trauma centers in the U.S. were legally intoxicated, and 20-25 percent of inpatients in a set of hospitals for treatment for trauma had alcohol-related difficulties (Rose, Zweben, & Stoffel, 1999). Clearly, alcohol use and abuse play major roles in trauma, much of it driving related, in this country.

Of 1,131 pregnant women aged 18 and older, 15% reported some alcohol use during pregnancy and 13% scored above the TWEAK cutoff of two (Flynn, Marcus, Barry, & Blow, 2003). (The TWEAK screening test is described below.) More generally, after a marked decline during the 1970s and 1980s, following the discovery of the nature and extent of the fetal alcoholism syndrome, alcohol consumption rates in the U.S. among pregnant women are increasing, with current rates estimated to be between 16-20% (National Pregnancy and Health Survey, 1996).

These findings cover a broad segment of primary care patients, including those visiting primary care physicians, those seen in hospital emergency rooms and on trauma wards, and those receiving prenatal care. All point to the same conclusion:

the prevalence of alcohol problems among primary care patients is substantial. Hence, efforts to detect and treat primary care patients for alcohol problems as early in the development of their problem drinking as possible makes a great deal of sense from the public health perspective.

Detecting Alcohol Problems in Primary Care Patients

DSM-IV Criteria

While most primary care patients - and even many primary care patients with alcohol problems - do not meet *DSM-IV* (APA, 1994) diagnostic criteria for alcohol abuse or dependence, some percentage of these patients do meet the following criteria.

Alcohol Abuse (one required)
1. Recurrent substance-related failure to fulfill major role obligations
2. Recurrent physically hazardous substance use
3. Recurrent substance-related legal problems
4. Continued substance use despite persistent or recurrent social or interpersonal problems caused or exacerbated by substance use

Alcohol Dependence (three or more required)
1. *Tolerance*: Increased consumption of alcohol to maintain initial effect, or
2. Diminished effect if consumption is not increased
3. *Withdrawal*: Characteristic withdrawal syndrome on cessation of consumption, or
4. Continued consumption to relieve or avoid withdrawal
5. *Loss of Control/Compulsive Use*: Consumption of alcohol in larger amounts or over a longer period than intended
6. Persistent desire or unsuccessful efforts to control use of alcohol
7. A great deal of time spent obtaining, using, or recovering from use
8. Important activities given up or reduced because of alcohol use
9. Consumption of alcohol is continued despite physical or psychological problems because of the consumption.

Screening Instruments

Several brief screening instruments designed to identify persons who may be experiencing alcohol problems have been used to screen for these individuals in primary care patients. All rely on self-report information, which limits their utility to individuals willing and able to tell the truth about their drinking behavior.

The CAGE Questionnaire (Ewing, 1984): A cut point of one detects about 90% of persons with alcohol-related disorder, although it also yields 48% false positives. In other words, while the sensitivity of this instrument is high, its specificity is only mediocre. The CAGE questions include the following:

1. Have you ever felt you should Cut down on your drinking?
2. Have people Annoyed you by criticizing your drinking?
3. Have you ever felt bad or Guilty about your drinking?
4. Have you ever had a drink first thing in the morning to steady your nerves or to get rid of a hangover (Eye opener)?

The TWEAK Test (Russell et al., 1991): This five-item self-report questionnaire was originally designed to screen for risky drinking during pregnancy. At a cut point of two, its sensitivity approximates and its specificity is distinctly better than the CAGE questions. TWEAK questions include the following:

1. (Tolerance): How many drinks can you "hold" or how many drinks does it take before you begin to feel the first effects of alcohol?
2. Have close friends or relatives Worried or complained about your drinking in the past year?
3. (Eye-Opener): Do you sometimes take a drink in the morning when you first get up?
4. (Amnesia/Blackouts): Has a friend or family member ever told you about things you said or did while you were drinking that you could not remember?
5. Could you sometimes feel the need to Cut down on your drinking?

The RAPS4 & RAPS4-QF (Cherpitel, 2002): The sensitivity of this instrument is better than either the CAGE or the TWEAK questions; its specificity equals the TWEAK and exceeds the CAGE. The addition of questions about quantity (Q) and frequency (F) of consumption enables the RAPS4-QF to outperform the CAGE at a cut point of one across a wide range of groups. RAPS4-QF questions include the following:

1. During the last year have you had a feeling of guilt or Remorse after drinking?
2. During the last year, has a friend or family member ever told you about things you said or did while you were drinking that you could not remember? (Amnesia)
3. During the last year, have you failed to do what was normally expected from you because of drinking? (Perform)
4. Do you sometimes take a drink in the morning when you first get up? (Starter)

F. On average, how many days a week do you drink?
Q. On average, how much do you drink on each drinking day?

The Michigan Alcoholism Screening Test (MAST; Selzer, 1971): The original MAST consisted of 25 questions, several briefer versions of the MAST have since been developed. The specificity and sensitivity of the instrument approximate the CAGE and TWEAK, although it takes a few minutes longer to administer than either of those questionnaires. The MAST is a quantifiable, self-report instrument that asks for yes-no responses to questions about a range of alcohol-related problems, diminished control over drinking, tolerance, and withdrawal.

The Alcohol Use Disorders Identification Test (AUDIT; Saunders, Aasland, Babor, de la Fuente, & Grant, 1993): This 10-item self-report core questionnaire assesses three domains, alcohol dependence, harmful drinking, and hazardous drinking. It was developed from the *ICD-10* criteria for harmful alcohol use. A sample item: "How often during the last year have you needed a first drink in the morning to get yourself going after a heavy drinking session?" (Never, scored 0; Less than monthly, 1; Monthly, 2, Weekly, 3; Daily or almost daily, 4)

Biological Markers

These markers are somewhat less sensitive and specific than screening instruments. They do not, however, require self-reports of drinking behavior.

- *Gamma-glutamyl transferase (GGT),* a blood protein, is the most commonly used biochemical measure of chronic drinking by alcoholics. However, because it is also elevated in nonalcoholic liver disease, its sensitivity is not high (Allen & Litten, 2001).
- *Carbohydrate-deficient transferrin (CDT),* another blood protein, is less commonly used than GGT, in part because of lower sensitivity in women and adolescents (Bearer, 2001).
- *Mean corpuscular volume (MCV),* an index of blood cell size, reflects excessive alcohol intake, although its sensitivity is low because it is also affected by other conditions (Helander, 2001).

Physical Disorders Commonly Comorbid with Alcohol Abuse

Chronic alcohol abuse is associated with a number of physical disorders. Hence, primary care patients who suffer from these disorders are more likely to suffer as well from alcohol problems.

- *Hepatitis C*: Alcohol exacerbates pre-existing liver damage caused by hepatitis C.
- *Coronary heart disease*: Alcohol increases the level of certain fat molecules associated with coronary heart disease.
- *Carcinoma*: Heavy alcohol consumption is strongly linked to cancers of the oral cavity, pharynx, esophagus, and larynx, and somewhat less strongly to cancers of the stomach, colon, rectum, liver, breast, and ovaries.

- *Disorders of the male and female reproductive systems*: Chronic alcohol abuse adversely affects a variety of hormone levels and functions.
- *Disorders of the central nervous system*: Chronic alcohol abuse heightens the adverse impact of HIV and other infections on brain function.

A recent study of the co-occurrence of the additional risk behaviors (RB) of smoking, poor diet and sedentariness among 479 high risk (HR) adult drinkers (Rosal, Ockene, Hurley, & Reiff, 2000) found that 67% of the HR drinkers reported at least one RB and 61% reported smoking, sedentariness, or both.

Comorbid Psychopathology

Alcohol Abuse/Dependence is more often comorbid with other *DSM-IV* disorders than any other *DSM-IV* condition. Thus, the authors of the multisite PRIME-MD 1000 Study of 1,000 primary care patients (Johnson et al., 1995) reported that AAD patients (persons diagnosed with alcohol or drug abuse or dependence) were significantly more likely to be diagnosed as well with major depressive disorder without dysthymia ($p < .02$) and more likely to experience any PRIME-MD psychiatric disorder ($p < .08$) than patients in the non-AAD comparison group. Moreover, investigators in the multisite ECA Study (Regier et al., 1990) reported that 47% of persons with schizophrenia and 56% of people with bipolar disorder also had a substance use disorder. However, Coyne, Thompson, Klinkman, and Nease (2002) observed that "individuals with emotional disorders are more likely to use primary medical care than specialty mental health services, but these disorders are likely to be undetected or inadequately treated."

Because of high base-rates overall, however, identification of alcohol problems solely from the presence of an array of *DSM-IV* disorders alone is unwise.

Violence and Aggression

Violence and aggression are very often linked with alcohol use and abuse. Thus:

- Up to 86% of homicide offenders, 37% of assault offenders, 60% of sexual offenders, 57% of men and 27% of women involved in marital violence, and 13% of child abusers reported in published studies were drinking at the time (Roizen, 1997).
- Up to 42% of violent crimes reported to police departments in selected cities nationwide involved alcohol; 51% of the victims interviewed believe their assailants had been drinking (Permanen, 1991).
- A strong correlation also appears to exist between alcohol use and physical violence in marital or partner relationships: it has been estimated that between 25 and 50% of persons who commit acts of domestic violence also have alcohol or other substance abuse problems (Fazzone, Holton, & Reed, 1997).

In other words, primary care patients with histories of violence, victimhood, or both are more likely to present with alcohol problems.

Suicide

A history of substance abuse is a major risk factor for suicide (CDC, 2000), in part because of the well-established link between depression and suicide. Alcohol abuse is a particular problem: "The combination of depression and alcohol use disorders is particularly lethal, conferring a higher risk of suicide than any other clinical or demographic predictor" (Kingree, Thompson, & Kaslow, 1999). When Beck, Steer, and Kovacs (1985) reviewed more than 19,000 deaths suspected of being homicides or suicides over a 10-year period, they found that 23% of these individuals were intoxicated at the time of death.

A suicide attempt or gesture by a primary care patient should be considered a manifestation of a substance abuse problem until or unless proven otherwise.

How Often Do Primary Care Physicians Ask About Alcohol Use?

A survey of 23,349 adults who visited primary care physicians during a three-year period (Arndt, Schultz, Turvey, & Petersen, 2002) revealed that the physicians asked the patients about alcohol use much less frequently than they asked about other health-related behaviors. They were least likely to ask white patients, women, and widows who drank significantly about alcohol use. Similarly, despite the well-recognized association between alcohol abuse and a range of medical conditions, only 55 percent of a group of Level I trauma centers regularly obtained measures of blood alcohol concentration for trauma patients and only a few centers routinely provided referrals for trauma patients with alcohol problems (Soderstrom & Cowley, 1987). Even more surprising, alcohol use by pregnant women seen by a large number of primary care physicians was neither routinely assessed nor identified, despite the well-known risk to the developing fetus that is associated with drinking during pregnancy (Serdula, Williamson, Kendrick, Anda, & Byers, 1991).

Primary Care Physicians' Views on Screening and Management

A recent survey of primary care physicians' views on substance abuse screening and management yielded information that helps explain some of these surprising screening lapses. The survey was designed to determine the extent to which primary care physicians follow National Institute on Alcohol Abuse and Alcoholism (NIAAA) guidelines for screening for alcoholism (primarily with the CAGE). It was mailed to a diverse group of 210 internists and family physicians (Spandorfer, Israel, & Turner, 1999). The response rate to the mailing was a respectable 68%. However, only 65 percent of the physicians screened 80-100 percent of their patients for substance abuse during the patients' initial visit, as NIAAA recommends, and only 34 percent screened during annual visits. Only 20 percent of the physicians rated treatment resources as adequate for early problem drinkers, which may help explain the low screening rates. Older physicians, those working in non-urban settings, and those with more years of practice were all less likely to believe that a primary care physician could have a positive impact on an alcohol abusers.

Brief Primary Physician Advice (Project TrEAT)

Notably, despite the belief that primary care physicians are unlikely to be able to help alcohol abusers, a recent well-designed study reported positive outcomes from brief physician-administered intervention for substance abuse among a group of primary care patients. Fleming and his colleagues (2002) reported the results of a 48-month efficacy and benefit-cost analysis of Project TrEAT (Trial for Early Alcohol Treatment), a randomized controlled trial of brief physician advice for the treatment of problem drinking jointly funded by NIAAA and the Robert Wood Johnson Foundation.

Almost 800 primary care patients (482 men, 292 women), aged 18-65, were randomly assigned to control ($n=382$) or intervention ($n=392$) groups. The intervention consisted of two visits with a primary care physician and two follow-up telephone calls by a primary care nurse. The brief intervention included physician review of normative drinking patterns with the patient in the effort to suggest behavioral alternatives to the patient's abusive pattern of alcohol use; discussion of patient-specific alcohol effects to help create reasons why the patient should moderate his or her drinking; a worksheet of drinking cues designed to alert the patient to situations associated with high risk drinking; drinking diary cards to help the patient keep a careful record of consumption; and a drinking agreement in the form of a prescription by which the patient and physician reached agreement on a plan for the patient gradually to bring his or her abusive drinking under control.

Patients in the physician-administered intervention condition significantly ($p<0.01$) reduced seven-day alcohol use, number of binge drinking episodes, and frequency of excessive drinking as compared to the control group within six months of the intervention. This change was maintained over the 48-month follow-up. Intervention patients also experienced fewer days of hospitalization and fewer emergency department visits. The benefit-cost analysis suggested a $43,000 reduction in future health care costs for every $10,000 invested in early intervention.

The results of this study represent the first direct evidence that brief physician advice can be associated with sustained reductions in alcohol use, health care utilization, motor vehicle events, and associated costs.

Brief Intervention for Alcohol Problems in Primary Care Settings

A number of the key elements of Project TrEAT derive from prior research on brief intervention strategies for alcoholism (Edwards et al., 1977), especially including Motivational Enhancement Therapy (Miller, Zweben, DiClemente, & Rychtarik, 1992) and Motivational Interviewing (Miller & Rollnick, 2002; Miller & Sanchez, 1993). For this reason, it makes sense to review briefly here some of the voluminous data on the techniques for and effectiveness of brief interventions for alcohol abuse and dependence.

Miller and Sanchez (1993) proposed the acronym FRAMES as an aid to remembering the following six essential elements of brief intervention.

1. *F*eedback of personal risk: The clinician shares detailed information on the results of his or her assessment of the patient's alcohol problem with the patient, focusing on details of the likely adverse consequences on health if the patient continues to abuse alcohol.
2. *R*esponsibility of the patient: The clinician emphasizes to the patient that primary responsibility for bringing about the desirable change in drinking is the patient's, rather than the clinician's, family members', friends' or others'.
3. *A*dvice to change: The clinician makes very clear to the patient that his or her advice is to reduce or stop drinking.
4. *M*enu of ways to reduce drinking: Clinician and patient together develop a set of practical approaches designed to reduce drinking. They include identifying situations in which (and drinking companions with which) the patient is at heightened risk to binge drink; adopting strategies to reduce the frequency with which the patient continues to come in contact with those high risk situations and individuals; and establishing a sequenced set of goals for reduced drinking designed to lead to reduction or cessation of drinking.
5. *E*mpathetic counseling style: The clinician's interactions with the patient are to be characterized, above all, by an empathetic counseling style. The clinician adopts a person-centered counseling style first described by Carl Rogers: The clinician strives to understand the patient's view of his or her situation and to develop and maintain a warm, understanding, and non-confrontational relationship with the client.
6. *S*elf-efficacy of the patient: The fundamental aim of the empathetic counseling style is to encourage the patient to develop self-efficacy for his or her ability to change his or her abusive drinking pattern.

Other factors that appear to contribute to successful outcomes of brief intervention include involving patients in goal setting (Ockene et al., 1988), providing regular professional follow-up (Persson & Magnusson, 1989), and identifying patients ready to change their abusive drinking (O'Connor & Schottenfeld, 1998).

Many studies have suggested that brief interventions can help non-alcohol-dependent patients reduce their drinking (Yahne & Miller, 1999). A meta-analysis of 32 brief invention studies (Bien, Miller, & Tonigan, 1993) indicated that the average positive change was about 27 percent. Among alcoholics identified in an emergency room setting, 65 percent of those receiving brief counseling kept a subsequent appointment for specialized treatment as against 5 percent who did not receive counseling (Chafetz et al., 1962).

Follow-up data from Project MATCH, the NIAAA-funded multisite trial of three psychosocial treatments for alcohol abuse and dependence, indicated that four sessions of brief intervention therapy was as effective as the two other more extended (12 session) comparison treatments in bringing about marked reductions in alcohol consumption (Project MATCH Research Group, 1997).

Primary Care Health Psychology Training

Given the substantial involvement of psychologists in the development of both screening methods and brief interventions for substance abusers in primary care settings, as well as the growth and development of health psychology in primary care settings as a major activity for many clinical and counseling psychologists, one could expect that many health psychology training programs would seek to train students in primary care settings. Surprisingly, though, only a single report published over the past several years described a training program in health psychology in primary care settings (Garcia-Shelton & Vogel, 2002).

The article described a 13-year-old fellowship approved by the APA in clinical health psychology that is explicitly designed to provide training in primary care health psychology. Since 1987, the Michigan State University Family Practice Residency in Flint, Michigan, has sponsored a two-year primary care health psychology postdoctoral fellowship. The program trains psychologists as consultants and teachers to family physicians in the behavioral sciences and in the care of patients. Unfortunately, nowhere in the article describing the program is training in screening and treating patients with alcohol problems mentioned.

Unresolved Issues

- *How can screening rates for alcoholism in primary care settings be increased?* It is clear that primary care physicians and nurses can screen successfully for substance abuse. When they do screen, they are able to detect significant numbers of alcohol problems in their patients. When those abusers are then treated, either by the primary care physician or a behavioral health provider, they often benefit from the treatment. So the key seems to be to develop strategies for increasing screening rates by primary care physicians, nurses, or others in primary care settings.

- *How can rates of referral of alcohol abusers to treatment by primary care physicians be increased?* Again, given the success physicians and behavioral health providers have had treating primary care patients with alcohol problems, how can primary care physicians be induced to increase their referral rates of these patients to treatment?

- *How can more of the alcohol abusers referred for treatment from primary care settings be helped actually to enter treatment with substance use professionals?* Relatively few primary care patients referred outside the primary care setting for additional assessment and possible treatment ever actually persevere and receive additional assessment and treatment. Given the promising outcomes of such referrals, what can be done to increase the rate of successful referrals?

- *How can more primary care physicians be induced to learn brief intervention for alcohol problems?* The extremely promising data from Project TrEAT that suggest that brief physician interventions with primary care patients with substance abuse problems yield surprisingly long-lasting positive changes in abusive drinking patterns strongly encourage additional efforts to increase the number of primary care physicians motivated and trained to deliver brief interventions with their own patients with substance abuse problems.

•   *Why aren't more psychologists involved in developing intervention systems for alcohol abusers in primary care, given their central role in developing screening methods and effective brief interventions?* Although some psychologists have begun providing behavioral health services in primary care settings, including brief interventions for alcohol problems, few training programs exist for psychologists who wish to work in primary care settings. It seems likely that, were more such training programs to be developed, more psychologists would choose to practice in primary care settings.

References

Allen, J.P. & Litten, R.Z. (2001). The role of laboratory tests in alcoholism treatment. *Journal of Substance Abuse Treatment, 20*, 81-85.

American Psychiatric Association. (1994). *Diagnostic and statistical manual of mental disorders* (4th ed.). Washington, DC: Author.

Arndt, S., Schultz, S.K., Turvey, C., & Petersen, A. (2002). Screening for alcoholism in the primary care setting: Are we talking to the right people? *Journal of Family Practice, 51*, 41-46.

Bearer, C.F. (2001). Markers to detect drinking during pregnancy. *Alcohol Research & Health, 25*, 210-218.

Beck, A.T., Steer, R.A., & Kovacs, M. (1985). Hopelessness and eventual suicide: A 10-year prospective study of patients hospitalized with suicidal ideation. *American Journal of Psychiatry, 142*, 559-563.

Bien, T.H., Miller, W.R., & Tonigan, J.S. (1993). Brief interventions for alcohol problems: A review. *Addiction, 88*, 315-336.

Centers for Disease Control (CDC). (2000). Suicide in the United States. www.cdc.gov/nipc/factsheets/suifacts.htm.

Chafetz, M.E., Blane, H.T., Abram, H.S., Golner, J., Lacy, E., McCourt, W.F., Clark, E., & Meyers, W. (1962). Establishing treatment relations with alcoholics. *Journal of Nervous and Mental Disease, 134*, 395-409.

Cherpitel, C.J. (2002). Screening for alcohol problems in the U.S. general population: Comparison of the CAGE, RAPS4, and RAPS4-QF by gender, ethnicity, and service utilization. *Alcoholism: Clinical and Experimental Research, 26*, 1686-1691.

Coyne, J.C., Thompson, R., Klinkman, M.S., & Nease, D.E., Jr. (2002). Emotional disorders in primary care. *Journal of Consulting and Clinical Psychology, 70*, 798-809.

Edwards, G., Orford, J., Egert, S., Guthrie, S., Hawker, A., Hensman, C., Mitcheson, M., Oppenheimer, E., & Taylor, O. (1977). Alcoholism: A controlled trial of "treatment" and "advice." *Journal of Studies on Alcohol, 38*, 1004-1031.

Ewing, J.A. (1984). Detecting alcoholism: the CAGE Questionnaire. *Journal of the American Medical Association, 252,* 1905-1907.

Fazzone, P.A., Holton, J.K., & Reed, B.G. (1997). Substance abuse treatment and domestic violence. Substance Abuse and Mental Health Services Administration. *Center for Substance Abuse Treatment.* Treatment Protocol (TIP) Series 25.

Fleming, M.F., Mundt, M.P., French, M.T., Manwell, L.B., Stauffacher, E.A., & Barry, K.L. (2002). Brief physician advice for problem drinkers: Long-term efficacy and benefit-cost analysis. *Alcoholism: Clinical and Experimental Research, 26,* 36-43.

Flynn, H.A., Marcus, S.M., Barry, K.L., & Blow, F.C. (2003). Rates and correlates of alcohol use among pregnant women in obstetrics clinics. *Alcoholism: Clinical and Experimental Research, 27,* 81-87.

Garcia-Shelton, L. & Vogel, M.E. (2002). Primary care health psychology training: A collaborative model with family practice. *Professional Psychology: Research and Practice, 33,* 546-556.

Helander, A. (2001). Biological markers of alcohol use and abuse in theory and practice. In Agarwal, D.P. & Seitz, H.K. (Eds.), *Alcohol in health and disease* (pp. 177-205). New York: Marcel Dekker.

Johnson, J.G., Spitzer, R.L., Williams, J.B.W., Kroenke, K., Linzer, M., Brody, D., DeGruy, F., & Hahn, S. (1995). Psychiatric comorbidity, health status, and functional impairment associated with alcohol abuse and dependence in primary care patients: Findings of the PRIME MD-1000 Study. *Journal of Consulting and Clinical Psychology, 63,* 133-140.

Kingree, J.B., Thompson, M.P., & Kaslow, N.J. (1999). Risk factors for suicide attempts among low-income women with a history of alcohol problems. *Addictive Behaviors, 24,* 583-587.

Miller, W.R. & Rollnick, S. (2002). *Motivational interviewing: Preparing people for change* (2nd edit.). New York: Guilford Publications, Inc.

Miller, W.R. & Sanchez, V.C. (1993). Motivating young adults for treatment and lifestyle change. In G. Howard & P.E. Nathan (Eds.), *Issues in alcohol use and misuse in young adults.* Notre Dame, IN: University of Notre Dame Press.

Miller, W.R., Zweben, A., DiClemente, C.C., & Rychtarik, R.G. (1992). Motivational enhancement therapy manual: A clinical tool for therapists treating individuals with alcohol abuse and dependence. *Project MATCH Monograph Series,* Vol. 2. Rockville, MD: U.S. Department of Health and Human Services and National Institute on Alcohol Abuse and Alcoholism.

National Institute on Alcohol Abuse and Alcoholism (NIAAA). (2000). *Tenth special report to the U.S. Congress on Alcohol and Health.* Washington, D.C.: U.S. Government Printing Office.

National Pregnancy and Health Survey. (1996). Drug abuse among women delivering live births: 1992. Rockville, MD: *NIH publication 96-3819.* DHHS, NIDA.

Ockene, J.K., Quirk, M.E., Goldberg, R.J., Kristeller, J.L., Donnelly, G., Kalan, K.L., Gould, B., Greene, H.L., Harrison-Atlas, R., Pease, J., Pickens, S., & Williams,

J.W. (1988). *A residents' training program for the development of smoking intervention skills. Archives of Internal Medicine, 148*, 1039-1045.

O'Connor, P.G., & Schottenfeld, R.S. (1998). Patients with alcohol problems. *New England Journal of Medicine, 338*, 592-602.

Permanen, K. (1991). *Alcohol in human violence.* New York: Guilford Press.

Persson, J. & Magnusson, P.H. (1989). Early intervention in patients with excessive consumption of alcohol: A controlled study. *Alcohol, 6*, 403-408.

Project MATCH Research Group. (1997). Matching alcoholism treatments to client heterogeneity: Project MATCH post-treatment drinking outcomes. *Journal of Studies on Alcohol, 58*, 7-29.

Regier, D.A., et al. (1990). Comorbidity of mental disorders with alcohol and other drug abuse: Results from the Epidemiological Catchment Area (ECA) Study. *Journal of the American Medical Association, 21*, 2511-2518.

Roizen, J. (1997). Epidemiological issues in alcohol-related violence. In M. Galanter (Ed.), *Recent developments in alcoholism,* Vol. 13 (pp. 7-40). New York: Plenum Press.

Rosal, M.C., Ockene, J.K., Hurley, T.G., & Reiff, S. (2000). Prevalence and co-occurrence of health risk behaviors among high-risk drinkers in a primary care population. *Preventive Medicine, 31*, 140-147.

Rose, S.J., Zweben, A., & Stoffel, V. (1999). Interfaces between substance abuse treatment and other health and social systems. In B.S. McCrady & E.E. Epstein (Eds.), *Addictions: A comprehensive guidebook* (pp. 421-436). New York: Oxford University Press

Russell, M., et al. (1991). Measures of maternal alcohol use as predictors of development in early childhood. *Alcoholism: Clinical and Experimental Research, 18*, 1156-1161.

Saunders, J.B., Aasland, O.G., Babor, T.F., de la Fuente, J.R., & Grant, M. (1993). Development of the Alcohol Use Disorders Identification Test (AUDIT): WHO Collaborative Project on Early Detection of Persons with Harmful Alcohol Consumption. II. *Addictions, 88*, 791-804.

Selzer, M.L. (1971). The Michigan Alcoholism Screening Test (MAST): The quest for a new diagnostic instrument. *American Journal of Psychiatry, 127*, 1653-1658.

Serdula, M., Williamson, D.F., Kendrick, J.S., Anda, R.F., & Byers, T. (1991). Trends in alcohol consumption by pregnant women: 1985-1988. *Journal of the American Medical Association, 265*, 876-879.

Soderstrom, C.B., & Cowley, R.A. (1987). A national alcohol and trauma center survey. *Archives of Surgery, 122*, 1067-1071.

Spandorfer, J.M., Israel, Y., & Turner, B.J. (1999). Primary care physicians' views on screening and management of alcohol abuse: Inconsistencies with national guidelines. *Journal of Family Practice, 48*, 899-902.

Yahne, C.E. & Miller, W.R. (1999). Enhancing motivation for treatment and change. In B.S. McCrady & E.E. Epstein (Eds.), *Addictions: A comprehensive guidebook* (pp. 235-249). New York: Oxford University Press.

Opportunities for Improved Detection and Treatment of Alcohol Misuse: Using Behavioral Health Consultants in Primary Care

Christine N. Runyan, Ph.D.

*Population Health Support Division, Air Force Medical
Operations Agency, Brooks Air Force Base*

Introduction

Alcohol misuse[1] is a substantial public health problem and is one of the top three causes of premature morbidity and mortality in the United States (McGinnis & Foege, 1993). Approximately 14 million Americans, or 7.4 percent of the population, meet diagnostic criteria for alcohol abuse or dependence (Grant et al., 1994). Moreover, alcohol misuse is a major cause of illness and death, responsible for the loss of over 100,000 lives each year. It also creates a sizable economic burden in health care costs, public safety and social welfare expenditures. In 1992, the measured economic cost of alcohol misuse was over $148 billion (Harwood et al., 1998). A more recent estimate, accounting for both population growth and inflation, puts this figure over $184 billion each year (Harwood, 2000). Interestingly, it is not only those individuals with alcohol dependence who create this burden. Individual who *misuse* alcohol account for a significant proportion of alcohol-related problems, such as motor vehicle crashes, other injuries, health problems, and family difficulties (Institute of Medicine, 1990).

Both research and applied clinical experiences have created a body of evidence on types of interventions that are most successful in treating and managing individuals with alcohol abuse and alcohol dependence. However, long-term success rates of these treatments remain modest. On the prevention front, both policy-level and community based prevention activities aim to reduce the overall prevalence of alcohol misuse. Unfortunately, national prevalence rates of both chronic alcohol use and binge drinking continue to rise (CDC, 2002). Alcohol misuse disorders pose a considerable dilemma in healthcare delivery as both patients and providers are reticent to discuss alcohol use during medical care visits. Thus, one of the missing links is the development, evaluation, and implementation of strategies targeted towards redesigning the delivery system in a manner that brings together the evidence on what works to identify potential alcohol misusers with effective intervention strategies. This chapter will present one such model for the systematic identification, assessment, and intervention for individuals with alcohol misuse problems in primary care clinics.

Why Primary Care?

Alcohol abuse and dependence have a long history of being treated in specialty mental health clinics, ranging from intensive outpatient to partial hospitalization and inpatient programs. Although specialized treatment centers are a critical component to building and sustaining an effective overall model of treatment for alcohol-related disorders, there are at least three significant flaws associated with relying on specialty mental health programs to manage the burden of alcohol abuse and dependence.

First, although current estimates on the effectiveness of various types of treatments for alcohol abuse and dependence range considerably, all suggest no more than moderate rates of long-term success. In fact, interventions for alcohol dependence are similar in effectiveness to those of other chronic health conditions. Although research on new approaches to improve these treatments is ongoing, new cases of alcohol abuse and dependence are also constantly emerging. Thus, in the absence of a "cure," the overall prevalence, and therefore the economic, societal, and healthcare burden, of alcohol misuse disorders is likely to continue to grow.

Secondly, delivering alcohol misuse treatment in a specialty mental health clinic almost necessarily implies that individuals are symptomatically impaired to the point of meeting diagnostic criteria. Because alcohol misuse disorders are progressive, often marked by months or years of problematic use long before an individual meets diagnostic criteria, there have been numerous missed opportunities to intervene at a time when the problem was less severe and perhaps easier to treat. Treatment programs focused exclusively on the severe alcohol abuse patient will necessarily fail to identify and treat persons with only problem drinking. By failing to focus on groups with elevated risk for alcohol disorders, the overall problem as well as the demand for more intensive services, will continue to grow beyond the nation's existing healthcare capacity.

Finally, with regard to personal and societal harms associated with alcohol use disorders, those with alcohol dependence are most likely to personally experience or cause harm, however, *problem drinking* is over five times more prevalent than alcohol dependence. Therefore, problem drinkers, as compared to alcoholics, actually cause more economic and societal harms on the whole (Institute of Medicine, 1990). The identification of such individuals, before they progress to more serious disorders, has the potential to not only reduce societal and economic costs, but minimize personal harm as well. One avenue to selectively target problem drinkers includes community-level prevention and education programs. However, with roughly 80% of all adult Americans visiting their primary care physician each year, primary care clinics are also one of the best sources for identifying individuals with patterns of alcohol misuse.

Nearly half of the adult U.S. population (aged 18 and over) are current drinkers who have consumed at least 12 drinks in the preceding year (Dawson et al. 1995). Although many current drinkers consume alcohol safely and in moderation, according to one study, roughly one in five men and one in ten women who visit their primary care providers meet the criteria for high-risk drinking, problem drinking, or alcohol dependence (Manwell et al. 1998). Another recent study found that 11% of patients in an adult primary care population met one or more of the following criteria in the past month: (a) more than two drinks per day, on average; (b) greater than two binge drinking episodes; or (c) one episode of driving following three or more alcoholic beverages (Curry et al., 2000). Still another study in community-based primary care clinics found a 13.8% prevalence of problem drinking as defined by either: (a) 14 or more drinks per week, on average, for men or 11 or more drinks per week, on average, for women; or (b) four or more binge drinking episodes in the past month (Fleming et al., 2002). Unfortunately, the vast majority of primary care physicians (PCPs) fail to recognize or address alcohol use and alcohol-related problems within their patients (Arndt, 2002; Buchsbaum et al., 1992). In fact, most estimates suggest fewer than one-third of PCPs routinely screen for alcohol use and alcohol-related problems; some evidence suggests that fewer than 10% of physicians successfully identify alcohol abuse in their patients (CASA, 2000). Use of biomedical indicators, if used as a screening mechanism, rarely reveal problems with alcohol since they are not sensitive and tend to be highly variable indicators of actual use or misuse. Even once screening is done, processes for additional assessment and intervention are rarely in place. To further complicate this dilemma, patients who engage in high-risk behaviors while under the influence of alcohol, or whose overall pattern of alcohol use may be problematic, are equally unlikely to raise this as a concern with their PCP. Primary care is therefore a setting in which routine screening of alcohol use and alcohol-related problems, coupled with effective intervention strategies, can help improve rates of timely identification and intervention (USPSTF, 1996).

Definition of Terms

Before talking more extensively about screening, identification, and intervention in primary care clinics, a few definitions are warranted. There are many types of primary care clinics and primary care providers, including family practice physicians, internists, and OB/GYN. For purposes of this discussion, *Primary Care*, as defined by the Institute of Medicine (Donaldson et al., 1996), refers to "the provision of integrated, accessible health care services by clinicians who are accountable for addressing a large majority of personal health care needs, developing a sustained partnership with patients, and practicing in the context of family and community."

There are multiple ways to conceptualize and define the misuse of alcohol, including, but not limited to "at risk" or high-risk drinking, hazardous or harmful consumption, problem drinking, binge drinking, or alcohol abuse/dependence as

defined by the *Diagnostic and Statistical Manual for Mental Disorders, 4ᵗʰ Edition.*
Depending on the definition used and the problem of interest, different mechanisms
of assessment and treatment may be warranted. In this chapter, for reasons that will
be later discussed, the focus will be on alcohol misuse.

Alcohol misuse is defined as any maladaptive pattern of alcohol use in a manner
that impairs one's physical, psychological, or social functioning, increases risk of
harm to self or others, or places an undue burden upon society. This definition
includes *Binge Drinking*, defined as 5 or more alcoholic beverages consumed in one
setting, as well as *Heavy Alcohol Use*, defined as frequent episodes (four or more times
in the past 30 days) of binge drinking.[2] This definition also necessarily includes all
types of alcohol abuse or dependence; however, these more severe disorders will not
be the focus of the proposed model in this chapter.

Finally, the term *Behavioral Health Consultant (BHC)* warrants definition. A
behavioral health consultant is a psychologist or clinical social worker that has received
additional specialized training in a consultative model of behavioral healthcare. The
BHC serves as a consultant to primary care providers and to patients, providing
additional assessment, curbside consultation and interventions regarding a wide
array of behavioral health needs within a primary care setting.[3]

Targeting Alcohol Misuse

A substantial amount of research, resources, and clinical treatment programs
focus on severe or diagnostic alcohol use disorders. The model proposed here takes
a complementary perspective in suggesting that screening and intervention among
those with *alcohol misuse* provides a unique opportunity to address this substantial
public health problem. Alcohol-related disorders, binge drinking, and high-risk
behaviors involving alcohol misuse are both prevalent and costly. The prevalence
of problem drinking varies from 10% to 25% depending on the definition used, sex,
age, and clinical setting (Fleming et al., 1998). Furthermore, problem drinking,
including binge drinking, is associated with a host of adverse outcomes including
unintentional injuries, suicide, sudden infant death syndrome, alcohol poisoning,
hypertension, acute myocardial infarction, gastritis, pancreatitis, sexually transmit-
ted diseases, interpersonal violence, fetal alcohol syndrome, and unintended
pregnancy (Chou, Grant, & Dawson, 1996). Among older persons, even relatively
low amounts of alcohol consumption can lead to deleterious health outcomes, due
to age-related physiological changes and the interaction of alcohol with medications
or otherwise impaired health status (Moore et al., 1999). A recent description of
binge drinking among US adults from the 1993-2001 Behavioral Risk Factor
Surveillance System data (Naimi et al., 2003) reported that rates of binge drinking
have been increasing since 1993 and that men aged 18-25 have the highest rates of
rates of binge drinking. However, 69% of binge drinking episodes occurred among
those 26 years old or older, suggesting that the majority of binge drinking episodes
are among older Americans. Moreover, 73% of binge drinkers were otherwise
moderate (i.e., not heavy) drinkers. Perhaps most noteworthy of this analysis was that
those classified as binge drinkers were nearly 14 times more likely to drive a vehicle

while impaired by alcohol. With such staggering statistics, it is not surprising, that reducing binge drinking among adults is one of the leading health indicators in Healthy People 2010 (United States Department of Health and Human Services, 2000).

Another advantage of targeting alcohol misuse is that this population often responds well to clinician counseling, brief interventions, and self-guided educational and motivational interventions. In fact, reductions in short-term alcohol use have been demonstrated in several randomized controlled clinical trials using brief interventions, many of which have been done using brief physician counseling in primary care (see Fleming, 2003 for a recent review). Referrals to more costly and more time-intensive specialty treatment may not be required or preferred among the majority of individuals who misuse alcohol. Although the data demonstrating the efficacy of brief interventions for more severe alcohol abusers is relatively new, the evidence on the effectiveness of preventive approaches to both screen and counsel adolescents and adults for problem drinking as a means to significantly reduce illness or injury has existed for several years. In fact, the United States Preventive Services Task Force (USPSTF) issued a recommendation in 1996 stating the following: *"Screening to detect problem drinking is recommended for all adult and adolescent patients. Screening should involve a careful history of alcohol use and/or the use of standardized screening questionnaires"* (USPSTF, 1996). Unfortunately, as previously noted, the vast majority of primary care providers and clinics do not comply with this screening and counseling recommendation, much less brief interventions for alcohol misuse. The next sections will address the various reasons why screening is not more commonplace in today's healthcare delivery system.

Screening and Primary Care Interventions

As the "gatekeepers" and "front line" medical providers in healthcare delivery, primary care providers and clinics are confronted with the ominous task of providing clinical preventive services, medical care for acute conditions, referrals and follow-up with specialty providers, as well as long-term management of chronic medical conditions for their patients. PCPs are bombarded with lengthy Clinical Practice Guidelines (CPGs) from various agencies that algorithmically detail evidenced-based approaches toward the assessment and management of various conditions. In addition, they are expected to comply with recommended preventive services, such as screening and counseling for a wide array of topics. A recent study reported that it would require 7.4 hours of every working day for a PCP to provide all recommended preventive services to a practice of 2500 patients with age and sex distributions based on the US population (Yarnall et al., 2003). With a typical PC appointment lasting 15 minutes, the low rates of screening and detection for alcohol misuse and other common behavioral health conditions that are reported for primary care are not surprising. Without redesigning the delivery system of primary care, PCPs will continue to be unable to meet the demand for providing quality care in addition to other recommend practices. As such, following a review of common barriers to screening, a process that decentralizes the work involved with screening and brief interventions for alcohol misuse within the primary care clinic will be presented.

Barriers to Screening

In the absence of focused and systematic efforts to improve screening for alcohol misuse, many primary care providers rely on indirect indicators or subtle cues to detect alcohol misuse among patients. While the most severe cases of alcohol abuse or dependence may be relatively easy to identify among patients in a medical setting, the inherent flaws with indirect indicators become apparent when trying to identify those patients that are not so clinically obvious. Specifically, signs of alcohol misuse are highly variable and often misleading, they are easy to ignore and they can be dependent upon a provider's own alcohol use in terms of what he/she may consider a problem. Moreover, strategies to systematically identify potential alcohol misuse may not be a part of most primary care providers training. All of these factors may lead to numerous *missed* opportunities.

One example of the difficulty in relying on provider identification and indirect cues comes from a well-designed study on the efficacy and cost-effectiveness of a physician-delivered brief intervention for problem drinking in a primary care setting. In this study by Fleming and colleagues (2002), individuals who were determined by researchers to meet their criteria for problem drinking were enrolled to either receive an intervention within primary care or to a "usual care" condition (i.e., whatever assessment or intervention their physician would typically provide related to their drinking patterns). The intervention proved to be both clinically effective and cost-effective. However, among the problem drinkers assigned to the usual care condition, less than 5% received physician advice to reduce their alcohol use during the four years of the study. This finding is one of many demonstrating that, in the absence of systematic screening tools, physicians in busy primary care clinics may not have the time to be effective at identifying individuals with problematic patterns of alcohol use.

There have been several surveys and summaries about why screening is not routinely done in primary care clinics, despite national recommendations to do so (CASA, 2000; WHO, 2001). The primary reasons for lack of screening as presented in Table 8.1 have been adopted from the World Health Organization's publication on *Brief Interventions in Primary Care* (2001) as well as the CASA report on *Missed Opportunities* (2000).

Goals of Screening

The overall goal of screening for alcohol misuse in primary care are to identify individuals who are (a) at elevated risk for developing alcohol related problems, (b) likely to have some type of alcohol misuse and require further assessment, and / or (c) need treatment and referrals. In order for a screening program for a particular disease or problem within primary care to be effective, it should meet the following criteria according to the US Preventive Services Task Force (1996). The problem

Barriers to Screening	Arguments for Screening
Lack of Time	Screening and scoring requires less than 5 minutes of time and can usually be done by someone other than the PCP. Approximately 5%-20% of PC population will require brief intervention, which can be initiated by the PCP and then implemented by a BHC.
Inadequate Training	Evidence does suggest the vast majority of PCPs receive little or no training related to alcohol misuse; however, it takes little time to effectively train PC staff for screening and PCPs for assessment and brief interventions
Fear of Patient's Response	Nearly half of PCPs report being uncomfortable with talking with patients about their alcohol use and roughly 25% feel they will anger their patients if they talk about it; however, data suggests that a provider trained to deliver feedback and advice to patients, without labels or judgments, will rarely alienate or anger a patient.
Belief that Alcohol Screening and Treatment is Not Compatible with Primary Healthcare	Alcohol misuse can adversely impact numerous health conditions and is associated with unintentional injuries, increased healthcare utilization, and worsening alcohol use. The sooner it is addressed, deleterious health consequences are fewer and less severe.
Belief that Treatment is Not Effective	Treatment for alcohol misuse is as effective as treatments for many other chronic diseases; many trials show fairly good long term effects of both brief intervention as well as specialty care once proper identification and referrals are made.
Competing Demands	Numerous guidelines related to screening, early identification, and clinical preventive services exist. The USPSTF selects only those screening and interventions with ample evidence. Screening for alcohol use in PC is one of these and is also one of the leading health indicators for Healthy People 2010.

*Table 8.1: Common Reasons Screening for Alcohol Use
is not Being Done in Primary Care*

should be: (1) prevalent; (2) reduce duration and quality of life; (3) have an effective treatment; (4) be detectable via effective screening methods and (5) the treatment should halt or delay the disease progression. Finally, the screening *process* must be acceptable to patients and cost-effective. Alcohol misuse clearly meets these criteria for a problem of interest in primary care. The screening and follow-up process described in the next section is designed to be acceptable, clinically effective and cost-effective. The model describes a process of healthcare delivery for responding and intervening with those individuals whose screening measure indicates further assessment and/or intervention is needed (i.e., they screen "positive").

Screening: Selecting a Screening Instrument

Although numerous screening instruments for alcohol use exist, a comprehensive review is outside the scope of this chapter. For additional information on useful screening instruments, readers are referred to published reviews in the literature, the National Institute on Alcohol Abuse and Alcoholism's website (http://

www.niaaa.nih.gov), or the Substance Abuse and Mental Health Services Administration, Center for Substance Abuse Treatment website (http://www.samhsa.gov/
centers/csat2002/).

The selection of a particular screening instrument should be linked to the
objective for screening, population of interest, the clinical setting, and the process
of care following screening. The screening measure recommended for integrated
primary care clinics (i.e., clinics with an on-site behavioral health consultant) is the
Alcohol Use Disorders Identification Test (AUDIT: Saunders et al., 1993). The
AUDIT was originally developed by investigators at the World Health Organization
for use in the PC setting, as a means to identify individuals with alcohol-related
problems. It is a 10-item scale that assesses three conceptual areas, including alcohol
consumption in the past year, signs of alcohol dependence in the past year, and
adverse consequences related to alcohol consumption either in the last year or ever.
The AUDIT is available at no cost and it is both easy and quick to administer and
score (generally takes less than 5 minutes). For a recent and thorough review of the
AUDIT, readers are referred to an article entitled *The Alcohol Use Disorders Identification Test (AUDIT): A Review of Recent Research* by Reinert and Allen (2002). The
AUDIT has been evaluated in numerous settings and with various patient populations. It has demonstrated sufficient patient acceptability as well as solid psychometric properties. Indices of reliability, such as the median Cronbach alpha value for the
AUDIT, are above .80 (Reinert & Allen, 2002). In fact, several studies have
systematically evaluated the performance of the AUDIT as a screening tool. Reinert
and Allen (2002) summarized these studies and, using fairly restrictive criteria,
calculated the median sensitivity of the AUDIT to be .86 across all eligible studies
and the median specificity to be .89. However, it has been noted by several
researchers that the AUDIT might not be the optimal screening measure among the
elderly, as it is likely to miss a level of alcohol use that can still be problematic among
older adults or those with co-morbid medical conditions.

Although the AUDIT was developed and tested as a single 10-item
instrument, there have been a few studies that have examined the performance of
a *modified AUDIT*. Specifically, a brief five-item version of the AUDIT has been
developed (AUDIT-PC), the first three items of the AUDIT have been used
(AUDIT-C), and a single-item version (consisting only of the third, binge
drinking, item – AUDIT-3) has been used and evaluated for detection of binge
drinking. These adaptations to the AUDIT perform at varying levels of
sensitivity and specificity and also appear to function differently for males and
females. Finally, when the AUDIT has been used as a structured interview, skip
out patterns after negative responses to the first three items have been used
(Babor et al., 2001).

For integrated clinics, the AUDIT can be used as a full 10-item screener
annually; however, rates of non-drinkers in a typical primary care clinic may be
as high as 45% potentially causing an undue burden on these individuals to
complete the entire screener. As such, a two-stepped screening process in which

only those persons endorsing the first three items will continue on for the remainder of the questionnaire (see Appendix A). This version of the AUDIT is recommended to streamline the screening process. However, there has not yet been a systematic evaluation of using the AUDIT in this way within an integrated care clinic. It has been chosen for use among some integrated care clinics primarily for its practical advantages. Rather than using the AUDIT-PC or AUDIT-C, this process allows the substantial proportion of abstainers that exist within any PC population to skip the remaining seven items of the questionnaire, without compromising the overall reliability, validity or predictive value of the full AUDIT for the alcohol users.

Screening: Process

The screening process recommended for use in integrated clinics (see Figure 8.1) starts with a technician, LVN, nurse's aide or nurse to initiate the screening in the PC clinic when the patient presents for their appointment. Often this can be incorporated into the other routine screening (pre-visit) measures that are taken in most PC settings, such as blood pressure, temperature, and other screening items. All patients are encouraged to complete the initial three item pre-screen; this should eliminate abstainers and infrequent, non-binge drinkers.

After the screening instrument is completed, the administrator can score it by summing each item. The total score and interpretation can be used to determine if the PCP should be notified. Generally, scores of 8 or higher warrant some additional questions and/or intervention. The initial assessment, which is primarily related to safety concerns, is conducted by the PCP who may also want to order labs and other medical work-ups, if indicated. An automatic referral to the BHC is then typically recommended for all patients who screen positive on the AUDIT. This process allows all patients who screen positive the opportunity for further assessment and exploration of drinking patterns that may not be feasible in the course of a 15 minute PC appointment that was presumably made for a reason other than alcohol use. BHCs begin by a more comprehensive assessment and will then discuss intervention options with patients, make recommendations and, most commonly, initiate a primary care based brief intervention. BHCs routinely provide feedback on their assessment findings and recommendations, in case the PCP believes further medical or other laboratory work-ups may be indicated.

What Do BHCs Do Once Patients are Referred?

The BHC Model of Integration

Before describing the role of the Behavioral Health Consultant (BHC) in assessing and intervening with alcohol misuse problems specifically, a few comments about the model of integrated care and the overall role of BHCs in the clinic are warranted. Integrated care differs from specialty mental health or collaborative healthcare in that the BHC becomes part of the primary care team. Behavioral health (BH) needs (either expressed by or suspected in patients) and BH care, become one

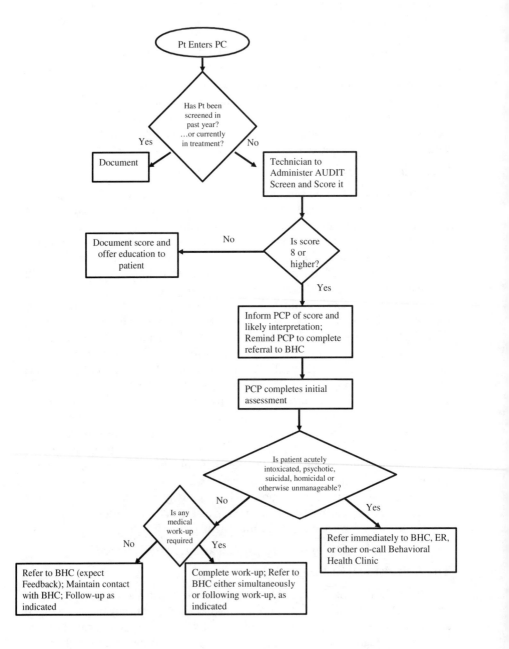

Figure 8.1: Patient Flow for Screening and Intervention in Primary Care

of the routine elements addressed in all primary care visits. This is perhaps the most critical component that distinguishes integrated care from other types of collaborative care. Other aspects of integrated care include the following:

- Patients are seen at the request of the PCP or PC nurse
- The BHC serves as a consultant to the PCP; the PCP remains responsible for patient's overall healthcare
- No written informed consent forms are required; no separate mental health record is maintained (documentation of visits are in the routine healthcare record)
- Assessments and interventions are brief and focused on patient's functioning, overall health status, and quality of life (less focus on disease specific complaints)
- Emphasis on shared decision-making with patients, options for alternate care delivery and treatment are presented
- PCPs are provided same day feedback from the BHC
- BHCs deliver patient education, and work with patients on self-management strategies and skill building techniques
- Appointments are shorter in length as compared with specialty mental health (30 minutes) and the total number of visits are typically limited, although there is no set maximum number of appointments

Within this model of care, there are several common services that BHCs provide to patients with potential alcohol misuse disorders. These include:

- Formal DSM-IV assessment of whether diagnostic criteria are sufficiently met for a diagnosis of substance abuse or dependence
- Assessment of whether detoxification is required or if acute intoxication exists
- Determine if the patient requires, or is willing to seek specialty care, if indicated
- Assess for imminent suicidality or other high-risk conditions warranting specialty care
- Assess patient's readiness to change alcohol use and patient's self-efficacy for change
- Assess reasons for drinking and typical patterns of use to help guide interventions

This model of integrating BHCs into primary care relies on the PCP to act upon the screening findings, conduct an initial assessment of the patient's alcohol use, and refer the patient to the BHC for a more thorough assessment. Then, unless laboratory tests are warranted or further medical work-ups are needed, the BHC and the patient devise a treatment and management plan that is reviewed by the PCP. BHCs routinely provide feedback (both verbal and written feedback) to PCPs on all referred patients, even when further medical work-ups may be happening simultaneously. In an integrated clinic that is adequately resourced with one or more BHCs, BHCs can provide same-day or next-day access for follow-up patient appointments.

An interesting by-product, if not a secondary goal, of this model is that the PCP is able to learn more about the assessment and interventions for alcohol disorders over time. The numerous competing demands and time constraints on PCP's time may never allow them to spend 30 minutes during a routine care appointment discussing a patient's alcohol use. However, they will gradually increase their knowledge, decrease any fear and discomfort, and increase their belief that effective interventions for alcohol misuse exist.

The proposed model relies on standardized and systematic process within the PC clinic, with well-defined roles for different types of providers. The model assumes that the PCP is not the optimal provider to screen, assess, and deliver brief interventions for alcohol misuse. The BHC model of integrated care allows for the PCP to be intimately involved and capitalizes on the patient-provider relationship by having all care take place within the PC clinic. This model also attempts to makes the most out of the education and training of behavioral health providers to deliver the interventions. Using BHCs releases time for the PCP to conduct other tasks that are unique to the scope of practice for physicians. This type of healthcare delivery redesign not only fulfills the recommendation for screening and clinical preventive services outlined by the USPSTF, but also uses a potentially less costly approach (it should be noted that the cost-effectiveness of this particular model of integration with respect to alcohol misuse remains unknown).

Specific Strategies Used by the BHC

Little research has been done to examine whether using alternate providers *in primary care* can be effective for delivering the same brief interventions that are known to be effective when delivered by physicians. However, BHCs rely on the cumulative evidence related to the common elements known to be effective across different types of brief interventions, regardless of setting or type of provider. These are often referred to using the acronym FRAMES and include the following components: (F) Feedback on Personal Risk and Education; (R) Emphasis on Personal Responsibility; (A) Clear Advice to Change; (M) Menu of Alternative Change Options; (E) Empathy; and (S) Enhancement of Patient's Self-Efficacy (Miller & Rollnick, 1991). BHCs routinely use follow-up appointments following the delivering brief interventions as well. This allows a determination of the clinical effectiveness of the intervention as well as an opportunity for referral to more specialized treatment when indicated.

Patient Education

BHCs include personalized patient education as part of their initial assessment visits. This is done for two primary reasons. First, it often engages patients to think about an area for change and allows them to leave the initial appointment with something to work on. Secondly, it is not uncommon for patients to be seen only once by a BHC, so if they do not return, they have at least received some personalized feedback coupled with a change message. Common elements of patient education include the following: information on safe limits of consumption, including typical myths and misconceptions about alcohol use; discussion to promote understanding about blood alcohol levels; education on the biphasic effect of alcohol; potential consequences of continuing to misuse alcohol (e.g., health, social, relationships, legal, occupational). BHCs also explore the patient's reasons for drinking to gain understanding on motivational factors, and may then use this information as an opportunity to clarify and myths or misconceptions.

Motivational Interviewing and Intervention Selection:

The role of the BHC in brief PC interventions for alcohol misuse is similar to what has been shown to be effective among brief interventions delivered by other providers in the PC setting. These include underscoring the patient's personal responsibility, while still advising them to change. A thorough assessment of readiness to change is conducted, along with a determination of whether the patient feels (1) that is important to change and (2) their level of confidence in their ability to change (self-efficacy). Guided from motivational interviewing strategies (Miller and Rollnick, 1991; 2002), the BHC initially targets the patient's perceived level of importance, when that is assessed to be low. When the level of importance of change is moderate to high, ensuring and supporting the patient's self-efficacy to change is then targeted.

In general, brief interventions are appropriately matched both to the patient's level of risk as well as their readiness to change. For patients who are either pre-contemplative or contemplative, the BHC's intervention is focused primarily on education, personalized feedback and discussions about risk and reasons for change. Once a patient is expressing more of an active desire or commitment towards change (preparation), interventions are geared towards skill building, choosing a goal, and negotiating specific behavioral strategies for meeting that goal. Among those actively working on a plan of behavior change (action or maintenance), typical BHC interventions include encouragement, feedback, problem-solving barriers to change, and building a relapse prevention plan. (For a more thorough review of matching interventions to stage of change/readiness to change, the reader is referred to several publications listed in the references by Prochaska and DiClemente).

Goals and strategies are continuously negotiated with patients, as their involvement and investment is considered critical. Specific goals that can be broken down into behavioral and measurable elements are developed, along with target dates for each goal. Common goals may be to reduce drinking to below some specified unsafe or hazardous levels or reducing risks when drinking (e.g., driving safety, etc.). Abstinence is a possible goal as well; however, because the majority of individuals seen by BHCs do not meet criteria for alcohol abuse or dependence, abstinence is rarely a recommended goal, unless the patient desires it. Finally, once goals are established, specific change strategies are developed and agreed upon to form the short-term plan; follow-up strategies are also developed. In general, common strategies used by the BHC include self-help materials, such as readings, personalized worksheets, and in-vivo practice of new skills. BHCs monitor the change progress through follow-up appointments, telephone contact, or through the patient's PCP. Pre-printed templates, handouts, and worksheets are routine aspects of BHC interventions.

For BHCs or other providers that do not have access to or have not yet developed standard intervention tools for brief interventions in primary care tailored to a particular setting, the World Health Organization's *Brief Intervention for Hazardous and Harmful Drinking: A Manual for Use in Primary Care*, outlines an easy-to-use process for developing a highly specific and individually tailored plan with the patient to either cut down or stop drinking (Babor & Higgins-Biddle, 2001). It is intended to be used by clinicians in primary care settings for individuals with alcohol misuse. Through a series of questions and discussion, the patient develops a specific habit-breaking plan that includes the following elements:

1. A list of several reasons to cut down or stop drinking (e.g., spend less money, avoid DUI).
2. A list of several dangerous situations that may increase likelihood of not meeting identified goals
3. For each situation, a list of several ways of coping with that situation to avoid a setback
4. A list of strategies for how to meet others who don't drink or drink in low-risk amounts/patterns
5. A list of strategies to combat boredom
6. A statement of how they plan to ensure that they will remember their plan

Barriers to Using BHCs in Primary Care

There are numerous reasons why integrated care is not yet commonplace, including historical roots, divergence in theoretical frameworks, and differences in the cultures and practices between physical and behavioral medicine. However, the most significant barrier to both researching and using BHCs in primary care for the early identification, assessment, and treatment of alcohol misuse in primary care is the financing structure of many healthcare institutions. With the exception of staff-model Health Maintenance Organizations or similar healthcare delivery models, behavioral healthcare coverage is often carved out from the physical healthcare benefit and therefore managed by a different company. In fact, the vast majority of mental health services in the U.S. are organized and financed this way (Findlay, 1999). This means that behavioral healthcare provided within the context of physical healthcare, is generally not reimbursed. In order for behavioral health services to be reimbursed under carve-out models, patients must be seen by a behavioral health provider in the network of providers identified by the company who manages the behavioral health benefit. This generally means that the behavioral health care is fragmented and nearly always offered in the specialty care setting by someone who has little to no affiliation with the patient's medical care provider. Even if care is provided by the PCP, it is not likely to be reimbursed because the money allocated for these types of services have been distributed to the Behavioral Health carve-out.

By way of example, consider Mrs. Gonzales, a 46 year-old single working mother of two children with daily alcohol use (3-4 drinks/day) to manage her stress. She pays her health insurance premiums to a company that her employer has selected to provide healthcare to its workers. Under this plan, Mrs. Gonzales has coverage for both her physical health conditions as well as for behavioral health disorders; however, two different companies manage her healthcare: one for her medical care and another manages the delivery of behavioral health care. Mrs. Gonzales' sees her PCP for sleep difficulties and is asked about alcohol use. She reports her typical use patterns and is referred to the behavioral health provider working in the PC clinic. Mrs. Gonzales is willing to see the BHC in the primary clinic because she believes they can help with her overall stress level and sleep problems as well. The BHC conducts an assessment and recommends Mrs. Gonzales learn other, more adaptive ways of managing her stress than drinking. The BHC is unable to receive any reimbursement for this assessment even though Mrs. Gonzales has "health coverage" because the company has carved out all of the coverage for her behavioral health care. If Mrs. Gonzales' behavioral health consultant were to bill the company that covers her medical care, they would not pay for the behavioral health services since it is not one of their covered services, by one of their preferred providers. If the behavioral health company were billed, they would not likely cover this care either. In order for the behavioral health insurance company to cover these services at the maximum rate, they would need to be provided by a recognized provider in their network and for "covered" services. The BHC would also be unable to receive reimbursement for any stress management interventions with Mrs. Gonzales so he recommends that she see a psychologist in her insurance carrier's network of providers. Mrs. Gonzales is fearful of losing her job or insurance if she sees a "shrink" and is not convinced she has a problem anyway. She has no intention of following through with this referral to a specialty care provider for such services and leaves the PC clinic.

This scenario illustrates perhaps the biggest reason integrated care, particularly consultative BH care, is not a routine component of most PC clinics. Although other barriers exist (lack of a clear model of care, lack of training and education. etc), organizational and financial barriers are inarguably a leading impediment to industry change. There is no mechanism for a BH provider within a PC clinic to financially support his/her services when carve out models of health insurance coverage predominate the industry. Only recently - in 2002 - have billing codes relevant to this type of consultative behavioral health activities in PC been approved for use and reimbursement under Medicare (the '96150 series' of CPT codes). While clearly a step in the right direction, the use of these codes is still in its infancy. In contrast, some staff-model HMOs that employ both the medical and behavioral health providers and provide coverage for both the physical and behavioral healthcare of all enrolled persons have been able to develop and sustain integrated care clinics. The rationale for integrated care in these settings is a function of providing high quality care, patient preference, and evidence that collaborative care is superior for nearly all chronic health conditions, including depression and alcohol misuse disorders, as well as an investment in prevention of other severe mental health disorders.

Summary

The use of BHCs in the primary care setting represents a paradigm shift in the traditional "identification and referral" model for alcohol and other substance problems in primary care. Although the majority of empirical studies conducted in PC settings have used physicians to conduct assessments and deliver brief interventions, the use of the BHC is potentially a more cost-effective model for involving the PCP and capitalizing on a team approach within the PC clinic. Furthermore, the use of the BHC assumes that behavioral health providers have more education and training in alcohol misuse as compared with most physicians, that they can allocate more time to any given patient, and that using BHCs allows the PCPs to dedicate their clinical time to PC activities that require a physician (whereas assessment and intervention of alcohol misuse problems is within the scope of care of BH providers). Finally, using a BHC who is located within the PC clinic also capitalizes on the patient's preference to be treated within the primary care clinic, which is not an insignificant point to consider since the patient's level of investment can determine the success or failure of interventions to reduce the misuse of alcohol. Above all else, the likelihood of integrated care taking root is contingent upon the elimination of the organizational and financial "silos" that currently exist between physical and mental healthcare throughout this country.

Acknowledgements

The views expressed in this article are those of the author and do not reflect the official position of the United States Air Force, the US Department of Veteran's Affairs, the Department of Defense, or the United States Government.

This material is based upon work supported, in part, by the Office of Research and Development, Health Services R&D Service, Department of Veterans Affairs and the University of Texas Health Science Center – San Antonio, Texas.

The author graciously acknowledges Vincent P. Fonseca, M.D. and Scott A. Schinaman, M.A. for their careful review and critique of this chapter.

Appendix A.
Revised AUDIT for Two-Step Screening Process with Interpretation

How often do you have a drink containing alcohol?	Never	Monthly or Less	2 – 4 Times/ Month	2 – 3 Times/ Week	4 or More Times/ Week	
	(0)	(1)	(2)	(3)	(4)	
How many drinks containing alcohol do you have on a typical day when you are drinking?	None	1-2	3-4	5-6	7, 8, 9	10 or more
	(0)	(0)	(1)	(2)	(3)	(4)
How often do you have six or more drinks on one occasion?	Never	Less than Monthly	Monthly	Weekly	Daily or Almost Daily	
	(0)	(1)	(2)	(3)	(4)	

If you answered **"NEVER / NONE"** to **ALL** *questions*, return form to technician.
If **two or more** of your answers above are in the **colored area**, continue below.

Put in "X" in the box that best describes how often you have had this problem.

Item	Never	Less than Monthly	Monthly	Weekly	Daily or Almost Daily
	0	**1**	**2**	**3**	**4**
How during the last year often had you failed to do what was normally expected of you because you had been drinking?					
How often during the last year have you needed a first drink in the morning to get yourself going after a heavy drinking session?					
How often during the last year have you had a feeling of guilt or remorse after drinking?					
How often during the last year have you been unable to remember what happened the night before because you had been drinking?					

Have you or someone else been injured as a result of your drinking?
> (0) - No
> (2) - Yes, but NOT in the last year
> (4) - Yes, during the last year

Has a relative, friend, doctor or other health worker been concerned about your drinking or suggested you cut down?
> (0) - No
> (2) - Yes, but NOT in the last year
> (4) - Yes, during the last year

SCORING INSTRUCTIONS:

On first three items and last two items, the numbers in parentheses indicate the score on that item. For items #4-8, the score for that item is the number at the top of the table that corresponds to the response option the patients pick. Sum all item scores for one overall total score.

TOTAL SCORE= SUM OF ALL 10 ITEMS. Range is 0-40

A score of **8 or more** indicates a strong likelihood of hazardous or harmful alcohol consumption. **Notify PCP if score is 8 or higher.**

References

Arndt, S., Schultz, S., Turvey, C., & Petersen, A. (2002). Screening for alcoholism in the primary care setting: Are we talking to the right people? *The Journal of Family Practice, 51(1)*, 41-46.

Babor, T. F., Higgins-Biddle, J. C., Saunders, J. B., & Monteiro, M. G. (2001). Brief Intervention for Hazardous and Harmful Drinking: A Manual for Use in Primary Care. *A Report from the World Health Organization, Department of Mental Health and Substance Dependence.*

Babor, T. F., & Higgins-Biddle, J. C. (2001). AUDIT: The alcohol use disorders identification test. Guidelines for use in primary care, second edition. *A Report from the World Health Organization, Department of Mental Health and Substance Dependence.*

Buchsbaum , D.G., Buchanan, R.G., Poses, R.M., Schnoll, S.H., & Lawton, M.J. (1992). Physician detection of drinking problems in patients attending a general medicine practice. *Journal of General Internal Medicine, 7(5)*, 517-21.

Center on Addiction and Substance Abuse at Columbia University (CASA). (2000). *Missed Opportunity: National Survey of Primary Care Physicians and Patients on Substance Abuse.* Conducted by the Survey Research Laboratory, University of Illinois at Chicago.

Centers for Disease Control and Prevention (CDC). (2002). *Behavioral Risk Factor Surveillance System Survey Questionnaire.* Atlanta, Georgia: U.S. Department of Health and Human Services, Centers for Disease Control and Prevention.

Chou S.P., Grant B.F., & Dawson D.A. (1992). Medical consequences of alcohol consumption-United States, 1992. *Alcoholism Clinical and Experimental Research, 20,* 1423-29

Curry, S. J., Ludman, E. Grothaus, L. Donovan, D., Kim, E., & Fishman, P. (2000). At-Risk drinking among patients making routine primary care visits. *Preventive Medicine, 31,* 595-602.

Dawson, D.A., Grant, B.F., Chou, S.P., & Pickering, R.P. (1995). Subgroup variation in U.S. drinking patterns: Results of the 1992 National Longitudinal Alcohol Epidemiologic Study. *Journal of Substance Abuse, 7,* 331–344.

Donaldson, M.S., Yordy, K.D., Lohr, K. N., &. Vanselow, N.A. (Eds.). (1996). Primary Care: America's Health in a New Era. Report of a study by a committee of the Institute of Medicine, *Division of Health Care Services.* Washington DC: National Academy Press.

Findlay, S. (1999) Managed behavioral healthcare in 1999: an industry at a crossroads. *Health Affairs (18)5,* 116-124.

Fleming, M.F. (2003). Brief interventions and the treatment of alcohol use disorders: current evidence. *Recent Developments in Alcoholism. 16,* 375-90.

Fleming M.F., Manwell L.B., Barry K.L., & Johnson, K. (1998). At-risk drinking in an HMO primary care sample: prevalence of health policy implications. *American Journal of Public Health, 88,* 90-93.

Fleming, M. F. Mundt, M.P., French, M. T. Manwell, L. B., Stauffacher, E. A., & Barry, K. L. (2002). Brief Physician Advice for Problem Drinkers: Long-Term Efficacy and Benefit-Cost Analysis. *Alcoholism Clinical and Experimental Research, 26(1)*, 36-43

Grant, B.F., Harford, T.C., Dawson, D.A., Chou, P., DuFour, M., & Pickering, R. (1994). Prevalence of DSM-IV alcohol abuse and dependence: United States, 1992. Epidemiologic Bulletin No. 35. *Alcohol Health Research World 18(3)*, 243–248.

Harwood, H. (2000). *Updating Estimates of the Economic Costs of Alcohol Abuse in the United States: Estimates, Update Methods and Data.* Report prepared by the Lewin Group for the National Institute on Alcohol Abuse and Alcoholism.

Harwood, H.J., Fountain, D., & Livermore, G. (1998). Economic costs of alcohol and drug abuse in the United States, 1992. *Report prepared by the Lewen Group for the National Institute on Drug Abuse*, Bethesda, MD. NIH Publication 98-4327.

Harwood, H., Fountain, D. & Livermore, G. (1999). The Economic Costs of Alcohol and Drug Abuse in the United States, 1992. *Report prepared for the National Institute on Drug Abuse and the National Institute on Alcohol Abuse and Alcoholism*, National Institutes of Health, U.S. Department of Health and Human Services. NIH Pub. No. 98-4327.

Institute of Medicine, Division of Mental Health and Behavioral Medicine. (1990). *Broadening the Base of Treatment for Alcohol Problems.* Washington, DC: National Academy Press.

McGinnis, J.M. & Foege, W.H. (1993). Actual causes of death in the United States. *JAMA, 270*, 2207-2212.

Manwell, L.B., Fleming, M.F., Johnson, K., & Barry, K.L. (1998). Tobacco, alcohol, and drug use in a primary care sample: 90-day prevalence and associated factors. *Journal of Addictive Disorders, 17*, 67–81.

Miller, W.R., & Rollnick, S. (1991). *Motivational Interviewing: Preparing people to change addictive behavior.* Guilford Press: New York.

Miller, W.R., & Rollnick, S. (2002). *Motivational Interviewing: Preparing people to change addictive behavior* (2nd ed.). Guilford Press: New York.

Moore A.A., Morton S.C., Beck J.C., Hays R.D., Oishi S.M, Partridge J.M., Genovese B.J., & Fink A. (1999). A new paradigm for alcohol use in older persons. *Medical Care, 37(2)*, 165-179.

Moyer A., Finney J. W., Swearingen C. E., & Vergun, P. (2002). Brief interventions for alcohol problems: A Meta-analytic review of controlled investigations in treatment and non-treatment-seeking populations. *Addiction, 97(3)*, 279-292.

Naimi, T.S., Brewer, R.D., Mokdad, A., Denny, C., Serdula, M.K., & Marks, J.S. (2003). Binge drinking among US adults, *JAMA, 289*, 70-75.

Prochaska, J.O., & DiClemente, C.C. (1983). Stages and processes of self-change of smoking: toward an integrative model of change. *Journal of Consulting & Clinical Psychology, 51(3)*, 390-395.

Prochaska, J.O., & DiClemente, C.C. (1992). Stages of change in the modification of problem behaviors. *Progress in Behavior Modification, 28*, 183-218.

Prochaska, J.O., DiClemente, C.C., & Norcross, J.C. (1992). In search of how people change: Applications to addictive behaviors. *American Psychologist, 47(9)*, 1102-1114.

Reinert, D., & Allen, J. (2002). The alcohol use disorders identification test (AUDIT): A review of recent research. *Alcoholism: Clinical and Experimental Research, 26(2)*, 272-279.

Saunders, J. B., Aasland, O.G., Babor, T. F., del la Fuente, J. R., & Grant, M. (1993). Development of the alcohol use disorders identification test (AUDIT): WHO collaborative project on early detection of persons with harmful alcohol consumption. II. *Addiction, 88*, 791-804.

United States Department of Health and Human Services. (2000). *Healthy People 2010: Understanding and Improving Health* (2nd ed.). Washington DC: U.S. Government Printing Office.

United States Department of Health and Human Services (1996). Guide to Clinical Preventive Services, 2nd ed. *Report of the U.S. Preventive Services Task Force.* Washington DC: US Government Printing Office.

Yarnall, K.S., Pollak, K.I., Ostbye, T., Krause, K.M., & Michener, J.L. (2003). Primary care: is there enough time for prevention?. *American Journal of Public Health, 93(4)*, 635-41.

Endnotes

1. Alcohol misuse, as later defined, incorporates *both* alcohol related problems that meet diagnostic criteria, such as alcohol abuse or alcohol dependence, as well as problems that do not meet diagnostic criteria. Alcohol-related problems that do meet diagnostic criteria for alcohol abuse or dependence have been given numerous labels, including problem drinking, binge drinking, hazardous drinking, heavy drinking, and harmful drinking. The term "problem drinking", when used in this chapter, necessarily connotes the absence of a diagnosis.

2. Some definitions of binge drinking or hazardous drinking are set at different thresholds for males and females. For example, binge drinking among females is often defined as four or more standard alcoholic drinks in one setting. According to the World Health Organization, hazardous drinking is defined as 14 or more drinks per week among males, and seven or more drinks per week among females.

3. The overall model of behavioral health integration into primary care and the role of BHCs has been described in detail elsewhere (see Runyan, CR, Fonseca, VP, and Hunter, CL (2003). Integrating Consultative Behavioral Healthcare into the Air Force Medical System. In N. A. Cummings, W. T. O'Donohue, & K. E. Ferguson (Eds.), *Behavioral Health as Primary Care: Beyond Efficacy to Effectiveness*. Reno, NV: Context Press). This chapter will discuss only how the model and the BHC pertain to the identification and intervention of individuals with alcohol misuse.

Late Life Alcoholism in Primary Care

David W. Oslin
University of Pennsylvania

Overview

Alcohol dependence is one of the leading causes of disability worldwide; however, alcohol misuse is often not appreciated as relevant to the care of older adults (Murray & Lopez, 1996). The public health impact of alcohol dependence as well as other substance use disorders will likely increase with the growing number of older adults. In addition to an increase in the elderly population, the prevalence of late life addiction has been predicted to increase because of cohort changes. The current cohort of 30 to 50 year old people, represents a group who were raised during the 1950's and 1960's and were exposed to increasing use of and addiction to heroin, cocaine, tobacco, and alcohol. Both continued substance dependence and a history of substance dependence will likely have physical and mental health consequences for this cohort as it ages.

Although research in late life addictions has developed slowly, recent research has underscored the prevalence and disability related to substance abuse in late life. Perhaps more importantly, recent research has demonstrated the efficacy of psychotherapeutic, social, and pharmacological treatments for older adults with alcohol abuse or dependence. Moreover, there is emerging evidence that reduction in alcohol use among older adults with alcohol dependence can lead to improvement in health related quality of life. This article will highlight the recent advances in understanding and treating late life alcoholism.

Diagnosis and Terms

Older adults pose special concerns when developing alcohol consumption guidelines. Compared with younger people, older adults have an increased sensitivity to alcohol as well as over-the-counter and prescription medications. There is an age-related decrease in lean body mass and total body water in relation to total fat volume, and the resultant decrease in total body volume increases the concentration of alcohol in the blood plasma space. Central nervous system sensitivity to alcohol also increases with age and interactions between medication and alcohol is a particular concern in this age group. For some patients, any alcohol use, coupled with the use of specific over-the-counter or prescription medications, can be problematic. Because of these issues, alcohol use recommendations for older adults are generally lower than those set for adults under age 65.

The National Institute on Alcohol Abuse and Alcoholism (NIAAA) and the CSAT Treatment Improvement Protocol on older adults recommend that persons age 65 and older consume no more than 1 standard drink/day or 7 standard drinks/

week (Blow, 1998; National Institute on Alcohol Abuse and Alcoholism, 1995). In addition, older adults should consume no more than 2 standard drinks on any drinking day. The drinking limit recommendations for older adults have been shown to be consistent with data regarding the relationship between consumption and alcohol-related problems within this age group (Chermack, Blow, Hill, & Mudd, 1996). Recommendations are also consistent with the current evidence on the beneficial health effects of drinking (Klatsky & Armstrong, 1993; Poikolainen, 1991).

Drinking guidelines also highlight an important distinction between problem drinking or at-risk drinking and alcohol dependence. "Alcohol dependence" refers to a medical disorder characterized by loss of control, preoccupation with alcohol, continued alcohol use despite adverse consequences, and physiological symptoms such as tolerance and withdrawal (*Diagnostic and statistical manual of mental disorders fourth edition*, 1994). Older adults engaging in "problem or at-risk" use are drinking at a level that either has already resulted in adverse medical, psychological, or social consequences or substantially increases the likelihood of such problems. Individuals engaging in problem or at-risk drinking often do not meet criteria for alcohol dependence. Because some of the classic symptoms of dependence such as employment or legal problems are not present, individuals and practitioners may underestimate the risks of this level of consumption. However, due to the risks associated with this level of drinking, problem and at-risk drinking do represent an appropriate target for interventions.

In addition to these categories of problematic drinking behavior, individuals may also consume alcohol at levels of low risk or be considered abstainers. "Abstinence" refers to drinking no alcohol in the previous year. Approximately 60-70% of older adults are abstinent. If an older patient is abstinent, it is useful to ascertain why alcohol is not used. Some individuals are abstinent because of a "previous history of alcohol problems". Some are abstinent because of recent illness, while others have life-long patterns of low risk use or abstinence. Patients who have a previous history of alcohol problems may require preventive monitoring to determine if any new stresses could exacerbate an old pattern. In addition, a previous history of at-risk drinking or alcohol dependence may increase the risks for developing other mental health problems in late life such as depressive disorders or cognitive problems. "Low risk or moderate use" is alcohol use that falls within the recommended guidelines for consumption and is not associated with problems. Older adults in this category drink within recommended drinking guidelines are able to employ reasonable limits on alcohol consumption, and do not drink when driving a motor vehicle or boat, or when using contraindicated medications.

Epidemiology

The most recent studies that have examined the epidemiology of substance use disorders among the elderly have focused on specialty care settings such as primary care physician practices, nursing homes, or hospitals. Barry and colleagues conducted an alcohol screening program in over 12 000 elderly primary care patients

(Barry et al., 1998). Among those evaluated, 15 % of the patients screened positive for at-risk or problem drinking based upon alcohol consumption, binge drinking, or the presence of alcohol related problems. A similar project conducted by Callahan and Tierney found 10.6 % of 3954 primary care patients over age 60 met criteria for problem drinking (Callahan & Tierney, 1995). Among clinical populations, estimates of alcohol problems are substantially higher because problem drinkers of all ages are more likely to present in health care settings (Beresford, 1979; Institute of Medicine, 1990). A consistent finding among all of these studies finds higher rates of alcohol use and dependence among men compared with women and among Caucasians compared with ethnic minorities (Blow, 1998; National Institute on Alcohol Abuse and Alcoholism, 1995).

The prevalence of alcohol dependence among community dwelling elderly has been estimated in two recent studies. Kandel and colleagues reported on symptoms of alcohol dependence using the National Household Survey on Drug Abuse (Kandel, Chen, Warner, Kessler, & Grant, 1997). The study was conducted between 1991 and 1993 and included 87 915 participants. Among those age 50 and over, the prevalence of alcohol use was common (54.9 % reported alcohol use in the last year). However, the prevalence of alcohol dependence was only 1.6 %. Black and colleagues reported on a cohort of 865 elderly adults living in a public housing project in Baltimore (Black, Rabins, & McGuire, 1998). The prevalence of current problem drinking (currently drinking and > 2 positive CAGE questions) was 4 % with a lifetime prevalence of 22%. These prevalence rates are similar to those previously reviewed by Liberto and colleagues focusing on literature from 1965 until 1993 (Liberto, Oslin, & Ruskin, 1992). Prevalence estimates of at-risk or problem drinking using community surveys have ranged from 1% to 15% (Adams, Fleming, & Barry, 1996; Gurland & Cross, 1982; Robins et al., 1984). These rates vary widely depending on the definition of at-risk drinking, and the methodology used in obtaining samples.

Despite the common occurrence of alcohol problems, most elderly patients have not been recognized as problem drinkers by health care personnel. Moreover, few elderly patients with alcohol problems seek help in specialized addiction treatment settings. Given the high utilization of general medical services by the elderly, physicians and other health care professionals can be crucial in identifying those in need of treatment and providing appropriate interventions based upon clinical need (Coulehan, Zettler-Segal, Block, McClelland, & Schulberg, 1987).

Consequences

Low risk alcohol use is often cited as having beneficial effects especially related to cardiovascular disease. There is a substantial body of epidemiological evidence that, among otherwise healthy adults, especially middle-aged adults, moderate alcohol use may reduce cardiovascular disease, may reduce the risk of some dementing illnesses, and may have benefits in reducing cancer risk when compared to risk in abstainers (Broe et al., 1998; DeLabry et al., 1992; Klatsky, Armstrong, & Friedman, 1990; Orgogozo et al., 1997; Scherr et al., 1992; Shaper, 1990; Stampfer,

Colditz, Willett, Speizer, & Hennekens, 1988; Thun et al., 1997). Alcohol is often consumed socially and may help to reduce stress, at least temporarily (Dufour, Archer, & Gordis, 1992). However, only a limited amount of this research on low risk use has focused on elderly individuals and there is very limited research on the effects of moderate alcohol use in the context of chronic medical and psychiatric diseases which are common in late life. To understand further the benefits of low risk drinking, a better understanding of the risks of developing an illness in the group of abstainers is also needed. Typically, morbidity and mortality for abstainers is higher than those with low risk use (the so-called "J" or "U" shaped morbidity curves). However, some of the individuals who are abstainers in late life formerly may have drank heavily or used other substances and thus may have increased their risk of illness based on past consumption patterns. The effect of past heavy alcohol use is highlighted in the findings from the Liverpool Longitudinal Study demonstrating a fivefold increase in psychiatric illness among elderly men who had a lifetime history of five or more years of heavy drinking (Saunders et al., 1991).

Negative Effects

The health related consequences of alcohol use and other drugs of abuse have been articulated in many articles and reviews. Alcohol dependence is associated with increased morbidity and mortality from disease specific disorders such as alcohol induced cirrhosis or alcohol related cardiomyopathy as well as increasing the risks for such diseases as hypertension or trauma related to falls or motor vehicle accidents. At-risk and problem drinking have also been demonstrated to impair driving-related skills, may lead to other injuries such as falls, depression, memory problems, liver disease, cardiovascular disease, diabetes, cognitive changes, and sleep problems (Gambert & Katsoyannis, 1995; Kivela, Nissinen, & Ketola, 1989; Liberto et al., 1992). Of particular importance to the elderly are the interactions between alcohol and both prescribed and over-the-counter medications, especially psychoactive medications such as benzodiazepines, barbiturates, and antidepressants. Alcohol use is one of the leading risk factors for adverse drug reactions and is known to interfere with the metabolism of medications such as digoxin and warfarin (Fraser, 1997; Hylek, Heiman, Skates, Sheehan, & Singer, 1998; Onder et al., 2002).

Screening and Diagnosis

To be able to practice prevention and early intervention with older adults, clinicians need to screen for alcohol use (frequency and quantity), drinking consequences, and alcohol/medication interaction problems. An important aspect to assessment is understanding the concept of standard drinks. It is generally accepted that the negative effects of alcohol is related to the alcohol content of a beverage. In order to improve assessment outcomes, clinicians should quantify alcohol in terms of standard alcohol drinks. Although it is not important to be exact in the ascertainment of quantity nor is it helpful to engage in debates with patient over exact amounts consumed, standard drinks do provide a useful method of quantifying alcohol intake.

Screening can be done as part of routine mental and physical health care and should be updated annually, before the older adult begins taking any new medications, or in response to problems that may be alcohol or medication-related. Screening questions can be asked by a verbal interview, by a paper-and-pencil questionnaire, or by a computerized questionnaire. All three methods have equivalent reliability and validity (Barry & Fleming, 1990; Greist, Klein, Erdman, & Bires, 1987). Any positive responses can lead to further questions about consequences. To successfully incorporate alcohol (and other drug) screening into clinical practice with older adults, it should be simple and consistent with other screening procedures already in place (Barry, Oslin, & Blow, 2001). In addition to quantity/frequency questions to ascertain use, the Short Michigan Alcoholism Screening Test-Geriatric version (SMAST-G), the CAGE, and the Alcohol Use Disorders Identification Test (AUDIT) are often used with older adults. Of these, the SMAST-G was developed specifically for older adults. The Short Michigan Alcoholism Screening Instrument - Geriatric Version (SMAST-G) (See Table 1) was developed at the University of Michigan (Blow, Gillespie, Barry, Mudd, & Hill, 1998) as an elderly alcoholism screening instrument for use in a variety of settings. Psychometric properties of this instrument are superior to other screening tests for the identification of elderly persons with alcohol abuse/dependence. Of note, the CAGE questionnaire (Mayfield, McLeod, & Hall, 1974) is the most widely used alcohol screening test in clinical practice. It contains four items regarding alcohol use: felt they should Cut down, felt Annoyed that people criticized their drinking, felt Guilty about their drinking, and had a drink upon waking in the morning to get rid of a hangover - an Eye-opener. The CAGE questionnaire is often modified to only ask about recent problems and the threshold is often reduced to one positive response as an indicator of problems in older adults. Under these conditions, the CAGE has high specificity for detecting alcohol abuse but relatively low sensitivity for alcohol dependence or problem drinking.

Clinicians can follow-up the brief questions about consumption and consequences such as those in the SMAST-G, AUDIT, and the CAGE with a few more in-depth questions about consequences, health risks, and social/family issues. To assess dependence, questions should be asked about alcohol-related problems, a history of failed attempts to stop or to cut back, or withdrawal symptoms such as tremors. Clinicians should refer any patient thought to be dependent for a diagnostic evaluation and possible specialized alcohol treatment with an emphasis on treatment targeted to older adults.

Treatments

Brief Interventions/Therapies

Low intensity, brief interventions, or brief therapies have been suggested as cost-effective and practical techniques that can be used as an initial approach to at-risk and problem drinkers in various clinical settings (Barry, 2001). Studies of brief interventions for alcohol problems have employed various approaches to change drinking behaviors. Strategies have ranged from relatively unstructured counseling and feedback to more formal structured therapy (Chick, Lloyd, & Crombie, 1985; Fleming, Barry, Manwell, Johnson, & London, 1997; Persson & Magnusson, 1989), and have relied heavily on concepts and techniques from the behavioral self-control training literature (Miller & Hester, 1986; Miller & Rollnick, 1991).

A number of large randomized controlled trials of brief alcohol interventions have demonstrated efficacy among younger adults in a variety of clinical settings (Barry, 2001). To date, there have been two brief alcohol intervention trials with older adults. Fleming, et al and Blow, et al have conducted randomized clinical brief intervention trials to reduce hazardous drinking with older adults using advice protocols in primary care settings (Blow, 2003; Fleming, Manwell, Barry, Adams, & Stauffacher, 1999). These studies have shown that older adults can be engaged in brief intervention protocols, the protocols are acceptable in this population, and there is a substantial reduction in drinking among the at-risk drinkers receiving the interventions compared to a control group.

The first study, Project GOAL, was a randomized, controlled clinical trial (sample size = 158) conducted in Wisconsin with 24 community-based primary care practices (43 practitioners) located in ten counties (Fleming et al., 1999). The intervention consisted of two, 10-15 minute, physician-delivered counseling visits which included advice, education, and contracting using a scripted workbook. At 12-month follow-up, the intervention group drank significantly less than the control group ($p<.001$). The second elder-specific study, the Health Profile Project randomized a total of 452 subjects to usual care or to a single brief intervention session (Blow, 2003). At 12 months, there were significant reductions in alcohol consumption among those receiving the brief intervention compared to usual care. While these trials were conducted in primary care settings, brief interventions for older adults are likely to be effective in other settings including mental health settings. As such, geriatric mental health providers should be familiar with delivering brief intervention therapy both as a primary treatment tool but also as a way to motivate patients for more formal addiction treatment.

Psychosocial Interventions

Relatively little formal research has been conducted on the comparative efficacy of various approaches to addiction treatment in older adults. Because traditional residential alcoholism treatment programs generally provide services to few older adults, sample size issues have been a barrier to studying treatment outcomes for elderly alcoholics in most settings. However, a recent study suggests that older adults who do engage in treatment can have substantially better outcomes compared to younger adults (Oslin, Pettinati, & Volpicelli, 2002). Thus in contrast to popular beliefs, older adults are quite amenable to treatment. Perhaps one of the reasons for the positive outcomes in this study was the type of psychotherapy used. This study used individualized treatment, delivered by a nurse practitioner or therapists familiar with treating older adults.

Most treatment outcome research on older adults with substance use disorders has focused on adherence with treatment program expectations, including drinking behavior (Atkinson, 1995). Results from adherence studies have shown that age-specific programming improved treatment completion and resulted in higher rates of attendance at group meetings compared to mixed age treatment (Kofoed, Tolson, Atkinson, Toth, & Turner, 1987). In addition, older adults with substance use disorders were significantly more likely to complete treatment than younger patients (Schuckit & Pastor, 1978; Wiens, Menustik, Miller, & Schmitz, 1982 - 1983). Atkinson et al. also found that the proportion of older male alcoholics completing peer-group oriented treatment was twice that of younger men (Atkinson, Tolson, & Turner, 1993). Age of onset of alcohol problems has been suggested as a risk factor for poor treatment outcomes. However, this has not been demonstrated in clinical trials. For example, a study by Schonfeld and Dupree using a matched-pairs, post hoc design, demonstrated no difference in completion rat for 148 subjects based on age of onset (Schonfeld & Dupree, 1991).

There are few prospective treatment outcome studies reported in the literature, in part due to the complexity of studying older adults in treatment, and in part due to difficulties in following them after completion of treatment. Thus, sample sizes tend to be too small to provide definitive results. An exception is a study of 137 male veterans (age 45-59 years, n=64; age 60-69 years, n=62; age 70 years and older, n=11) with alcohol problems who were randomly assigned after detoxification to age-specific treatment or standard mixed-age treatment (Kashner, Rodell, Ogden, Guggenheim, & Karson, 1992). Outcomes at 6 months and 1 year showed that elder-specific program patients were 2.9 times more likely at 6 months, and 2.1 times more likely at 1 year to report abstinence compared to mixed-age group patients. Treatment groups, however, could not be compared at baseline because baseline alcohol consumption and alcohol severity data were not included in the study.

Pharmacotherapy of Addiction

Pharmacologic treatments have not traditionally played a major role in the long-term treatment of older alcohol dependent adults. Until recently, disulfiram was the only medication approved for the treatment of alcoholism, but was seldom used in older patients because of concerns related to adverse effects. In 1995, the opioid antagonist naltrexone was approved by the FDA for the treatment of alcoholism. The FDA approval of naltrexone was based upon studies by Volpicelli and colleagues and O'Malley and colleagues demonstrating the efficacy of naltrexone for the treatment of middle age patients with alcohol dependence (O'Malley et al., 1992; Volpicelli, Alterman, Hayashida, & O'Brien, 1992). In both studies, naltrexone was found to be safe and effective in preventing relapse and reducing the craving for alcohol. The use of naltrexone was based on studies demonstrating an interaction between endogenous endorphin activity and alcohol intake.

Oslin and colleagues have extended this line of research by studying a group of older veterans age 50 to 70 (Oslin, Liberto, O'Brien, Krois, & Norbeck, 1997). The study was designed as a double blind placebo controlled randomized trial with naltrexone 50 mg per day. The results were similar to the other clinical trials with half as many naltrexone treated subjects relapsing to significant drinking compared to those treated with placebo. It is important to note that there was no improvement in total abstinence but improvement in relapse to heavy drinking. Thus, failure to achieve abstinence should not be seen as a failure of treatment. Although this study did not include many elderly subjects, it does raise the hope that opioid antagonists may have clinical efficacy among older alcoholics.

Recently, acamprosate has been studied as a promising agent in the treatment of alcoholism. Although, the exact action of acamprosate is still unknown, acamprosate is thought to reduce glutamate response, but not as a typical NMDA blocker (Pelc I et al., 1997). The clinical evidence favoring acamprosate is impressive. Sass and colleagues have studied 272 alcohol dependent subjects in Europe for up to 48 weeks using a randomized placebo controlled study of acamprosate. Forty-three percent of the acamprosate treated group was abstinent at the conclusion of the study compared to 21 % in the placebo group (Sass, Soyka, Mann, & Zieglgansberger, 1996). There have been no studies of the efficacy or safety of acamprosate among elderly patients.

Detoxification and Withdrawal

Alcohol withdrawal symptoms commonly occur in patients who stop drinking or markedly cut down their drinking after regular heavy use. Alcohol withdrawal can range from mild and almost unnoticeable symptoms to severe and life-threatening ones. The classical set of symptoms associated with alcohol withdrawal includes autonomic hyperactivity (increased pulse rate, increased blood pressure, and increased temperature), restlessness, disturbed sleep, anxiety, nausea, and tremor. More severe withdrawal can be manifested by auditory, visual, or tactile hallucinations, delirium, seizures, and coma. Other substances of abuse such as benzodiazepines, opioids and cocaine have distinct withdrawal symptoms that are also potentially life threatening. Elderly patients have been shown to have a longer duration of withdrawal symptoms and withdrawal has the potential for complicating other medical and psychiatric illnesses. However, there is no evidence to suggest that older patients are more prone to alcohol withdrawal or need longer treatment for withdrawal symptoms (Brower, Mudd, Blow, Young, & Hill, 1994).

Highlighted by the potential for life threatening complications, all clinicians caring for patients who abuse substances need to have a fundamental understanding of withdrawal symptoms and the potential complications. All clinicians should demonstrate knowledge of the most common withdrawal symptoms and the anticipated time course of the symptoms. In addition, all clinicians should be able to complete a standardized assessment of withdrawal such as the Clinical Institute Withdrawal from Alcohol-version A, revised (Sullivan, Sykora, Schneiderman, & Naranjo, 1989). Those clinicians in settings in which withdrawal management or treatment is available need also to be competent in providing detoxification management. This includes the use of benzodiazepines for the management of alcohol withdrawal.

Treatment Matching

Further studies will need to clarify the point at which patients are unable to be treated in primary care or mental health clinics but rather need referral for specialty addiction care. To highlight this point, a recent study compares the engagement of older primary care patients referred to specialty mental health providers to an integrated care model using a brief intervention. In this study of 560 at-risk and problem drinkers, 65.4% of patients attended at least one visit in the integrated care model. In contrast, only 37.9 % of patients attended at least one visit to a specialty provider despite elimination of copayments and insurance claims at most sites and assuring appointments within 2 weeks of being identified with at-risk drinking (Bartels et al., Submitted). Thus in terms of a public health perspective, there is no one best treatment option, rather it is likely that patients with less severe disease can and should be treated in primary and mental health care settings and patients with more severe disease should be treated by their principal clinician in conjunction with specialty care.

Comorbity with Other Mental Health Problems

Epidemiologic studies have clearly demonstrated that comorbidity between alcohol use and other psychiatric symptoms is common in younger age groups. Less is known about comorbidity between alcohol use and psychiatric illness in late life. A few studies do indicate that dual diagnosis with alcoholism is important among the elderly. Blow et al. reviewed the diagnosis of 3,986 VA patients between ages 60 - 69 presenting for alcohol treatment (Blow, Cook, Booth, Falcon, & Friedman, 1992). The most common comorbid psychiatric disorder was an affective disorder found in 21 % of the patients. Of these patients, 43 % had major depression. Blazer and Williams studied 997 community dwelling elderly of whom only 4.5 % had a history of alcohol abuse (Blazer, Hughes, & George, 1987). However, of these subjects almost half had a comorbid diagnosis of depression or dysthymia.

Comorbid depressive symptoms are not only common in late life but are also an important factor in the course and prognosis of psychiatric disorders. Depressed alcoholics have been shown to have a more complicated clinical course of depression with an increased risk of suicide and more social dysfunction than non-depressed alcoholics (Conwell, 1991; Cook, Winokur, Garvey, & Beach, 1991). Moreover, they were shown to seek more treatment. However, relapse rates for alcoholics did not appear to be influenced by the presence of depression. Alcohol use prior to late life has also been shown to influence treatment of late life depression. Cook and colleagues found that a prior history of alcohol abuse predicted a more severe and chronic course for depression (Cook et al., 1991).

The relationship between alcohol use and dementing illnesses such as Alzheimer's disease is complex. Alcohol-related dementia may be difficult to differentiate from Alzheimer's disease. Although the rates of alcohol-related dementia in late life differ according to diagnostic criteria used and the nature of the population studied, there is a consensus that alcohol contributes significantly to the acquired cognitive deficits of late life. For example, among subjects over the age of 55 evaluated in the ECA study, the prevalence of a lifetime history of alcohol abuse or dependence was 1.5 times greater among persons with mild and severe cognitive impairment than those with no cognitive impairment (George, Landerman, Blazer, & Anthony, 1991). Similarly, Finlayson et al. found that 49 of 216 (23 %) elderly patients presenting for alcohol treatment had dementia associated with alcoholism (Finlayson, Hurt, Davis, & Morse, 1988). As might be expected, patients with alcohol related dementia who become abstinent do not show a progression in cognitive impairment compared to those with Alzheimer's disease (Oslin & Cary, 2003). Cognitive screening of subjects will be included in the clinical study as a source of psychiatric disability.

Sleep disorders and sleep disturbances represent another group of comorbid disorders associated with excessive alcohol use. Alcohol causes well-established changes in sleep patterns such as decreased sleep latency, decreased stage IV sleep, and precipitation or aggravation of sleep apnea (Wagman, Allen, & Upright, 1977). There are also age-associated changes in sleep patterns including increased REM episodes, a decrease in REM length, a decrease in stage III and IV sleep, and increased awakenings. The age associated changes in sleep can all be worsened by alcohol use and depression. Moeller and colleagues demonstrated in younger subjects that alcohol and depression had additive effects upon sleep disturbances when occurring together (Moeller et al., 1993). Wagman and colleagues also demonstrated that abstinent alcoholics did not sleep well because of insomnia, frequent awakenings, and REM fragmentation (Wagman et al., 1977). However, when these subjects ingested alcohol, sleep periodicity normalized and REM sleep was temporarily suppressed suggesting that alcohol use could be used to self-medicate for sleep disturbances. A common anecdote from patients is that alcohol is used to help with sleep problems.

Summary

Over the last several years there has been a growing awareness that addictive disorders among the elderly are a common public health problem. Epidemiological studies suggest that alcoholism is present in up to 4 % of community dwelling elderly and there is at least one report suggesting that the prevalence of alcoholism among older adults is on the rise (Liberto & Oslin, 1995; Osterling & Berglund, 1994). Moreover, problem or hazardous drinking is estimated to be even more common among the elderly than alcoholism (Barry et al., 1998; Liberto & Oslin, 1995). However, there continues to be a gap in the number of older adults who are referred for treatment or who receive treatment for addictive disorders. Although, there are many reasons for patients not to be engaged in treatment, recommending treatment is partially based upon the availability of effective treatment. Towards this end, there needs to be better dissemination of information regarding currently available and efficacious treatments for alcoholism and other addictive disorders as well as continued development of more effective treatments. There is also a greater need for further research as there are major gaps in understanding the effectiveness of treatments and the economic and social benefits gained from treatment.

	YES	NO
1. When talking with others, do you ever underestimate how much you actually drink?	(1)	(0)
2. After a few drinks, have you sometimes not eaten or been able to skip a meal because you didn't feel hungry?	(1)	(0)
3. Does having a few drinks help decrease your shakiness or tremors?	(1)	(0)
4. Does alcohol sometimes make it hard for you to remember parts of the day or night?	(1)	(0)
5. Do you usually take a drink to relax or calm your nerves?	(1)	(0)
6. Do you drink to take your mind off your problems?	(1)	(0)
7. Have you ever increased your drinking after experiencing a loss in your life?	(1)	(0)
8. Has a doctor or nurse ever said they were worried or concerned about your drinking?	(1)	(0)
9. Have you ever made rules to manage your drinking?	(1)	(0)
10. When you feel lonely, does having a drink help?	(1)	(0)

TOTAL SMAST-G SCORE (0-10) _____

A score of 3 or more is indicative of problem drinking.

Reprinted with permission of the
University of Michigan Alcohol Research Center
© The Regents of the University of Michigan, 1991

Table 9.1. Short Michigan Alcohol Screening Test-Geriatric

References

Adams, W. L., Fleming, M., & Barry, K. (1996). Screening for problem drinking in older primary care patients. *JAMA, 276*, 1964-1967.

American Psychiatric Association. (1994). *Diagnostic and statistical manual of mental disorders* (4th ed.). Washington, DC: Author.

Atkinson, R. (1995). Treatment programs for aging alcoholics. In T. Beresford & E. Gomberg (Eds.), *Alcohol and Aging*. New York: Oxford University Press.

Atkinson, R., Tolson, R., & Turner, J. (1993). Factors affecting outpatient treatment compliance of older male problem drinkers. *Journal of Studies on Alcohol, 54*, 102-106.

Barry, K., Consensus Panel Chair. (2001). *Brief Alcohol Interventions and Therapies in Substance Abuse Treatment*. Washington, DC: US Government Printing Office.

Barry, K., & Fleming, M. (1990). Computerized administration of alcoholism screening tests in a primary care setting. *Journal of the American Board of Family Practice, 3*, 93-98.

Barry, K. L., Blow, F. C., Walton, M. A., Chernack, S. T., Mudd, S. A., Coyne, J. C., & Gomberg, E. S. L. (1998). Elder-specific brief alcohol intervention: 3-month outcomes. *Alcoholism: Clinical and Experimental Research, 22*, 32 A.

Barry, K. L., Oslin, D. W., & Blow, F. C. (2001). *Prevention and management of alcohol problems in older adults*. New York: Springer Publishing.

Bartels, S., Coakley, E., Zubritsky, C., Ware, J., Areán, P., Chen, H., Oslin, D., Llorente, M., Miles, K., Costantino, G., Quijano, L., McIntyre, J., Linkins, K., Oxman, T., & Levkoff, S. (Submitted). Engaging Older Primary Care Patients with Depression, Anxiety Disorders, or At-risk Alcohol Use in Mental Health Services: A Comparison of Integrated and Referral Care. *JAMA*.

Beresford, T. (1979). Alcoholism consultation and general hospital psychiatry. *General Hospital Psychiatry, 1*, 293-300.

Black, B. S., Rabins, P. V., & McGuire, M. H. (1998). Alcohol use disorder is a risk factor for mortality among older public housing residents. *International Psychogeriatrics, 10*, 309-327.

Blazer, D. G., Hughes, D. C., & George, L. K. (1987). The epidemiology of depression in an elderly community population. *Gerontologist, 27*, 281-287.

Blow, F. (1998). *Substance abuse among older Americans* (DHHS No. (SMA) 98-3179). Washington DC: US Government Printing Office.

Blow, F. (2003). Brief interventions in the treatment of at-risk drinking in older adults. Personal communication.

Blow, F., Cook, C. L., Booth, B., Falcon, S., & Friedman, M. (1992). Age-related psychiatric comorbidities and level of functioning in alcoholic veterans seeking outpatient treatment. *Hospital and Community Psychiatry, 43*, 990-995.

Blow, F., Gillespie, B., Barry, K., Mudd, S., & Hill, E. (1998). Brief screening for alcohol problems in elderly population using the Short Michigan Alcoholism Screening Test-Geriatric Version (SMAST-G). *Alcoholism: Clinical and Experimental Research*, 20-25.

Broe, G. A., Creasey, H., Jorm, A. F., Bennett, H. P., Casey, B., Waite, L. M., Grayson, D. A., & Cullen, J. (1998). Health habits and risk of cognitive impairment and dementia in old age: a prospective study on the effects of exercise, smoking and alcohol consumption. *Australian & New Zealand Journal of Public Health, 22*(5), 621-623.

Brower, K. J., Mudd, S., Blow, F. C., Young, J. P., & Hill, E. M. (1994). Severity and Treatment of Alcohol Withdrawal in Elderly Versus Younger Patients. *Alcoholism: Clinical and Experimental Research, 18*, 196-201.

Callahan, C. M., & Tierney, W. M. (1995). Health services use and mortality among older primary care patients with alcoholism. *Journal of the American Geriatrics Society, 43*, 1378-1383.

Chermack, S. T., Blow, F. C., Hill, E. M., & Mudd, S. A. (1996). The relationship between alcohol symptoms and consumption among older drinkers. *Alcoholism: Clinical and Experimental Research, 20*, 1153-1158.

Chick, J., Lloyd, G., & Crombie, E. (1985). Counselling problem drinkers in medical wards: a controlled study. *British Medical Journal Clinical Research Ed., 290*(6473), 965-967.

Conwell, Y. (1991). Suicide in elderly patients. In L. S. Schneider & C. F. Reynolds & B. D. Lebowitz & A. J. Friedhofff (Eds.), *Diagnosis and Treatment of Depression in Late Life* (pp. 397-418). Washington, DC: American Psychiatric Press, Inc.

Cook, B., Winokur, G., Garvey, M., & Beach, V. (1991). Depression and previous alcoholism in the elderly. *British Journal of Psychiatry, 158*, 72-75.

Coulehan, J., Zettler-Segal, M., Block, M., McClelland, M., & Schulberg, H. (1987). Recognition of alcoholism and substance abuse in primary care patients. *Archives of Internal Medicine, 147*, 349-352.

DeLabry, L. O., Glynn, R. J., Levenson, M. R., Hermos, J. A., LoCastro, J. S., & Vodonas, P. S. (1992). Alcohol consumption and mortality in an American male population: Recovering the U-shaped curve—findings from the normative aging study. *Journal of Studies on Alcohol, 53*, 25-32.

Dufour, M. C., Archer, L., & Gordis, E. (1992). Alcohol and the elderly. *Clinics in Geriatric Medicine, 8*, 127-141.

Finlayson, R., Hurt, R., Davis, L., & Morse, R. (1988). Alcoholism in elderly persons: a study of the psychiatric and psychosocial features of 216 inpatients. *Mayo Clinics Proceedings, 63*, 761-768.

Fleming, M., Barry, K., Manwell, L., Johnson, K., & London, R. (1997). Brief physician advice for problem alcohol drinkers: A randomized controlled trial in community-based primary care practices. *Journal of the American Medical Association, 277*, 1039-1045.

Fleming, M. F., Manwell, L. B., Barry, K. L., Adams, W., & Stauffacher, E. A. (1999). Brief physician advice for alcohol problems in older adults: a randomized community-based trial. *Journal of Family Practice, 48*(5), 378-384.

Fraser, A. G. (1997). Pharmacokinetic interactions between alcohol and other drugs. *Clinical Pharmacokinetics, 33*(2), 79-90.

Gambert, S., & Katsoyannis, K. (1995). Alcohol-related medical disorders of older heavy drinkers. In T. Beresford & E. Gomberg (Eds.), *Alcohol and Aging* (pp. 70-81). New York: Oxford University Press.

George, L. K., Landerman, R., Blazer, D. G., & Anthony, J. C. (1991). Cognitive impairment. In L. N. Robins & D. A. Regier (Eds.), *Psychiatric Disorders in America: The Epidemiologic Catchment Area Study* (pp. 291-327). New York: The Free Press.

Greist, J., Klein, M., Erdman, H., & Bires, J. (1987). Comparison of computer- and interviewer-administered versions of the Diagnostic Interview Schedule. *Hospital & Community Psychiatry, 38*, 1304-1311.

Gurland, B., & Cross, P. (1982). Epidemiology of psychopathology in old age. Some implications for clinical services. *Psychiatric Clinics of North America, 5*, 11-26.

Hylek, E. M., Heiman, H., Skates, S. J., Sheehan, M. A., & Singer, D. E. (1998). Acetaminophen and other risk factors for excessive warfarin anticoagulation. *JAMA, 279*(9), 657-662.

Institute of Medicine. (1990). Who provides treatment? Committee of the Institute of Medicine (Division of Mental Health and Behavioral Medicine) *Broadening the ease of treatment for alcoholism*. Unpublished manuscript, Washington, DC.

Kandel, D., Chen, K., Warner, L., Kessler, R., & Grant, B. (1997). Prevalence and demographic correlates of symptoms of last year dependence on alcohol, nicotine, marijuana and cocaine in the U.S. population. *Drug & Alcohol Dependence, 44*(1), 11-29.

Kashner, T. M., Rodell, D. I., Ogden, S. R., Guggenheim, F. G., & Karson, C. N. (1992). Outcomes and Costs of Two VA Inpatient Treatment Programs for Older Alcoholic Patients. *Hospital and Community Psychiatry, 43*(10), 985-989.

Kivela, S. L., Nissinen, A., & Ketola, A. (1989). Alcohol consumption and mortality in aging or aged Finnish men. *Journal of Clinical Epidemiology, 42*, 61-68.

Klatsky, A. L., & Armstrong, A. (1993). Alcohol Use, Other Traits and Risk of Unnatural Death: A Prospective Study. *Alcohol: Clinical and Experimental Research, 17*, 1156-1162.

Klatsky, A. L., Armstrong, M. A., & Friedman, G. D. (1990). Risk of cardiovascular mortality in alcohol drinkers, ex-drinkers and nondrinkers. *American Journal of Cardiology, 66*, 1237-1242.

Kofoed, L. L., Tolson, R. L., Atkinson, R. M., Toth, R. L., & Turner, J. A. (1987). Treatment compliance of older alcoholics: an elder-specific approach is superior to "mainstreaming". *Journal of Studies on Alcohol, 48*, 47-51.

Liberto, J. G., & Oslin, D. W. (1995). Early versus late onset of alcoholism in the elderly. *International Journal of the Addictions, 30*(13-14), 1799-1818.

Liberto, J. G., Oslin, D. W., & Ruskin, P. E. (1992). Alcoholism in older persons: a review of the literature. *Hospital & Community Psychiatry, 43*(10), 975-984.

Mayfield, D., McLeod, G., & Hall, P. (1974). The CAGE questionnaire: Validation of a new alcoholism instrument. *American Journal of Psychiatry, 131*, 1121-1123.

Miller, W., & Hester, R. (1986). *Treating Addictive Behaviors: Processes of Change*. New York: Plenum Press.

Miller, W., & Rollnick, S. (1991). *Motivational interviewing: preparing people to change addictive behavior*. New York: The Guilford Press.

Moeller, F. G., Gillin, J. C., Irwin, M., Golshan, S., Kripke, D. F., & Schuckit, M. (1993). A Comparison of Sleep EEGs in Patients with Primary Major Depression and Major Depression Secondary to Alcoholism. *Journal of Affective Disorders, 27*, 39-42.

Murray, C., & Lopez, A. (1996). *The global burden of disease: A comprehensive assessment of mortality and disability from diseases, injuries, and risk factors in 1990 and projected to 2020* (Vol. 1). Boston: Harvard University Press.

National Institute on Alcohol Abuse and Alcoholism. (1995). Diagnostic criteria for alcohol abuse. *Alcohol Alert, 30*(PH 359), 1-6.

O'Malley, S. S., Jaffe, A. J., Chang, G., Schottenfeld, R. S., Meyer, R. E., & Rounsaville, B. (1992). Naltrexone and coping skills therapy for alcohol dependence: a controlled study. *Archives of General Psychiatry, 49*, 881-887.

Onder, G., Pedone, C., Landi, F., Cesari, M., Della Vedova, C., Bernabei, R., & Gambassi, G. (2002). Adverse drug reactions as cause of hospital admissions: results from the Italian Group of Pharmacoepidemiology in the Elderly (GIFA). *Journal of the American Geriatrics Society, 50*(12), 1962-1968.

Orgogozo, J. M., Dartigues, J. F., Lafont, S., Letenneur, L., Commenges, D., Salamon, R., Renaud, S., & Breteler, M. B. (1997). Wine consumption and dementia in the elderly: a prospective community study in the Bordeaux area. *Revue Neurologique, 153*(3), 185-192.

Oslin, D., & Cary, M. (2003). Alcohol related dementia - validation of diagnostic criteria. *American Journal of Geriatric Psychiatry, 11*(4), 441-447.

Oslin, D., Liberto, J. G., O'Brien, J., Krois, S., & Norbeck, J. (1997). Naltrexone as an adjunctive treatment for older patients with alcohol dependence. *American Journal of Geriatric Psychiatry, 5*(4), 324-332.

Oslin, D. W., Pettinati, H. M., & Volpicelli, J. R. (2002). Alcoholism treatment adherence: older age predicts better adherence and drinking outcomes. *American Journal of Geriatric Psychiatry, 10*, 740-747.

Osterling, A., & Berglund, M. (1994). Elderly first time admitted alcoholics: a descriptive study on gender differences in a clinical population. *Alcoholism: Clinical and Experimental Research, 18*, 1317-1321.

Pelc I, Verbanck P, Le Bon O, Gavrilovic M, Lion K, & Lehert P. (1997). Efficacy and safety of acamprosate in the treatment of detoxified alcohol-dependent patients. A 90-day placebo-controlled dose-finding study. *British Journal of Psychiatry, 171*, 73-77.

Persson, J., & Magnusson, P. H. (1989). Early intervention in patients with excessive consumption of alcohol: a controlled study. *Alcohol, 6*(5), 403-408.

Poikolainen, K. (1991). Epidemiologic assessment of population risks and benefits of alcohol use. *Alcohol and Alcoholism, Supplement 1*, 27-34.

Robins, L., Helzer, J., Weissman, M., Orvaschel, H., Gruenberg, E., Burke, J., & Regier, D. (1984). Lifetime prevalence of specific psychiatric disorders in three sites. *Archives of General Psychiatry, 41*, 949-958.

Sass, H., Soyka, M., Mann, K., & Zieglgansberger, W. (1996). Relapse prevention by acamprosate: results from a placebo-controlled study in alcohol dependence. *Archives of General Psychiatry, 53*, 673-680.

Saunders, P. A., Copeland, J. R., Dewey, M. E., Davidson, I. A., McWilliam, C., Sharma, V., & Sullivan, C. (1991). Heavy drinking as a risk factor for depression and dementia in elderly men. *British Journal of Psychiatry, 159*, 213-216.

Scherr, P. A., LaCroix, A. Z., Wallace, R. B., Berkman, L., Curb, J. D., Cornoni-Huntley, J., Evans, D. A., & Hennekens, C. H. (1992). Light to Moderate Alcohol Consumption and Mortality in the Elderly. *Journal of the American Geriatrics Society, 40*, 651-657.

Schonfeld, L., & Dupree, L. W. (1991). Antecedents of drinking for early - and late - onset elderly alcohol abusers. *Journal of Studies on Alcohol, 52*, 587-592.

Schuckit, M., & Pastor, P. (1978). The elderly as a unique population. *Alcoholism: Clinical and Experimental Research, 2*, 31-38.

Shaper, A. G. (1990). Alcohol and mortality: A review of prospective studies. *British Journal of Addiction, 85*, 837-847.

Stampfer, M. J., Colditz, G. A., Willett, W. C., Speizer, F. E., & Hennekens, C. H. (1988). A prospective study of moderate alcohol consumption and the risk of coronary disease and stroke in women. *New England Journal of Medicine, 319*, 267-273.

Sullivan, J. T., Sykora, K., Schneiderman, J., & Naranjo, C. A. (1989). Assessment of alcohol withdrawal: the revised clinical institute withdrawal. *British Journal of Addiction, 84*(11), 1353-1357.

Thun, M. J., Peto, R., Lopez, A. D., Monaco, J. H., Henley, S. J., Heath, C. W., & Doll, R. (1997). Alcohol consumption and mortality among middle-aged and elderly US adults. *New England Journal of Medicine, 337*, 1705-1714.

Volpicelli, J. R., Alterman, A. I., Hayashida, M., & O'Brien, C. P. (1992). Naltrexone in the treatment of alcohol dependence. *Archives of General Psychiatry, 49*, 876-880.

Wagman, A. M., Allen, R. P., & Upright, D. (1977). Effects of alcohol consumption upon parameters of ultradian sleep rhythms in alcoholics. *Advances in Experimental Medicine and Biology, 85A*, 601-616.

Wiens, A. N., Menustik, C. E., Miller, S. I., & Schmitz, R. E. (1982 - 1983). Medical-Behavioral Treatment for the Older Alcoholic Patient. *American Journal of Drug and Alcohol Abuse, 9*, 461-475.

Early Detection and Treatment of Prescription Drug Abuse in Primary Care

J. Harry Isaacson, M.D.
Department of General Internal Medicine, Cleveland Clinic Foundation

When a patient is in physical or emotional pain, prescribing controlled substances often appears to be the simplest and most efficient path to relieving suffering and distress. However, in a minority of cases, this approach leads to prescription drug abuse and patient harm. This article will review the epidemiology of prescription drug abuse, legal policies designed to safeguard against prescription drug abuse, physician and patient factors associated with prescription drug abuse, and finally practical solutions the primary care physician can implement to minimize the risk of prescription drug abuse.

Definitions

Determining when prescription drug abuse is present clinically is admittedly imprecise, in part because of variable physician and societal beliefs about what constitutes appropriate use of medication. Finch has outlined a useful terminology related to prescription drug abuse, which is adapted below (Finch, 1993). *Appropriate use of controlled substances* is defined as a patient who receives a prescription for and uses controlled substances as prescribed for a defined condition with no signs of misuse or abuse. *Misuse/Inappropriate use* refers to use of a controlled substance for a reason other than that for which it was prescribed, or in a dosage different than that prescribed. Misuse can be *unintentional* and result from a lack of communication between physician and patient, resulting in dosage escalation. Misuse may also be *intentional*, such as using a controlled substance that was not prescribed for that patient, for example using a family member's narcotic or psychotropic medication. Using a previous prescribed controlled substance for a new clinical problem would also represent *intentional* misuse of medication. An example of this would be someone using an oral narcotic previously prescribed after surgery, for a new problem such as headache or back pain. Implied in this definition is the fact that the patient's inappropriate use of a controlled substance is infrequent, and does not represent a pattern of misuse leading to disability or dysfunction. *Prescription drug abuse* refers to use of a controlled substance outside the normally accepted standards of use, resulting in disability and/or dysfunction. Such a pattern may be manifest by escalating use of a substance, use of a substance for medication effects independent of a defined medical condition, drug-seeking behavior directed at one or more physicians, and continued use of substances despite negative consequences from their use. These patients demonstrate a preoccupation with obtaining the controlled substance. Table 10.1 summarizes an overview of Prescription Drug Abuse.

Term	Definition	Clinical Examples	Intervention Strategies
Appropriate Use	Use of a controlled substance as prescribed for a defined condition with no signs of misuse or abuse.	-10-day course of post-operative narcotics taken as prescribed.	Explain in advance to the patient narcotics will be used only for a limited time.
Misuse/Inappropriate Use	Use of a controlled substance for a reason other than that for which it was prescribed or in a dosage different than that prescribed. No pattern of misuse leading to disability or dysfunction.	-Single episode of narcotic used twice as often as prescribed. -Use of an old prescription for a new clinical problem without consulting a physician.	Educate the patient on proper use of the medication.
Prescription Drug Abuse	Use of a controlled substance outside the normally accepted standards of use, resulting in disability and/or dysfunction.	-Continued misuse despite interventions. -Use of narcotic for recreational purposes unrelated to a medical condition.	-Express concerns in an empathic manner. -Discontinue the medication of abuse. -Consult with expert (chemical dependency, pain management).
Catastrophic Use	Use of a controlled substance that involves illegal activity or places the patient in immediate harm.	-Altering a prescription or selling a controlled substance. -Overdose of a controlled substance.	-Immediately stop prescribing any controlled substances. -Consult with chemical dependency expert. -Notify legal authorities if indicated.

Table 10.1: Overview of Prescription Drug Abuse

Chapter 10

Physical dependence does not equal abuse

Physical dependence, refers to the pharmacological principle that abrupt cessation of intake of a substance leads to characteristic withdrawal symptoms. *Tolerance* refers to the fact that escalating doses of a substance must be ingested in order to attain the same clinical effect. A patient treated chronically with a controlled substance may exhibit physical dependence or tolerance (biologic phenomenal) to a medication without any misuse or abuse (behavioral phenomena). For example, a patient with metastatic cancer on high dose narcotics for pain relief will develop physical dependence and experience acute opioid withdrawal if the medication is abruptly stopped. In these situations, the patient must be educated about the benefits of the medication and the difference between physical dependence and drug abuse. In contrast, it is important to recognize that patients may meet criteria for prescription drug abuse without having any physical dependence on a substance. This may occur when the use of a substance is intermittent yet still significantly interferes with function. A substance can also be ingested for reasons other than a defined medical condition without being continuous or at a high enough dose to develop physical dependence. Finally, it is important to recognize that some patients may be denied *appropriate* use of controlled substances for medical conditions for a variety of reasons and be mislabeled as having a problem when in fact none exists.

Epidemiology

The lack of a universally agreed upon definition of prescription drug abuse has led to limitations in epidemiologic research. Although many classes of medications are subject to misuse, physicians are most often concerned with intentional abuse of prescription controlled substances. Prescription stimulants, sedatives, tranquilizers and analgesics are all subject to use for purposes other than intended. Prescription analgesics are the most widely misused of the prescription psychoactive medications, followed by tranquilizers, stimulants, and sedatives. The National Household Survey on Drug Abuse (NHSDA) provides our best insight into the scope of psychoactive medication misuse in the United States. According to the 1998 NHSDA, an estimated 5.7 million people aged 12 and older used psychoactive drugs for non-medical purposes in the twelve months prior to 1998 (Substance Abuse and Mental Health Services Administration, 1999). The 1998 NHSDA estimated that 1.7 million Americans were "current" non-medical users of prescription analgesics. Stimulant and sedative/tranquilizer misuse was estimated at about one-third of that for analgesics. In the United States, it is known that women are nearly 50% more likely to use any controlled prescription drug (primarily opiates and anxiolytics) (Simoni-Wastila, 2000). Despite the greater exposure of women to medications of abuse, rates of prescription drug misuse are similar for women and men. (Substance Abuse and Mental Health Services Administration, 1999). Patients with psychiatric disorders are more likely than the general population to have co-morbid substance abuse disorders (Regier et al., 1990).

NHSDA data from 1990 to 1998 showed the number of new non-medical users of opioid analgesics increased by 181 percent, with approximately 1.5 million new users (National Institute on Drug Abuse, 2001). Oxycodone related emergency department visits increased 352%, from 4,069 to 18,409 reports between 1994 and 2001 (Substance Abuse and Mental Health Services Administration, 2001). New use of tranquilizers, sedatives and stimulants for non-medical purposes increased 132, 90 and 165 percent respectively (National Institute on Drug Abuse, 2001). This rise in prescription drug abuse has resulted in the National Institute on Drug Abuse (NIDA) launching a campaign against prescription drug abuse (Vastag, 2001).

The Drug Abuse Warning Network (DAWN), operated by the Substance Abuse and Mental Health Services Administration (SAMHSA) tracks drug-related emergency department visits and deaths in the U.S. Data is from a sample of metropolitan areas and hospitals, and does not represent the prevalence of drug related incidents. Information from DAWN can be used to describe trends and patterns in the non-medical use of licit drugs. In the 1999 DAWN data revealed that codeine, diazepam, methadone, amitriptyline, and propoxyphene were in the top eleven for *drug-related deaths* in the U.S. (Substance Abuse and Mental Health Services Administration, 1999). The prescription drugs alprazolam, clonazepam, and hydrocodone were in the top ten for *drug-related emergency department visits* in the 1999 DAWN data (Substance Abuse and Mental Health Services Administration, 2001).

Beyond the NHSDA and DAWN data, epidemiologic studies are limited. Some generalizations can be made about the role of gender, age, and psychiatric co-morbidity in the subsequent development of prescription drug misuse. The most dramatic new misuse of prescription drugs has been seen among 12 to 25 year olds (Vastag, 2001). The elderly are a group at high risk for substance abuse in the United States. It is estimated that up to 17% of persons 60 years and older may be affected by prescription drug abuse (Substance Abuse and Mental Health Services Administration, 2000b).

A recent study of patients using opioid medications for noncancer pain in primary care settings found prescription drug abuse behavior in up to 31% of patients. A lifetime history of a substance use disorder and decreasing age were significantly associated with prescription drug abuse (Reid et al., 2002).

Legal Issues

Physicians are legally responsible when prescribing controlled drugs and should be knowledgeable of federal and state prescribing laws and regulations. In all cases the most stringent law whether it is federal or state takes precedence. Drugs are categorized according to federal and state laws as either "over the counter" (i.e. aspirin), "prescription" (i.e. antibiotics) or "controlled substances" (i.e. opioids, benzodiazepines). Controlled substances are considered drugs with potential for physical and/or psychological dependence (addiction). The U.S. Food and Drug Administration (FDA) under the Food, Drug and Cosmetics (FD&C) Act approves drugs established to be safe and effective. Physicians may choose to use drugs for indications other than their approved labeling if based on acceptable medical practice. The FDA is not meant to regulate medical practice (Joranson & Gilson, 1994). The federal Controlled Substances Act (CSA) of 1970, is the legal foundation by which the federal government regulates the use and availability of controlled drugs. The CSA legislation places all controlled drugs into one of five scheduled classes. (Table 10.2) The schedules are based on the degree of medicinal value, potential for abuse, and relative safety (Joranson & Gilson, 1994). Each schedule carries different penalties for unlawful use. The Schedule I class contains drugs that have no acceptable medical use and are illegal except for approved research use. Schedules II-V have accepted medical uses and have decreasing potentials for abuse.

Schedule I	high abuse potential and no accepted medical indications	Examples: heroin, marijuana, LSD, mescaline
Schedule II	high abuse potential and accepted medical indications with severe restrictions; may lead to severe psychological or physical dependence	Examples: morphine, codeine, methadone, onycodone, hydromorphone, meperidine, fentanyl, cocaine, amphetamines, dronabinol, and secobarbital
Schedule III	abuse potential less than Schedule II and accepted medical use	Examples: compounds with limited quantities of controlled substances i.e. acetaminophen when combined with codeine, acetaminophen with hydrocodone, and buprenorphine
Schedule IV	abuse potential less than Schedule III and accepted medical use	Examples: propoxyphene, pentazocine, phentermine, phenobarbital, bensodiazepines
Schedule V	abuse potential considered less than Schedule IV and accepted medical use	Examples: preparations with limited quantities of certain opioids and stumulants including many of the antitussive and antidiarrheal medications, with often are available without a prescription; examples include diaphenoxylate and propylhexedrine

Table 10.2: Schedules of Controlled Drugs

Schedule II drugs must be prescribed using a written prescription and refills are prohibited. However, in cases of medical emergencies, limited amounts of Schedule II medications may be telephoned or faxed to the pharmacy with a written prescription delivered with in 72 hours. Up to five refills are allowed with Schedule III - V medications. The CSA allows for the addition and elimination of drugs from various schedules as well as the rescheduling of medications. Federal laws do not limit the amount or the duration of prescriptions for controlled substances. Under the CSA it is unlawful to prescribe opioids for detoxification or maintenance treatment of opioid dependence. For example, methadone may be prescribed for analgesia as a Schedule II medication. However, under the 1974 Narcotic Addict Treatment Act if a physician is not affiliated with a Narcotic Treatment Program it is unlawful to prescribe methadone for purposes of outpatient detoxification or maintenance treatment (U.S. Department of Justice, 1990).

The Department of Justice's Drug Enforcement Agency (DEA) was established in 1973. The DEA's mission is to enforce all controlled substance laws and regulations including investigating cases of diversion. Physicians must register with the DEA in order to prescribe controlled substances.

States and not the federal government are responsible for regulating medical practice. Most states have adopted a version of the 1970 Uniform Controlled Substance Act (UCSA) which uses the same scheduling classification system as the federal Controlled Substances Act. Various state agencies including medical and pharmacy boards regulate physician-prescribing practices through licensing and monitoring systems. Of note, state medical boards report that controlled substance overprescribing is the leading cause of physician investigations and subsequent licensure loss (Parran, 1997). Monitoring programs vary from state to state and include such systems as Multiple Copy Prescription Programs (MCPP), and Electronic Data Transfer (EDT) programs. Which scheduled drugs are monitored also varies, with some states monitoring only Schedule II substances while others monitor all schedules. Most state regulatory boards emphasize the importance of balancing both drug control and drug availability. However, studies have shown that some state monitoring systems actually discourage physicians from using controlled drugs for legitimate indications (Hill, 1993). The Federation of State Medical Boards (FSMB) develops guidelines for state boards. One such guideline is the "Model Guidelines for the Use of Controlled Substances for the Treatment of Pain" which was developed in 1998 and serves as a framework for the use of opioids in the management of chronic pain (Federation of State Medical Boards of the United States, 1998). These guidelines serve to improve physician practice and protect legitimate medical use of controlled drugs.

Drug Factors

Since prescription medications are FDA approved, patients often consider abuse of these substances as safer than the abuse of illicit "street" drugs. The medications most commonly abused have mood altering effects such as opioids, benzodiazpines, barbiturates, and stimulants. The medications within these classes that are the most abused and have the greatest value for diversion have rapid onset of action and have high intensity of effect such as hydrocodone, oxycodone and alprazolam. Long acting/sustained release preparations have historically been less commonly abuse because of their slow onset of action. However, when a sustained release preparation is crushed, dissolved and injected its onset of action becomes rapid with a high intensity of effect. Brand name medications are more desirable among prescription drug abusers because they are more readily recognizable as the "real thing".

Patient Factors

There are a number of patient factors that may put the patient at risk or be clues to increased chance of prescription drug abuse. As noted, patients with a history of alcohol or drug problems in the past are clearly at increased risk when exposed to controlled substances (Reid et al., 2002). As patients become desperate to obtain medications, they may engage in a number of "scams" designed to dupe the unwary physician (Parran, 1997). Examples of such scams include patients presenting for care with pain syndromes such as toothache, renal colic (in some cases pricking their finger and dropping blood in the urine sample to mimic hematuria), or migraine headache. Such presentations are often to new physicians, emergency departments, or after hour phone calls when a primary physician is unavailable. Patients may seek out multiple physicians, claiming to be new to the area. Additional red flags are noted in Table 10.3.

1. More concern about medication than the problem
2. Multiple medication sensitivities.
3. "Can't take generics."
4. Refusal of diagnostic work-up or consultation.
5. Sophisticated knowledge of drugs.
6. "You are the only one who can help me."
7. Lost prescriptions.

Table 10.3: Red flags for drug seeking by patients

Physician Factors

A number of factors affecting physicians can increase the chance of prescription drug abuse. We live in a culture of "a pill for every ill", often with an expectation by both patients and physicians that a medication will be prescribed at the end of a visit. As a result, conflicts may ensue between providing symptom relief and limit setting. Smith has labeled physician factors associated with prescription drug abuse the "four D's." (Smith & Seymore, 1980). *Dated* refers to physicians who have not kept up with new medical knowledge and prescribe older medications with higher abuse potential and without regard to safe prescribing practices. *Duped* refers to physicians who fall victim of patient scams mentioned earlier. *Dishonest* refers to that small minority of physicians who divert controlled substances for their own proprietary gain. Finally, *disabled* physicians include those who prescribe substances for themselves because of their own abuse problems and those who prescribe for family members with similar problems. There are several other physician characteristics that contribute to prescription drug over-prescribing. These include a general societal emphasis on prescribing as the best response to all patient complaints ("medication mania"), the urge on the part of physicians to always help patients with all problems (hypertrophied enabling), and the lack of the ability to say "no" to patients on the part of physicians (confrontation phobia) (Parran, 1997). These issues increase the tendency to prescribe the frequency of prescribing for vague indications and the difficulty physicians have in extracting themselves from controlled drug prescribing once it has been initiated.

Prevention

There are a number of strategies to help prevent prescription drug abuse. (Table 10.4) First, the physician must screen patients for substance use disorders prior to prescribing controlled substances. A full discussion of screening strategies is beyond the scope of this article, and there are excellent reviews on this topic (Weaver, Jarvis, & Scholl, 1999; Isaacson & Schorling, 1999). The CAGE questionnaire is useful in screening for alcohol problems and can be adapted to screen for drug problems as well. (Table 10.5) The physician should inquire about prior problems with any substances and review records of prior physicians if available. The physician must carefully document the diagnosis, rationale, and anticipated time course and symptom endpoint when initiating a controlled prescription. A physician should not provide controlled substances without examining and diagnosing a patient. The physician must feel empowered to say no when request for medications are inappropriate, despite conflict with the physician's natural desire to partner with the patient to relieve suffering. Finally, the physician must avoid prescribing any psychotropic medication for him or herself or family members (avoid becoming *disabled*).

Careful Prescribing Practices

A number of guidelines for office practice can limit prescription drug abuse. (Table 10.6) Prescription pads should be locked away to limit patient access. A group practice policy should be formulated that defines rules for after hour prescription of controlled substances so that all members practice consistently. As noted earlier, such practice rules can be stated up front to patients when providing substances in order to avoid conflicts in the future. Finally, meticulous records must be kept of all controlled substances that are prescribed both during routine office hours and after hours. Use of a controlled drug refill flow chart can be very helpful. The advent of computerized medical records may make documentation of refills easier, especially for those at multiple practice sites.

1.   Screen for alcohol and drug abuse before prescribing controlled substances
2.   Physician knowledge about controlled substances
3.   Physician knowledge about anxiety, depression and pain syndromes
4.   Documentation in the medical record
5.   Careful prescribing practices
6.   Use of controlled substance contracts

Table 10.4: Prevention Strategies

•   Have you ever felt the need to **C**ut down or limit your use of alcohol (or drugs)?
•   Have you ever been **A**nnoyed by criticism of your use of alcohol (or drugs)?
•   Have you ever felt **G**uilty about your use of aocohol (or drugs)?
•   Do you ever need alcohol (or drugs) to help you get started in the morning or calm your nerves (**E**ye-opener)?

Table 10.5: CAGE Questionaire
(Adapted from Ewing, J.A. "Detecting Alcoholism: The CAGE Questionnaire."
JAMA 252(14): 1905-1907, 1984.)

1.   Clear clinical indication must be present
2.   Defined therapeutic endpoint should be present
3.   State refill policy up front
4.   Avoid prescribing multiple substances
5.   Avoid multiple refills without office visits

Table 10.6: Prescribing Practices for Controlled Substances

Many pain management programs routinely use "pain contracts", although their efficacy for limiting prescription drug abuse is not well established. However there are no standard or validated contracts for patients using controlled substances. Fishman et al reviewed opioid contracts from 39 academic pain centers and found substantial diversity (a Fishman, Bandman, Edwards, & Bosook, 1999). If used, the contract should include clear expectations of proper medication use, methods for monitoring appropriate use (e.g. pill counts, toxicology screens) as well as the consequences of improper use (e.g. taper off medication). Since the contract is intended to improve the therapeutic alliance between patients and providers, a less pejorative term such as a patient agreement form is recommended. Others may prefer to use an informed consent form, which serves to educate the patient about the controlled substance as well as the likelihood of physical dependence and the risk of psychological dependence (addiction). Examples of consent forms for chronic opioid therapy can be found from professional organizations. (American Academy of Pain Medicine, 1999).

Interventions for Prescription Misuse or Abuse

Table 10.1 outlines intervention strategies for misuse, abuse and catastrophic use of prescription drugs. For patients who meet criteria for prescription drug misuse or inappropriate use, the proper intervention is to *educate* the patient. This includes clear instructions about how to take medicine and clear expectations that medications will only be used for that condition for which it was prescribed. Patients who fail to change behavior after such education are moving into the area of abuse. For those with abuse detected, it is important to maintain professional demeanor and convey direct empathic concern in a nonjudgmental fashion. It is important to give advice relative to the patient's primary complaint such as "I know you have been suffering with your back pain and I want to help you, but I am concerned that your use of narcotics has become a problem." In most instances, when prescription drug abuse is documented or highly suspected, the offending drug should be discontinued. The use of consultants (see below), may be very helpful in confirming the diagnosis and developing alternative strategies for symptom relief. Clinicians are often faced with patients new to their practice who are using controlled substances for unclear reasons. In these situations a reasonable strategy is to provide the patient with enough medication until they can be evaluated by a consultant with expertise in chemical dependency. There should be a clear message that failure to follow through with the consultant will result in discontinuation of the medication in question. The clinician must continuously emphasize that the patient's health and welfare are their priorities. Such statements can help to diffuse anger and hostility that occurs in some patients. There are some clinical behaviors related to the use of controlled prescription drugs, which although uncommon, should precipitate immediate cessation of prescribing. These include commission of felonies (altering a prescription or selling controlled drugs), intentional or unintentional overdoses and the threatening of the physician or staff.

Use of Consultants

Use of consultants with expertise in prescribing controlled substances and treatment of substance use disorders can be invaluable when prescription drug abuse is suspected or for patients at risk for prescription drug abuse. Pain management experts may also be useful in developing opioid-sparing strategies for such patients. Direct communication with the consultant can allow the physician to maintain the role as a primary care physician but obtain help from an expert in much the same way a primary care physician might consult a cardiologist or endocrinologist for a specific problem. If controlled substances are to be continued, the primary care physician must clarify with consultants who will be responsible for prescribing.

Use of Controlled Substances for Chronic Non-Cancer Pain Syndromes

Much controversy exists regarding the use of controlled substances for chronic non-cancer pain syndromes. A full discussion of this topic is beyond the scope of this article, however, it is important for the clinician who engages in such practice to closely follow guidelines from their state medical board and keep meticulous records in their office. Some states have strict guidelines that must be met before controlled substances can be prescribed on an ongoing basis. More extensive initial screening for chemical dependency disorders and monitoring efforts are indicated. Portenoy has outlined the relevant issues related to this topic in a recent review. (Portenoy, 1996)

Conclusion

Prescription drug abuse occurs in a small but significant number of patients for whom controlled substances are prescribed. The clinician must maintain a balance that allows for appropriate relief of patient suffering without undue risk. A number of patient and physician factors increase the risk for prescription drug abuse. Recognition of these factors, as well as implementation of prevention strategies can allow physicians to prescribe controlled substances in a safe, effective manner.

[Note: Material adapetd from Isaacson J. H., Hopper, J. A., Alford, D. P., Parran, T., Prescription Drug Abuse: What Primary Care Physicians Need to Know. Accepted for publication, *Postgraduate Medicine 2003*]

References

American Academy of Pain Medicine. (1999). *Consent for chronic opioid therapy.* http://www.painmed.org/productpub/statements/pdfs/opioid_consent_form.pdf

Federation of State Medical Boards of the United States. (1998). *Model Guidelines for the Use of Controlled Substances for the Treatment of Pain.*

Finch, J. (1993). Prescription drug abuse. *Primary Care: Clinics in Office Practice, 20,* 231-9.

Fishman, S. M., Bandman, T. B., Edwards, A., & Bosook, D. (1999). The opioid contract in the management of chronic pain. *Journal of Pain Symptom Manage,18,* 27-37.

Hill, C. S. (1993). The negative influence of licensing and disciplinary boards and drug enforcement agencies on pain treatment with opioid analgesics. *Journal of Pharmaceutic Care in Pain and Symptom Control,1,* 43-61.

Isaacson, J., & Schorling, J. (1999). Screening for alcohol problems in primary care. *The Medical Clinics of North America – Screening, 83,* 1547-1563.

Joranson, D. E., & Gilson, A. M. (1994). Policy issues and imperatives in the use of opioids to treat pain in substance abusers. *The Journal of Law, Medicine and Ethics, 22,* 215-223.

National Institute on Drug Abuse Research Series. (2001). *Prescription Drugs, Abuse and Addiction*. Bethesda, MD.

Parran, T. V. (1997). Prescription drug abuse: a question of balance. *Medical Clinics of North America,81,* 967-978.

Portenoy R. K. (1996). Opioid therapy for chronic non-malignant pain: a review of critical issues. *Journal of Pain Symptom Manage, 11,* 203-217.

Regier, D. A., Farmer, M. E., Rae, D. S., et al. (1990). Co-morbidity of mental disorders with alcohol and other drug abuse. Results from the Epidemiologic Catchment Area (ECA). *JAMA,264,* 2511-18.

Reid, M. C., Eagles-Horton, L. L., Weber, M. B., et.al. (2002). Use of Opioid Medications for Chronic Noncancer Pain in Primary Care. *Journal of General Internal Medicine, 17,* 173-179.

Simoni-Wastila L. (2000). The use of abusable prescription drugs: the role of gender. *Journal of Women's Health and Gender-Based Medicine, 9,* 289-97

Smith, D. E., & Seymore, R. B. (1980). Prescribing Practices: The educational alternative for the misprescriber. *Proceedings of the White House Conference on Prescription Drug Abuse.* Washington, DC.

Substance Abuse and Mental Health Services Administration, Office of Applied Studies. (1999). *Summary of Findings from the 1998 National Household Survey on Drug Abuse.* Rockville, MD.

Substance Abuse Mental Health Services Administration. (2000a). *Drug Abuse Warning Network Annual Medical Examiner Data 1999.* Rockville, MD.

Substance Abuse Mental Health Services Administration. (2000b). *Substance Abuse among Older Adults (TIP #26): Physician's Guide.* Rockville, MD.

Substance Abuse Mental Health Services Administration. (2001). *Mid-Year 2000 Preliminary Emergency Department Data from the Drug Abuse Warning Network.* Rockville, MD.

Substance Abuse and Mental Health Services Administration. (2002). *Emergency Department Trends From the Drug Abuse Warning Network, Final Estimates 1994-2001.* Rockville, MD.

U.S. Department of Justice. (1990). *Drug Enforcement Administration. Physician's Manual: An Informational Outline of the Controlled Substances Act of 1970.*

Vastag, B. (2001). Mixed Message on Prescription Drug Abuse. Medical News and Perspectives. *JAMA,17,* 2183-4.

Weaver, M. F., Jarvis, M. A. E., & Schnoll, S. H. (1999). Role of the Primary Care Physician in Problems of Substance Abuse. *Archives of Internal Medicine,159,* 913-924.

Integrating Behavioral Interventions for Smoking into Primary Care

David Antonuccio, Ph.D.
Reno V.A. Medical Center and University of Nevada School of Medicine

Introduction

In this chapter, we will provide a brief overview of behavioral theory and a practical guide to empirically validated behavior therapy (BT) interventions for smoking. These interventions include self-control strategies, nicotine fading, contingency management, partner support, hypnosis, aversive procedures, cognitive strategies, and relapse prevention skills (Antonuccio, Boutilier, Ward, Morrill, & Graybar, 1992; Lichtenstein, 2002). We will also show how these behavioral strategies can be integrated into the primary care environment where smokers will be most likely to encounter a professional who can help them quit.

Epidemiology of Tobacco Use

Currently, about 23% of adult Americans smoke cigarettes (CDC, 2002). Somewhere between 2% and 9% of adult Americans use smokeless tobacco (CDC, 1993), a practice that has been on the rise. About 13% of middle schoolers and as many as 29% of college students report using tobacco (Rigotti, Lee, & Wechsler, 2000). As many as 30% of senior high school girls smoke. Lung cancer deaths have exceeded breast cancer deaths for women since 1987. About 44% of all adult Americans who had ever smoked have become former smokers. More than 1.3 million Americans quit smoking each year while more than 1 million people, mostly teenagers, take up smoking for the first time each year. Smoking prevalence in the United States has declined steadily since 1974, but has leveled off in recent years (CDC, 2002). While U.S. smoking rates have declined, smoking rates are increasing in third world countries. An AMA review of worldwide smoking reported that the use of tobacco has increased worldwide by almost 75% over the previous 20 years (Council on Scientific Affairs, 1990). There are about 1.1 billion smokers world-wide and this is expected to rise to 1.6 billion by 2025 (WHO, 2003).

Consequences of Smoking and Nicotine Use

The detrimental health effects of smoking have been well documented. Cigarettes kill about half of all lifetime users (WHO, 2003). About half of these deaths occur in middle age (between 35 and 69 years old). Every cigarette smoked is estimated to cost smokers on average, 11 minutes of life (Shaw, Mitchell, & Dorling, 2000). Worldwide there are an estimated 4.9 million premature deaths (about 5% of all deaths) per year directly attributable to tobacco consumption (WHO, 2003). To put this in perspective, this is the equivalent of 25 fully loaded Boeing 747s (with a maximum capacity of 524 passengers) crashing with everyone on board being killed, every day. The worldwide annual death toll from smoking is expected to rise to about 10 million by 2030 (WHO, 2003). Risk is correlated with the number of cigarettes smoked, but even smoking as few as 1-4 cigarettes per day can substantially increase risk (Willett, Green, Stampfer et al., 1987).

Every recent report of the Surgeon General has identified smoking as the primary cause of preventable morbidity and mortality in the United States (CDC, 2002). Smoking is one of the leading causes of cancer in the United States, including lung, laryngeal, oral, esophageal, cervical, pancreatic, and bladder cancer. Smoking accounts for 30% of all cancer related deaths (Bartechhi, Mackenzie, & Schrier, 1994). Smoking increases the risk of wound infections even for simple wounds (Sorensen, Karlsmark, & Gottrup, 2003). Smoking is also the most important modifiable risk factor for the development of coronary artery disease, stroke, and peripheral vascular disease (U.S. Department of Health and Human Services, 1983). Some of the cardiotoxic effects of smoking are attributable to nicotine, while others are caused by different components of cigarette smoke. Nicotine has sympathomimetic effects that lead to an increase in heart rate and blood pressure and cause coronary vasoconstriction (Joseph, Norman, Ferry, Prochaska, Westman, Steele, Sherman, Cleveland, Antonuccio, Hartman, & McGovern, 1996). Nicotine may also contribute to endothelial cell injury (Davis, 1990; Pittilo & Woolf, 1993).

The individual smoker who quits may expect to benefit in many ways (USDHHS, 1990). For example, quitting smoking 4 weeks prior to surgery reduces the risk of wound infection to that of never-smokers (Sorensen, Karlsmark, & Gottrup, 2003). Quitting smoking is associated with about a 36% decrease in of mortality for patients with coronary heart disease compared with those who continue smoking (Critchley & Capewell, 2003). Smokers who quit before the age of 50 have half the risk of dying in the subsequent 15 years compared to continuing smokers. This decrease in risk is due to decreased risk of cancer, coronary disease, stroke, pulmonary disease, arterial disease, and peptic ulcer. These benefits have been shown to be present regardless of age or presence of smoking-related illness. Therefore, programs aimed at helping smokers quit should not be restricted to the young, nor to patients who have not developed smoking-related illness.

The smoker is not the only person exposed to the hazards of tobacco smoke. Environmental tobacco smoke is estimated to kill 53,000 people per year in the U.S. (Glantz & Parmley, 1991). Information about the hazards of second hand smoke has been reaching smokers, with as many as 72% indicating awareness that sidestream smoke is a lung cancer risk factor (Price & Everett, 1994). Although we could find no data about its impact, clinically this awareness does seem to motivate some smokers to consider quitting in order to help lower the risks to family members, if not friends. Evidence suggests that smoking during pregnancy increases the risk for attention deficit disorder and reduces childhood IQ scores (Milberger Biederman, Faraone, Chen, & Jones, 1996). Smoking during pregnancy also accounts for 10%

of infant deaths in the U.S. (American Lung Association, 2002). Parents who quit smoking before their child reaches third grade are 39% less likely to have their child start smoking in adolescence compared with parents who continue to smoke (Bricker et al., 2003).

Behavioral Theory

The most prevalent smoking cessation programs have employed behavioral principles in concert with other strategies (Lichtenstein, 1982; Lichtenstein, 2003). "Typical" behavioral treatment programs focus on antecedents and consequences of smoking and include cognitive techniques that promote coping during and after treatment (Lichtenstein & Mermelstein, 1985; Lichtenstein, 2003). The behavioral perspective is that smoking is a learned behavior, originally initiated by psychosocial variables (e.g., adult modeling, curiosity, peer pressure, availability, and rebelliousness) and maintained by physiological dependence on nicotine in combination with conditioned environmental stimuli that elicit the urge to smoke once the behavior has been firmly established. In this sense, smoking is a highly overlearned behavior. An average pack a day smoker puffs an estimated 160 times each day (Lichtenstein & Antonuccio, 1981), providing ample opportunity for internal cues (e.g., anxiety, hunger) and environmental cues (e.g., drinking coffee, talking on the phone) to become associated with the urge to smoke. The act of smoking can also be heavily reinforced operantly by both internal (e.g., pleasure, craving reduction) and external (e.g., social approval from other smokers, handling the cigarette) consequences (Lichtenstein & Brown, 1980).

The aversiveness of withdrawal from nicotine must be considered in any model of smoking behavior. Self-monitoring has revealed that coughing, craving for tobacco, feelings of aggression, increased appetite, irritability, nervousness, and restlessness increase in severity during the first week after quitting followed by a decrease in severity thereafter (Lawrence, Amodei, & Murray, 1982). Constipation and craving for sweets are at higher levels than baseline for 6 weeks after quitting. Other symptoms showed no clear trends. Patients who maintain abstinence for six weeks experience fewer symptoms during the initial two weeks after quitting than those who don't. Additionally, at 6 weeks abstinent patients tend to experience symptoms at baseline or lower levels of severity. Clearly, many individuals experience the act of quitting smoking as aversive. The role of expectations in the experience of withdrawal symptoms has yet to be adequately evaluated.

A comprehensive bio-behavioral theory of smoking must include biological factors as well. Pomerleau and Pomerleau (1985) specified several biological factors that help to maintain smoking behavior. They hypothesized that smokers smoke to cause temporary improvements in performance and affect. They identified a periodic pattern of arousal and alertness during smoking, followed by calming and tension reduction after smoking. They showed that smoking stimulates the production of betaendorphins and vasopressin. These neurotransmitters are known to reduce pain, increase tolerance to stress, improve memory, increase concentration, and speed up information processing. Therefore smoking is maintained by both powerful negative (e.g., reduction of craving) and positive inducements (Pinto & Morrell, 1988). There may even be an inherited predisposition with regard to susceptibility to these inducements (Hughes, 1986; Pomerleau, Collins, Shiffman, & Pomerleau, 1993).

Behavior Therapy

Cognitive-behavioral methods often employ strategies designed to counteract these negative and positive inducements to smoke. These interventions include (1) aversive strategies such as smoke holding, rapid smoking, and noxious imagery, (2) nicotine fading and controlled smoking techniques, (3) self-control and self-monitoring strategies which help smokers identify and modify situations, cognitions, feelings, and other cues which promote urges to smoke, and (4) relapse prevention strategies (Antonuccio et al., 1992). Reports of initial cessation from behavioral programs have ranged from 50% to 100%, with relapse rates of 70% to 80% among studies which provided three-month follow-up data (Marlatt & Gordon, 1985). This dramatic decline from initial cessation to immediate relapse among the majority of smokers has caused a shift in emphasis toward relapse prevention among smoking researchers. In a selective review of controlled studies conducted between 1977 and 1987, Glasgow and Lichtenstein (1987) concluded that behavioral approaches have generally been found to be superior to control conditions. They concluded that all successful treatment approaches, including behavioral interventions, are more successful with light smokers and obtain abstinence rates that range between 25% and 33%. In his comprehensive review, Lichtenstein (1982) observed that at 6 and 12-month follow-ups, the "average" participant in the "average" smoking control program has a 20% chance of being abstinent. He suggests that involvement in one of the more successful programs may increase these odds to between 30% and 40%. It should be noted that most smokers quit without the help of an organized program (Cohen, Lichtenstein, Prochaska, Rossi, Gritz, Carr, Orleans, Schoenbach, Biener, Abrams, DiClemente, Curry, Marlatt, Cummings, Emont, Giovino, & Ossip-Klein, 1989), perhaps leaving the programs to deal with the smokers who have the most difficulty quitting.

Helping Smokers Quit in Primary Care

Somewhere between 70 and 85% of smokers indicate that they would like to quit (e.g., Gallup Organization, 1999). Counseling to quit smoking is second only to childhood vaccination in terms of prevention benefits. There has been an increasing emphasis on intervening at the point of contact with medical professionals (Lichtenstein, 2002) in an effort to "strike while the iron is hot". The U.S. Public Health Service recommends a "5 As approach" to treatment (Fiore et al., 2000) in the primary care setting. This approach involves (1) asking about tobacco use, (2) advising tobacco users to stop, (3) assessing the tobacco user's willingness to quit, (4) assisting the tobacco user who is willing to quit, and (5) arranging for follow-up. Below we offer some practical strategies for how to go about this with patients.

Addressing myths about quitting. Many smokers will come to the primary care environment with inaccurate beliefs about quitting that may interfere with motivation to quit. They may believe that because they have been unsuccessful in quitting in the past, that they are unable to quit. Older smokers may believe that because they have smoked for so long, there will be no benefit to quitting. These myths must be addressed directly by informing smokers that past quit attempts actually increase the likelihood that they'll be able to quit, especially if they've quit for at least 2 weeks in the past (Kenford, Fiore, Jorenby, Smith, Wetter, & Baker, 1994; Garvey, Bliss, Hitchcock, Heinold, & Rosner, 1992). Also, smokers must be told that even after many years of smoking and serious medical problems, they can benefit medically almost as soon as they quit. For example, those who've had a heart attack can reduce their risk for a second heart attack to less than half compared with someone who continues to smoke.

Matching intervention strategies with stage of change. In addressing smoking, physicians need to consider the smoker's stage of quitting. As outlined by DiClemente et al. (1991), the stages include precontemplation, contemplation, preparation, action, maintenance, and termination. About 15% of smokers are in the precontemplation stage and are not currently considering quitting. Precontemplators are unaware, unwilling, or discouraged about quitting smoking. They may believe they have their smoking under control. For whatever reasons, they are not considering quitting in the near future and they are the least likely to benefit from intensive smoking cessation training. In order to move to the next stage, precontemplators need to identify smoking as a problem, increase awareness of the negative aspects of smoking, and learn to accurately evaluate their ability to quit smoking. Motivational interviewing strategies using biomarker feedback (e.g., carbon monoxide feedback) might be the most useful intervention at this stage (Hatsukami, Hecht, Hennrikus, Joseph, & Pentel, 2003).

Contemplators are actively thinking about quitting. Contemplators are interested in gathering information about smoking and how to quit. Contemplators are more upset about their smoking than precontemplators. They tend to consider the advantages and disadvantages of quitting smoking. They are weighing their options but they are not quite ready to take action. Contemplators can benefit from advice and information about smoking cessation (e.g, Antonuccio, 1993a; Antonuccio, 1993b) because it provides the necessary information they need to move to the preparation stage of quitting. Patients may be taught about the medical consequences of smoking and the medical benefits of quitting. Patients may be taught about the normal stages of quitting so they will understand that quitting smoking is not an "all-or-none" phenomenon. Patients are shown how to use "wrap sheets" (structured tracking sheets that wrap around a pack of cigarettes) so they will have accurate baseline smoking data and to reinforce progressive reductions in smoking rate.

Patients may be given the Reasons for Quitting Scale (Curry, Wagner, & Grothaus, 1990) to evaluate intrinsic and extrinsic motivation. The Therapeutic Reactance Scale (Dowd, Milne, & Wise, 1991) may be used to evaluate resistance to instruction. The Partner Interaction Questionnaire (Mermelstein, Lichtenstein, & McIntyre, 1983) evaluates the impact of the smoker's partner. The Fagerstrom Nicotine Dependence Scale (Fagerstrom, 1978) can help determine the strength of the smoker's addiction. These questionnaires help the therapist tailor information, feedback, and interventions to an individual smoker's needs.

In the preparation stage, smokers feel ready to change. They are about to take action and are in the process of setting goals. Setting a target quit day moves someone into the preparation stage. It is a good idea to have the smoker pick a target date that is 2 to 4 weeks into the future. This is a good time to begin asking the smoker to track cigarettes on a wrap sheet. Patients may be taught relaxation and/or self-hypnosis to reduce anxiety and harness the power of self-suggestion. Smokers' partners may be encouraged to eliminate nagging, shunning, and punishing behaviors while increasing supportive and reinforcing behaviors.

The action stage involves actually changing smoking behavior. During the action stage, smokers actually practice some of the strategies designed to limit and eliminate smoking such as substitution, taste aversion, and self-rewards for not smoking. They may be taught strategies for avoiding or altering smoking cues or substituting alternatives to smoking. It is helpful for patients to practice using a nonsmoking strategy in a specific targeted situation (e.g., putting sugarless candy in the ashtray and keeping cigarettes in the trunk of the car while driving) to get practice at being a nonsmoker in one situation prior to quit day. Patients may be taught about "nicotine fading" by switching to a brand of cigarettes that has about half the nicotine of their normal brand to help reduce nicotine dependence prior to the quit date. Taste aversion or "smoke holding" may prove useful to interested smokers to help associate a negative taste with smoking. Individuals in the action stage must learn strategies to deal with relapse in order to progress to the maintenance stage. Patients may be asked to set a short-term goal (usually between 1 day and 2 weeks) and create a written contract in which they agree to send money (usually from $1 to $100 dollars) to their least favorite politicians only if they fail to achieve their short-term goal.

Maintenance is the final stage in quitting smoking and begins on quit day. This is perhaps the most challenging stage. Even 6 months after quitting smoking, there are often still psychological triggers for an urge to smoke. To enhance relapse prevention, patients may be asked to predict the situations in which they are most likely to relapse and devise plans for coping with those situations and for addressing "relapse" thoughts. To assist in this process, patients may fill out the Smoking Self-Efficacy Questionnaire (Baer, Holt, & Lichtenstein, 1986). It is rare that someone quits for good on their first try. Most people relapse and move back to an earlier stage. In other words, in the process of changing a powerful addictive behavior like smoking, it must be considered normal to move back and forth between stages rather than go smoothly from precontemplation to maintenance. This seems to be a normal part of the learning process. In fact, relapse itself may actually be an important part of the learning process. The individual can use relapse as an opportunity to learn about how to handle the factors that led to the relapse. The maintenance stage is the time when patients start weaning off nicotine replacement or other pharmacological treatment if they are using it.

Prochaska and DiClemente have speculated there is a sixth stage they call the termination stage during which nonsmoking is firmly established and no more time and energy are needed to maintain nonsmoking. It is difficult to say how long it takes for the average person to get to the termination stage. For most people, this may be several years.

Addressing resumption thoughts. Most smokers must deal with resumption thoughts, thoughts that contribute to the urge to resume smoking. Below are some common examples and some ways to challenge them. It is sometimes helpful to roleplay with the patient, with the physician playing "devil's advocate" and asking the patient to challenge each of these common resumption thoughts.

1.   *I remember when I used to smoke. I think I was happier then. Those were the days.*
     I may fondly remember when I used to smoke but I wasn't necessarily happier. In fact, I may have even felt more stressed. Besides, I have a lot of negative memories about my smoking as well, like burning holes in my clothes or the carpet, or chronic bronchitis. (Make a list of all the negative, unpleasant, or embarrassing memories you have about smoking).

2.   *Since I've been quit for a while now, I bet I can have one cigarette and enjoy it without starting smoking all over again.*
     Wait a minute! I know for sure this is not true. I've quit for a time before and all it took was one cigarette to start me on a gradual road to smoking as much as I was before. Besides, the possible enjoyment of one cigarette is not worth the risk of going back to smoking and having to quit all over again. I'm enjoying the benefits of not smoking too much at this point. (Make a list of all the benefits you have noticed since you quit smoking).

3.   *I need a cigarette to help me get through this personal crisis* (e.g. crashed car, fight with spouse, job stress, etc.).
     How is a cigarette going to help me deal with this crisis? After I smoke the cigarette, I'll still have the crisis plus I'll be smoking again. I can find another way to deal with the stress. I can practice my relaxation skills, go for a walk, or talk with a friend. Those are all better coping strategies for me to use than smoking a cigarette. (Make a list of ways for coping with the crisis that don't involve smoking).

4.   *I better go back to smoking because I notice I'm coughing more and I've gained some weight. I think I was better off when I was smoking.*
     I read that the coughing may actually be a good sign because it shows that my lungs are healing themselves and bringing up the garbage that has accumulated all these years. A few extra pounds is a lot better than

the smoking according to my doctor. Most of the negative changes I notice are temporary. I just need to be patient and focus on the positive things I notice about my not smoking. I notice I can smell and taste better and have more energy. Plus I really have a sense of accomplishment at having quit smoking. I can exercise a little more and eat better to help manage my weight. I don't want to go back to smoking just to lose a few pounds. (Make a list of all the benefits you have noticed since you quit smoking).

5. *I don't know if I really have what it takes to stay away from cigarettes.*
   Sure I do. I read that more than a million Americans quit smoking every year. I can too. There are many things I do on a daily basis that take a certain amount of willpower, like taking care of my personal hygiene or getting to work on time. Just because quitting smoking is challenging, doesn't mean I can't do it. No pain, no gain. I just need to keep at it.

6. *What difference does it make if I go back to smoking? We all have to die sometime.*
   Of course we all have to die. But the quality of my life is important to me as well as the length of it. I would like to live as healthy a life as possible. I'd rather not die a slow death due to severe emphysema.

Adding Nicotine Replacement to Behavior Therapy

Nicotine replacement therapies, particularly nicotine gum and transdermal nicotine patches, have become standard components of many behavioral treatment programs. Nicotine replacement is featured prominently in clinical practice guidelines for smoking cessation (e.g., Fiore et al., 1996). One of the difficulties in interpreting the effectiveness of nicotine replacement independently of behavioral treatment is that it is designed to be combined with behavior therapy, and the vast majority of published studies include some form of behavioral intervention when nicotine replacement is used (Klesges, Ward, & DeBon, 1996). Comparison studies involving nicotine replacement and behavior therapy rarely have single intervention conditions. This makes it difficult to determine how behavior therapy alone (i.e., without the nicotine replacement or placebo) would fare in a direct comparison with nicotine replacement alone or the combination treatment.

Outcome with nicotine gum has been summarized (Lam, Sze, Sacks, & Chalmers, 1987) in a meta-analysis of 14 randomized, controlled trials of nicotine gum. In specialized smoking cessation clinics that included intense behavioral interventions, abstinence rates at 6 months with BT plus nicotine gum vs. BT plus placebo were 27% and 18%, and the 12 month rates were 23% and 13%, respectively. In general medical practice with "minimal interventions" the results were less promising. The abstinence rate at 6 months in the nicotine gum group was 11.4% and in the placebo group was 11.7%. These trials demonstrate the benefit of combining nicotine gum with behavior therapy, while use of nicotine gum as the sole intervention is unlikely to be of significant benefit (Lam et al., 1987).

In a meta-analysis (Fiore, Smith, Jorenby, & Baker, 1994) of 17 double-blind, placebo-controlled studies, where the nicotine patch was applied as an adjunct to behavioral management, abstinence rates favor the active patch (22% abstinence) as opposed to placebo patch (9% abstinence) at six month follow-up. This is consistent with a recent meta-analysis showing that nicotine replacement increases quit rates 1.5 to 2 fold over control conditions at six-month follow-up (Silagy, Lancaster, Stead, Mant, & Fowler, 2003). The results with BT plus transdermal nicotine were generally in the range reported for other successful smoking cessation programs. The optimal duration of transdermal nicotine therapy remains an empirical question, although one review concluded that its use beyond six weeks (but no more than eight weeks) may be indicated only for the most dependent smokers (Fiore, Douglas, Jorenby, Baker, & Kenford, 1992). One study found that behavior therapy combined with 3 weeks of transdermal nicotine therapy resulted in similar outcome (28% abstinence) as behavior therapy combined with 12 weeks of transdermal nicotine therapy (29% abstinence) at one month following termination of nicotine replacement (Bolin, Antonuccio, Follette, & Krumpe, 1999). In general, use of the active patch without behavior therapy has been disappointing compared with the placebo patch. For example, one well-controlled double-blind multi-site study involved 584 cardiac patients randomly assigned to 12 weeks of active patch or placebo patch (Joseph et al., 1996). In this study, there was only about 15 minutes of behavioral counseling at the beginning of treatment. The placebo patch was scented to smell like nicotine to help ensure the integrity of the double blind. At 48 week follow-up, 10% of the patients assigned to active patch were abstinent compared with 12% of the patients assigned to placebo, a nonsignificant difference (Joseph & Antonuccio, 1999). Another controlled study found a 5% quit rate for the patch alone at very long-term (8 years after treatment) follow-up (Yudkin, Hey, Roberts, Welch, Murphy, & Walton, 2003). A meta-analysis of the efficacy of over-the-counter nicotine replacement (Hughes, Shiffman, Callas, & Zhang, 2003) found modest quit rates of about 7% at long term (i.e., 6 months or greater) follow-up. Another recent effectiveness study found that over-the-counter patch was not more effective than an unaided quit attempt (Pierce & Gilpin, 2002), possibly because most of the patch users were not systematically using behavioral strategies. Quit rates up to 22% at 6 month follow-up have been found when the patch was combined with a behavioral selfl-help book and information about area smoking cessation classes (Jolicoeur, Richter, Ahluwalia, Mosier, & Resnicow, 2003).

There are a number of clinical benefits from adding the nicotine patch to behavioral treatments. More people are willing to try to quit smoking when this combination treatment is used. More people trying to quit means more people quitting. The "Butt Out" smoking cessation groups at the Reno V.A. Medical Center, that now incorporate the patch, have consistently had 2 to 3 times more patients enroll compared to enrollment before the patch became available. There is evidence the patch helps reduce craving and other withdrawal symptoms. Also, patients appear to have reduced anxiety about quitting with nicotine replacement. In one of the few studies (Cinciripini, Cinciripini, Wallfisch, Haque, & Van Vunakis,

1996) to use a behavior therapy alone condition, BT plus patch had significantly higher abstinence than BT alone at the end of treatment through the 3-month follow-up. These effects weakened and did not attain statistical significance at the 6 and 12-month follow-ups. There was evidence that BT plus patch group experienced less general distress and more self-efficacy that the BT alone group. Unfortunately, due to bad luck during random assignment, the BT alone group had significantly heavier smokers, casting some doubt on the advantage of the combined condition. Also, there was not a BT plus placebo condition to help control for the expectation of receiving nicotine replacement. We were unable to find any studies with what we consider the ideal design, BT alone, BT plus patch, BT plus placebo, and patch alone.

Adding Bupropion to Behavioral Interventions

Recently, an antidepressant, particularly bupropion, has been added to behavior therapy as an aid to smoking cessation. In a study funded by the manufacturer, one year abstinence rates (23%) with buproprion combined with behavior therapy (Hurt et al., 1997) were similar to those found with the patch and behavior therapy. Another study found quit rates as high as 35% at 1 year follow-up when bupropion was combined with the patch and behavioral counseling (Jorenby et al., 1999). As with nicotine replacement, bupropion alone is rarely evaluated and when it has been the results have been very disappointing. For example, one study (Gifford et al., 2002) found less than a 5% quit rate at one year follow-up when bupropion was utilized without behavioral counseling. Also, bupropion failed to reduce or delay relapse to smoking in smokers who quit while on nicotine patch (Hurt et al., 2003). So while there is some evidence that bupropion can aid smoking cessation (Hughes, Stead, & Lancaster, 2001), there are really too few safety and efficacy studies with long-term follow-up to recommend it as a first line treatment at this time.

Suggested Practice Guidelines

As an adjunct to the recently published practice guidelines for smoking cessation (Fiore et al., 2000), based on our review of the cessation literature, we offer the following suggestions regarding the addition of nicotine replacement to behavior therapy for smoking cessation:

1. Require compliance with some form of self-help, individual, or group cognitive-behavioral treatment (e.g., "Butt Out", "Quit Smart", "Freedom from Smoking", or "Freshstart" programs) in order to access pharmacological interventions. These programs are generally relatively cheap, well packaged, and effective.
2. Build in maintenance sessions and withdrawal from nicotine replacement.
3. Strongly warn patients not to smoke on the patch if for no other reason than it significantly decreases their chances of quitting.
4. Use carbon monoxide monitoring to give feedback, reinforce success, and verify abstinence.

5. Encourage termination of the patch if there is evidence the patient is still smoking after two weeks. Have the patient set a new target quit date and try again later.
6. Consider encouraging most patients to use a three week "rapid deployment" nicotine replacement schedule because it appears to be cheaper and equally effective as a longer regimen.
7. In all cases, encourage termination of the patch after 6 weeks because there is no evidence of improved outcome with a longer regimen.
8. Do not routinely prescribe buproprion as a smoking cessation aid until more safety and efficacy data are available.

Following such guidelines will likely make the combination of nicotine replacement and behavior therapy safer, less costly, and more effective. Ultimately, these are issues that can be addressed by future studies.

References

American Lung Association (2002). *American Lung Association Fact Sheet: Smoking and Pregnancy.* http://www.lungusa.org/tobacco/pregnancy_factsheet99.html.

Antonuccio, D. O. (1993a). *Butt Out, The Smoker's Book: A Compassionate Guide to Helping Yourself Quit Smoking, with or without a Partner.* Saratoga, CA: R and E Publishers.

Antonuccio, D. O. (1993b). *Butt out, The Partner's Book: A compassionate quide to helping your friend or loved one quit smoking without nagging.* Saratoga, CA: R & E Publishers.

Antonuccio, D. O., Boutilier, L. R., Ward, C. H., Morrill, G. B., & Graybar, S. R. (1992). The behavioral treatment of cigarette smoking. In M. Hersen, R. M. Eisler, & P. M. Miller (Eds.) *Progress in Behavior Modification.* Dekalb, Illinois: Sycamore Publications.

Baer, J. S., Holt, C. S., & Lichtenstein, E. (1986). Self-efficacy and smoking reexamined: Construct validity and clinical utility. *Journal of Consulting and Clinical Psychology, 54(6)*, 846-852.

Bartecchi, C. E., Mackenzie, T. D., & Schrier, R. W. (1994). The human costs of tobacco use (first of two parts). *New England Journal of Medicine, 330*, 907-912.

Bolin, L, Antonuccio, D, Follette, W., & Krumpe, P. (1999). Transdermal nicotine: The long and the short of it. *Psychology of Addictive Behaviors, 13*, 152-156.

Bricker, J. B., Leroux, B. G., Peterson, A. V., Kealey, K. A., Sarason, I. G., Andersen, M., & Marek, P. M. (2003). Nine-year prospective relationship between parental smoking cessation and children's daily smoking. *Addiction, 98*, 585-593.

Centers for Disease Control and Prevention (1993). *Use of smokeless tobacco among adults–United States, 1991, Morbidity and Mortality Weekly Report, 42*, 263-266.

Centers for Disease Control and Prevention (2002). *Tobacco information and prevention* source: OSH summary for 2002. http://www.cdc.gove/tobacco/overview/oshsummary02.htm.

Cinciripini, P. M., Cinciripini, L. G., Wallfish, A., Haque, W., & Van Vunakis, H. (1996). Behavior therapy and the transdermal nicotine patch: Effects on cessation outcome, affect, and coping. *Journal of Consulting and Clinical Psychology, 64(2)*, 314-323.

Cohen, S., Lichtenstein, E., Prochaska, J. O., Rossi, J. S., Gritz, E. R., Carr, C. R., Orleans, K. C. T., Schoenbach, V. J., Biener, L., Abrams, D., DiClemente, C., Curry, S., Marlatt, G. A., Cummings, K. M., Emont, S. L., Giovino, G., & Ossip-Klein, D. (1989). Debunking myths about self-quitting. Evidence from 10 prospective studies of persons who attempt to quit smoking by themselves. *American Psychologist, 44*, 1355-1365.

Council on Scientific Affairs (1990). The worldwide smoking epidemic: Tobacco trade, use, and control. *JAMA, 263(24)*, 3312-3318.

Critchley, J. A. & Capewell, S. (2003). Mortality risk reduction associated with smoking cessation in patients with coronary heart disease: A systematic review. *JAMA, 290*, 86-97.

Curry, S. J., Wagner, E. H., & Grothaus, L. C. (1990). Intrinsic and extrinsic motivation for smoking cessation. *Journal of Consulting and Clinical Psychology, 58(3)*, 310-316.

Davis, J. W. (1990). Some acute effects of smoking on endothelial cells and platelets. *Advanced Experimental Medical Biology, 273*, 107-118.

DiClemente, C. C., Prochaska, J. O., Fairhurst, S. K., Velicer, W. F., Velasquez, M. M., & Rossi, J. S. (1991). The process of smoking cessation: An analysis of precontemplation, contemplation, and preparation stages of change. *Journal of Consulting and Clinical Psychology, 59(2)*, 295-304.

Dowd, E. T., Milne, C. R., & Wise, S. L. (1991) The Therapeutic Reactance Scale: A measure of psychological reactance. *Journal of Counseling and Development., 69*, 541-545.

Fagerstrom, K.O. (1978). Measuring degree of physical dependence to tobacco smoking with reference to individualization of treatment. Addictive Behaviors, 3, 235-241.

Fiore, M. C., Bailey, W. C., Cohen, S. J., Dorfman, S. F., Goldstein, M. G., Gritz, E. R., Heyman, R.B., Holbrook, J., Jaen, C.R., Kottke, T.E., Lando, H.A., Mecklenburg, R., Mullen, P. D., Nett, L. M., Robinson, L., Stitzer, M. L., Tommasello, A. C., Villejo, L., & Wewers, M. E. (1996). Smoking Cessation. Clnical Practice Guideline No. 18. Rockville, MD: U.S. Department of Health and Human Services, Public Health Service, Agency for Health Care Policy and Research. *AHCPR Publication No. 96-0692.*

Fiore, M. C., Douglas, E., Jorenby, D. E., Baker, T. M., & Kenford, S. L. (1992). Tobacco dependence and the nicotine patch: Clinical Guidelines for effective use. *Journal of the American Medical Association, 268(19)*, 2687-2694.

Fiore, M. C., Smith, S. S., Jorenby, D. E., & Baker, T. B. (1994). The effectiveness of the nicotine patch for smoking cessation: A meta-analysis. *JAMA, 271(24)*, 1940-1947.

Fiore, M. C. et al. (2000). *Treating tobacco Use and Dependence. Clinical Practice Guidelines*. Rockville, Md.: U.S. Department of Health and Human Services.

Gallup Organizastion, 1999. *Majority of smokers want to quit, consider themselves addicted* (http://www.gallup.com/poll/releases/pr991118.asp)

Garvey, A. J., Bliss, R. E., Hitchcock, J. L., Heinold, J. W., & Rosner, B. (1992). Predictors of smoking relapse among self-quitters: A report from the normative aging study. *Addictive Behaviors, 17*, 367-377.

Gifford, E. V., Kohlenberg, B. S., Piasecki, M. P., Palm, K. M., Antonuccio, D. O., & Hayes, S. C. (2002). *Bupropion SR in combination with acceptance-based behavioral therapy for smoking cessation: Results from a radomized controlled trial*. Paper presented at the annual meeting of the Asociation for the Advancement of Behavior Therapy, Reno, Nevada.

Glantz, S. A., & Parmley, W. W. (1991). Passive smoking and heart disease: epidemiology, physiology and biochemistry. *Circulation, 83*, 1-12.

Glasgow, R. E., & Lichtenstein, E. (1987). Long-term effects of smoking cessation interventions. *Behavior Therapy, 18*, 297-324.

Hatsukami, D. K., Hecht, S. S., Hennrikus, D. J., Joseph, A. M., & Pentel, P. R. (2003). Biomarkers of tobacco exposure or harm: Application to clinical and epidemiological studies. *Nicotine & Tobacco Research, 5*, 387-396.

Hughes, J. R. (1986). Genetics of smoking: A brief review. *Behavior Therapy, 17*, 335-345.

Hughes, J. R., Shiffman, S., Callas, P., & Zhang, J. (2003). A meta-analysis of the efficacy of over-the-counter nicotine replacement. *Tobacco Control, 12*, 21-27.

Hughes, J. R., Stead, L. F., & Lancaster, T. (2001). Antidepressants for smoking cessation (Cochrane Review). *The Cochrane Library, 4*.

Hurt R. D., Sachs, D. P., Glover, E. D., Offord, K. P., Johnston, J. A., Dale, L. C., Khayrallah, M. A., Schroeder, D. R., Glover, P. N., Sullivan, C. R., Croghan, I. T., & Sullivan, P. F. (1997). A comparison of sustained-release buproprion and placebo for smoking cessation. *New England Journal of Medicine, 337*, 1195-1202.

Hurt, R. D., Krook, J. E., Croghan, I. T., Loprinzi, C. L, Sloan, J. A., Novotny, P. J., Kardinal, C. G., Knost, J. A., Tirona, M. T., Addo, F, Morton, R. F., Michalak, J. D., Schaefer, P. L., Porter, P. A., Stella, P. J. (2003). Nicotine patch therapy based on smoking rate followed by bupropiron for prevention of relapse to smoking. *Journal of Clinical Oncology, 21*, 914-920.

Jolicoeur, D. G., Richter, K.P., Ahluwalia, J. S., Mosier, M. C., Resnicow, K. (2003). The use of nicotine patches with minimal intervention. *Substance Abuse, 24*, 101-106.

Jorenby, D. E., Leischow, S. J., Nides, M. A., Rennard, S. I., Johnston, J.A., Hughes, A. R., Smith, S. S., Muramoto, M. I, Daughton, D. M., Doan, K., Fiore, M. C., & Baker, T. B. (1999). A controlled trial of sustained release bupropion, a nicotine patch, or both for smoking cessation. *New England Journal of Medicine, 340*, 685-691.

Joseph, A. M., & Antonuccio, D. O. (1999). Lack of efficacy of transdermal nicotine in smoking cessation. *New England Journal of Medicine, 341*, 1157-1158.

Joseph, A. M., Norman, S., Ferry, L., Prochazka, A., Westman, E., Steele, B., Sherman, S., Cleveland, M., Antonuccio, D. O., Hartman, N., McGovern, P. (1996). The safety of transdermal nicotine therapy as an aid to smoking cessation in patients with cardiac disease. *New England Journal of Medicine, 335(24)*, 1792-1798.

Kenford, S .L., Fiore, M. C., Jorenby, D. E., Smith, S. S., Wetter, D., & Baker, T. B. (1994). Predicting smoking cessation: Who will quit with and without the nicotine patch. *JAMA, 271(8)*, 589-594.

Klesges, R. C., Ward, K. D., & DeBon, M. (1996). Smoking cessation: A successful behavioral/pharmacologic interfface. *Clinical Psychology Review, 16(6)*, 479-496.

Lam, W., Sze, P. C., Sacks, H. S., & Chalmers, T. C. (1987). Meta-analysis of randomised, controlled trials of nicotine chewing-gum. *Lancet, 2*, 27-30.

Lawrence, P. S., Amodei, N., & Murray, A. L. (1982). *Withdrawal symptoms associated with smoking cessation*. Paper presented at the 21st convention of the Association for Advancement of Behavior Therapy, Los Angeles.

Lichtenstein, E. (2002). From rapid smoking to the Internet: Five decades of cessation research. *Nicotine & Tobacco Research, 4*, 139-145.

Lichtenstein, E. (1982). The smoking problem: A behavioral perspective. *Journal of Consulting and Clinical Psychology, 50*, 804-819.

Lichtenstein, E., & Antonuccio, D.O. (1981). Dimensions of smoking. *Addictive Behaviors, 6*, 365-367.

Lichtenstein, E., & Brown, R. A. (1980). Smoking cessation methods: Review and recommendations. In W.R. Miller (Ed.), *The addictive behaviors: Treatment of alcoholism, drug abuse, smoking, and obesity*. Oxford: Pergamon Press.

Lichtenstein, E., & Mermelstein, R. (1985). Behavior modification strategies. In J. Matarazzo, N. E. Miller, S. M. Weiss, J. A. Herd, & S. M. Weiss (Eds.), *Behavioral health: A handbook of health enhancement and disease preventers*. New York: Wiley & Sons.

Marlatt, G. A., & Gordon, J. R. (1985). *Relapse prevention: Maintenance strategies in the treatment of addictive behaviors*. New York: Guilford Press.

Mermelstein, R., Lichtenstein, E., & McIntyre, K. (1983). Partner support and relapse in smoking-cessation programs. *Journal of Consulting and Clinical Psychology, 51(3)*, 465-466.

Milberger, S., Biederman, J., Faraone, S.V., Chen, L., & Jones, J. (1996). Is maternal smoking during pregnancy a risk factor for attention deficit hyperactivity disorder in children? *American Journal of Psychiatry, 153(9)*, 1138-1142.

Pierce, J. P, & Gilpin, E. A. (2002). Impact of over-the-counter sales on effectiveness of pharmaceutical aids for smoking cessation. *JAMA, 288*, 1260-1264.

Pierce, J. P., Fiore, M. C., Novotny, T. E., Hatziandreu, E. J., & Davis, R. M. (1989). Trends in cigarette smoking in the United States: Projections to the year 2000. *Journal of the American Medical Association, 261 (1)*, 61-65.

Pinto, R. P., & Morrell, E. M. (1988). Current approaches and future trends in smoking cessation programs. *Journal of Mental Health Counseling, 10(2)*, 95-110.

Pittilo, R. M., & Woolf, N. (1993). Cigarette smoking, endothelial cell injury and atherosclerosis. *Journal of Smoking Related Diseases, 4*, 17-25.

Pomerleau, O. F., & Pomerleau, C. S. (1985). Neuroregulators and the reinforcement of smoking: Towards a biobehavioral explanation. *Neuroscience and Boibehavioral Reviews, 8*, 503-513.

Pomerleau, O. F., Collins, A. C., Shiffman, S., & Pomerleau, C. S. (1993). Why people smoke and others do not: New perspectives. *Journal of Consulting and Clinical Psychology, 61(5)*, 723-731.

Price, J. H., & Everett, S. A. (1994). Perceptions of lung cancer and smoking in an economically disadvantaged population. *Journal of Community Health, 19 (5)*, 361-375.

Rigotti, N. A., Lee, J. E., & Wechsler, H. (2000). U.S. college students' use of tobacco products: Results of a national survey. *Journal of the American Medical Association, 284*, 699-705.

Shaw, M., Mitchell, R., & Dorling, D. (2000). Inequalities in health continue to grow despite government's pledges. *British Medical Journal, 320*, 53.

Silagy, C., Lancaster, T., Stead, L., Mant, D., Fowler, G. (2003). Nicotine replacement therapy for smoking cessation (Cochrane Review). *The Cochrane Library, 3*.

Sorensen, L. T., Karlsmark, T., & Gottrup, F. (2003). Abstinence from smoking reduces incisional wound infection: a randomized controlled trial. *Annals of Surgery, 238*, 1-5.

U.S. Department of Health and Human Services (1983). *The Health Consequences of Smoking: Cardiovascular Disease*. U.S. Department of Health and Human Services, Public Health Service, Office of the Assistant Secretary for Health, Office on Smoking and Health.

U.S. Department of Health and Human Services (1990). The Health Benefits of Smoking Cessation. U.S. Department of Health and Human Services, Public Health Service, Centers for Disease Control, Center for Chronic Disease Prevention and Health Promotion, Office on Smoking and Health. *DHHS Publication No.* (CDC) 90-8416.

Willett, W. C., Green, A., Stampfer, M. J., et al. (1987). Relative and absolute risks of coronary heart disease among women who smoke cigarettes. *New England Journal of Medicine, 317*, 1303-1309.

World Health Organization (2003). *Tobacco Free Initiative: The Tobacco Atlas*. http://www.who.int/tobacco/statistics/tobacco_atlas/en/

Yudkin, P., Hey, K., Roberts, S., Welch, S., Murphy, M., & Walton, R.. (2003). Abstinence from smoking eight years after participation in randomized controlled trial of nicotine patch. *British Medical Journal, 327*, 28-29.